Praise for *The Law (in Plain English) for Nonprofit Organizations*

"We work with the boards and senior leadership of nonprofits at every life cycle stage, and there are always complex legal questions facing organizations as they grow, scale up, merge, rebuild, etc. I have yet to find a reference book as comprehensive, concise, and easy to digest as *The Law (in Plain English)® for Nonprofit Organizations*. It offers practical legal guidance for nonprofit leaders without any of the usual lawyer jargon that frustrates us laypeople. This will be a top recommendation for our clients, and I know I'll be keeping a copy close at hand for my own purposes!"

—Xander Subashi, director of programs,
Support Center for Nonprofit Management

"*The Law (in Plain English)® for Nonprofit Organizations* is a very good read for organizations that are about to start up or are in the emerging phase. Founders and senior managers will find that the information provided, though it deals with complex issues, avails the reader of the right questions and considerations to be thinking through before delving into or expanding operations. In easy to understand language, the book walks one through the many different foundational aspects of running a nonprofit—an important tool to have handy on one's bookshelf!"

—Michael Royce, executive director,
New York Foundation for the Arts (NYFA)

"*The Law (in Plain English)® for Nonprofit Organizations* is a wonderful resource for nonprofit leaders. Our organization has worked with Leonard and Mary Ann DuBoff for more than twenty-six years and have benefited from their wealth of knowledge—from copyright, trademark, and contracts to other areas of legal expertise. This book is a great reference no matter where your organization may be in its life cycle."

—Lori Pourier, president and CEO, First Peoples Fund

"This is a magisterial and comprehensive overview of the variety and constant stream of legal issues faced by nonprofit organizations. I highly recommend it."

—Susan Crawford, consultant to nonprofits and
author of *Managing the Future: A Leader's Guide*

"An essential guide and wonderful resource, *The Law (in Plain English)®
for Nonprofit Organizations* is, as the title indicates, an easy-to-understand
explanation of key issues faced by nonprofits. I recommend this comprehensive guide to all nonprofit executives, volunteers, and board members alike."
—Matthew Devore, CEO, Cascade Pacific Council
of the Boy Scouts of America

"The Law (in Plain English)® for Nonprofit Organizations is the best resource
for the executive leadership of any nonprofit organization; it addresses the
important issues all nonprofits face as they grow and expand to accomplish
their stated missions. The authors have done an outstanding job of taking
a very complex subject and making it engaging and easy to understand. As
the executive director of a professional nonprofit association, I will encourage all of my board members to keep this excellent resource close to them
so it can be readily referred to and guide their decision-making on many
topics."
—Phillip Harris, executive director, Association
for Educational Communications and Technology

"An important resource for nonprofit managers, board members, advisers,
and consultants. This book offers a wealth of information about legal issues
affecting nonprofits, with especially important coverage of copyrights, trademarks, advertising, and the Internet."
—Cynthia Cumfer, attorney, adjunct professor, Lewis & Clark Law School,
author of *The Oregon Nonprofit Corporation Handbook*

The **Law**

(in Plain English)®

for

Nonprofit Organizations

The **Law**

(in Plain English)®

for
Nonprofit
Organizations

Leonard D. DuBoff *and* **Amanda Bryan**

Attorneys-at-Law

ALLWORTH PRESS
NEW YORK

Allworth Press books may be purchased in bulk at special discounts for sales promotion, corporate gifts, fund-raising, or educational purposes. Special editions can also be created to specifications. For details, contact the Special Sales Department, Allworth Press, 307 West 36th Street, 11th Floor, New York, NY 10018 or info@skyhorsepublishing.com.

23 22 21 20 19   5 4 3 2 1

Published by Allworth Press, an imprint of Skyhorse Publishing, Inc. 307 West 36th Street, 11th Floor, New York, NY 10018. Allworth Press® is a registered trademark of Skyhorse Publishing, Inc.®, a Delaware corporation.

www.allworth.com

Cover design by Mary Belibasakis

Library of Congress Cataloging-in-Publication Data

Names: DuBoff, Leonard D., author. | Bryan, Amanda, author.
Title: The law (in plain English) for nonprofit organizations / Leonard D.
    DuBoff and Amanda Bryan, Attorneys-at-Law.
Description: New York, New York: Allworth Press, an imprint of Skyhorse
    Publishing, 2019. | Includes index.
Identifiers: LCCN 2018061686 (print) | LCCN 2019000442 (ebook) | ISBN
    9781621536888 (eBook) | ISBN 9781621536864 (pbk.: alk. paper)
Subjects: LCSH: Nonprofit organizations—Law and legislation—United States.
Classification: LCC KF1388 (ebook) | LCC KF1388 .D83 2019 (print) | DDC
    346.73/064—dc23
LC record available at https://lccn.loc.gov/2018061686

Print ISBN: 978-1-62153-686-4
eBook ISBN: 978-1-62153-688-8

Printed in the United States of America

Dedication

To my mother, Millicent, and my father, Rubin, who provided me with the gift of life and the desire to use that gift effectively. To my mother-in-law, Cumi Elena Crawford, for her faith, trust, and inspiration, and to my wife, Mary Ann, for her enduring love and continuing support.

—Leonard D. DuBoff

To my children, Random, Grey, and Scout. You are as delightful, quirky, and compassionate as I could have wished for. Your love is my greatest treasure. And to my husband, Josh, for being my safe place and my other half.

—Amanda Bryan

Table of Contents

Acknowledgments   xv
Introduction   xvii

Chapter 1: Organizing Your Nonprofit   1
Legal Structure   2
Internal Structure of Charitable Trusts and Charitable Corporations   9
Trustees and Directors   10
Liability of Trustees and Directors   11
Co-Ops   12

Chapter 2: Nonprofit Organization Checklist   15
Accountant   15
Business Name   15
Structure   16

Chapter 3: Applying for Tax-Exempt Status   23
Federal Tax Exemption   23

Chapter 4: Developing Your Fund-raising Plan and Fund-raising   37
Charitable Auctions   39
Precious Metal Collection   41
Borrowing from Banks   43
Tax Shelters   43

Chapter 5: Liability of Members and Organizational Liability   45
Organizational Liability for the Wrongful Acts of Individuals   45
Issues to Consider   47
Agency   47
Liability Waivers   53
Conclusion   53

Chapter 6: Contracts   55
Contract Basics   55
Types of Contracts   56

Understanding Contract Principles   57
Proving an Agreement   58
When Written Contracts Are Necessary   59
Additional Terms   63
Contracting Online   64
Consumer Protection Laws   64
Mail-Order Sales   66

Chapter 7: Trademarks   **67**
Definition   69
Prohibited Trademarks   69
Certification Marks   70
Protecting a Trademark   71
Federal Registration   72
Infringement   78
International Protection   79
State Registration   80
Using an Attorney   80
Conclusion   80

Chapter 8: Copyrights   **81**
Copyright Law Foundation   81
Publication   82
Copyrightable Material   82
Scope of Protection   83
Ownership   84
Copyright Protection for Utilitarian Objects   87
Notice Requirement   88
Application Process   89
Delaying Registration   90
Period of Protection   91
Infringement   91
International Protection   94
Conclusion   95

Chapter 9: Advertising   **97**
Government Regulation   97
Comparative Advertising   98
Publicity and Privacy   99
Unauthorized Use of Trademark   100
Geographic Locations   100
Trade Dress   101

Insurance   102
Conclusion   103

Chapter 10: Licensing   **105**
General Consideration   106
Licensing Opportunities   106
Licensing Considerations   107
Trade Secrets   111
Misappropriating Trade Secrets   114

Chapter 11: The Internet   **115**
Protecting Organization Property   115
Protecting Consumer Information   116
Domain Names   116
Framing   119
Linking   119
Online Advertising   120
Keywords   120
Disclosures   120
Audits   121
Liability Insurance   121
International Concerns   121
Copyright Concerns   122
Permissions   122
Peer-to-Peer Problems   123
Server Protection   124
Email   124
Spam   125
Viruses, Worms, and Ransomware   125
Cyberterrorism   125
Security for Online Commerce   126

Chapter 12: Insurance   **127**
Basics of Insurance Law   127
Ascertaining Risk   129
Additional State Regulations   129
Expectations vs. Reality   129
Overinsuring and Underinsuring   130
Unintentional Undervaluing   131
Property Covered   132
Scheduling Property   132
Valuing Scheduled Property   133

When and How to Insure   133
Keeping the Cost Down   134

Chapter 13: Employees, Contractors, and Members   137
Employees   137
Independent Contractors   143
Volunteers   144
Discrimination   145
Harassment   146
Age Discrimination   147
Disabilities Discrimination   148
Employee Handbooks   149
Zero Tolerance Policies   149
The Family Medical Leave Act   150
Termination of Employment and Membership   150

Chapter 14: Taxes   153
Unrelated Business Income   153
Donations   155
Appraisals   157
Joint Ventures, Partnering, and Umbrella Organizations   159
Tax Shelters   159

Chapter 15: Zoning   165
Local Zoning Restrictions   165
Federal Regulations   166
Telecommuting and Web-Based Organizations   167

Chapter 16: Renting Space   169
Premises   169
Cost   170
Term   170
Restrictions   171
Remodeling   171
Americans with Disabilities Act   171
Environmental Laws   172
Utilities   172
Security and Zoning   173
Written Document   174
Donated Facilities   174

Chapter 17: Estate Planning   177

The Will   178
Payment of Testator's Debts   179
Disposition of Property Not Willed   179
Intestate Succession   180
Spouse's Elective Share   180
Advantages to Having a Will   181
Estate Taxes   182
Gross Estate   182
Valuation   183
The Taxable Estate   183
Distributing Property Outside the Will   185
Trusts   186
Probate   188

Chapter 18: Finding a Lawyer and an Accountant   191

Finding a Lawyer   192
Evaluating a Lawyer   193
Using a Lawyer   193
Finding an Accountant   194

Glossary   197
About the Authors   221
Index   223

Acknowledgments

In order to assemble the vast quantity of statutes, cases, articles, and books that have become available on this topic, it was necessary to enlist the aid of numerous friends and colleagues. Their help is greatly appreciated, and some deserve special recognition. I would, therefore, like to express my sincere thanks to my collaborator, Amanda Bryan, Esq., for her extraordinary help with this book. She has sacrificed many evenings and weekends to bring this project to fruition.

Amanda and I would like to thank Greg Rogers of the accounting firm of Rogers Financial Services; Greg O'Keefe; and Gregory R. Roer, CPA of Roer & Company, Inc. for their time and expertise in reviewing the tax chapter.

I am indebted to Tad Crawford of Skyhorse Publishing and his staff for their help in publishing this volume.

Thanks also to my paralegal, Sara Poehler, for all of her assistance and numerous recommendations.

We are very grateful for the recommendations and suggestions provided by Cynthia Cumfer, an adjunct law profession at Lewis & Clark Law School and author of a well-respected text on nonprofit law. Cynthia was also kind enough to write a blurb for this book, which appears on the back cover.

We are also indebted to Phillip Harris, the Executive Director of the Association for Educational Communications and Technology, for his review of the manuscript and very useful recommendations. He, too, was kind enough to write a blurb for this book.

We are also sincerely grateful to Therese Brown, Executive Director of the Association of Catholic Publishers, for the flattering blurb that she wrote.

Matthew Devore, Chief Executive Officer at Boy Scouts of America, Cascade Pacific Council, was kind enough to review the manuscript of this text and prepare a blurb for us as well. We really appreciate his contribution.

Not only was Tad Crawford instrumental in the publication of this work, but he was also willing to review numerous copies of the manuscript and provide many valuable recommendations and suggestions. His contributions to this work are significant. His wife, Susan Crawford, was also involved, and she was kind enough to write a blurb as well. Susan is the author of a book for nonprofits on which we relied for much of our research.

Lori Pourier, Executive Director of First People's Fund, was kind enough to review the manuscript for this book and provide us with a very thoughtful blurb. We appreciate her contribution.

Amanda would like to thank her children, Random Gomm, Grey Gomm, and Scout Gomm, and her husband Josh Congdon for their patience and support during the writing process, giving up weekends and evenings with her and being okay with unfolded laundry and macaroni and cheese dinners until this book was complete.

I am grateful for the support of my children and grandchildren. My son Robert has been very helpful with technology issues, and my daughter Colleen has been extremely creative with her graphic design skills. Her husband, Rudy, a lawyer who has recently joined our law firm, has been very helpful with research. I am also grateful to my grandson Brian and his fiancée, Megan Randall, for their personal assistance, and to the newest member of my family, my granddaughter Athena, for her cheerfulness. I would like to acknowledge my appreciation to my daughter Sabrina and my grandsons Tony and Grant for their support.

My late sister, Candace DuBoff Jones, JD, Northwestern School of Law, Lewis & Clark College, 1977; my late father, Rueben R. DuBoff; and my late mother, Millicent Barbara DuBoff, all provided me with the inspiration to create works such as this. I valued my mother-in-law Cumi Elena Crawford's faith, trust, and inspiration, which helped me create this project.

Finally, I would like to express my sincere gratitude and acknowledge the contribution to this project by my partner in law and in life, Mary Ann Crawford DuBoff. Without her, *The Law (in Plain English)® for Nonprofit Organizations* would never have become a reality.

—Leonard D. DuBoff

Introduction

When I first began writing the Law (in Plain English)® series more than a quarter-century ago, my goal was to educate nonlawyers on the business aspects of their businesses and professions. At the time, I was a full-time law professor, and as an educator, I felt that one of my missions was to provide educational tools. Later, as a full-time lawyer, I realized the importance of this series in educating my clients so that they could more effectively communicate with me. It became clear that the more knowledgeable my clients were about the myriad legal issues that they faced in their businesses and professions, the more effectively they could aid me in helping them. It is for this reason that I continue this series, and today, there are In Plain English® books for writers, high-tech entrepreneurs, healthcare professionals, craftspeople, gallery operators, photographers, small businesses, publishers, collectors, restaurants, and this volume for those who are involved with every aspect of nonprofit organizations.

It is important to understand the genesis of this book. When Amanda Bryan and I were working on the revision for *The Law (in Plain English)® for Small Business*, we realized that nonprofit organizations were not adequately considered in that book and that individuals involved in nonprofits would likely not expect to find useful information for their particular needs in it. Amanda then suggested that we write another book that focuses on nonprofit organizations, and as a result, this book emerged.

This book is not intended to be a substitute for the advice of a professional. Rather, it is designed to sensitize you to the issues that may require the aid of a skilled attorney or another expert. It is my sincere hope that this book will, like its predecessors in the series, be practical, useful, and readable. One of my goals in preparing this book is to enable the reader to identify problem areas and seek the aid of a skilled professional when necessary—or preferably before it becomes necessary—because it is quite common for those involved in nonprofit organizations to become embroiled in legal problems before they are able to appreciate the problem.

The law is quite complex and rapidly evolving. The Internet has become a vehicle for communication and commerce, and the law has been scrambling to keep pace. In writing this book, it was my intention to chronicle the changes and convert them into a clear and understandable text that will aid the reader in understanding the current state of nonprofit law. It is hoped that by my doing so, readers will be able to more effectively communicate with their associates and legal advisors when inevitable legal issues arise.

—Leonard D. DuBoff
Portland, Oregon, July 2019

CHAPTER 1

Organizing Your Nonprofit

When individuals or organizations desire to provide a public benefit, create an educational institution, start a religious organization such as a church, mosque, or synagogue, or engage in some other activity that is not intended to create a profit but instead is intended to provide others with enrichment, they can engage in these activities on their own, but they may wish to have an organizational structure and a liability shield.

Every organization requires a form best suited to it. When we counsel people on creating an organization, we usually adopt a two-step approach. First, we discuss various aspects of *taxes* and liability in order to decide which of the basic legal structures is best. There are only a handful of basic forms—the nonprofit *corporation*, the public trust, and the co-op. Once we have decided which of these is most appropriate, we go into the organizational documents such as corporate *bylaws*, *trust* documents, and *partnership agreements*. These documents define the day-to-day operations of the organization and must be tailored to individual situations.

What we offer here is an explanation of the features of each of these kinds of organizations, including their advantages and disadvantages. This should give you an idea of which form might be best for your organization. We will discuss potential problems, but since we cannot go into a full discussion of the more intricate details, you should consult an experienced *attorney* before deciding to adopt any particular structure. Our purpose is to facilitate your communication with your lawyer and to enable you to better understand the choices available.

The vast majority of these nonprofit organizations are structured as nonprofit corporations, which must comply with the law of the state in which the organization is created. The other forms discussed in this chapter are occasionally used for that reason, so we are discussing them as well.

LEGAL STRUCTURE

The two methods by which the legal structure of a nonprofit organization may be created are governed by statutory schemes that differ from *jurisdiction* to jurisdiction. Before deciding which legal form a nonprofit organization will adopt, the reader should compare the treatment accorded each in the relevant jurisdiction. The earliest form of public benefit organizations was the public trust.

Charitable Trusts

According to the Uniform Trust Code, a charitable trust is one created for a charitable purpose, namely, the relief of poverty, the advancement of education or religion, the promotion of health, governmental or municipal purposes, or other purposes the achievement of which is beneficial to the community.[1]

The commentary to the Restatement (Third) of Trusts explains:

> The discussion in this Section of dispositions that are charitable does not necessarily provide a complete enumeration of charitable purposes. Other purposes of the same general character are likewise charitable. The common element of charitable purposes is that they are designed to accomplish objects that are beneficial to the community—i.e., to the public or indefinite members thereof—without also serving what amount to private trust purposes (see a(1) of this Comment). As long as the purposes to which the property of the trust is to be devoted are charitable, however, the motives of the settlor in creating the trust are immaterial.[2]

A trust purpose is charitable if its accomplishment is of such social interest or benefit to the community as to justify permitting the property to be devoted to the purpose in perpetuity and to justify the various other special privileges that are typically allowed to charitable trusts.

---

1   National Conference of Commissioners on Uniform State Laws, Uniform Trust Code §§ 103, 405(a) (2010), available at http://www.uniformlaws.org/shared/docs/trust_code/utc_final_rev2010.pdf.
2   Restatement (Third) of Trusts §28 (2003).

There is no fixed standard to determine what purposes are of such interest to the community, for the interests of the community vary with time and place.[3]

Case law has also furnished some helpful definitions. For example, a public trust is one in which the public at large, or some undetermined portion of it, has a direct interest or property right, or in which the beneficiaries cannot be ascertained with certainty.[4] The term "public trust" is synonymous with "charitable trust."[5]

Trusts that have the purpose of educating a substantial portion of the public have been considered charitable in nature.

A charitable trust must be created in compliance with the law of trusts. Generally, this requires an owner of the property (referred to as the settlor) to manifest an intent to create the trust. The settlor must transfer the property's legal title to *trustees*, who administer it for the benefit of the public. A charitable trust is usually created by a written instrument, which may be either created during one's lifetime or created by a will after one's death. This document must comply with the applicable state laws.

The document will generally set forth the trustees' names or criteria for their selection, a description of the trust property, any limitations or restrictions imposed by the settlor (person creating the trust), and the trust's purpose.

The Cy Pres Doctrine

If the trust's objective, as described in the trust instrument, cannot be fulfilled, or if its purpose is unclear, a court may use the cy pres doctrine, which essentially means "next nearest," to apply the trust *assets* to a similar purpose. Before doing so, however, the court must be satisfied that the creator of the trust had a general charitable purpose in mind when the trust was created.

Until recently, the party seeking cy pres relief was required to prove this element, but, as noted above, the trend is to presume that the creator of the

---

3   Restatement (Third) of Trusts §28 (2003), cmt. a.
4   *Holman v. Renaud*, 141 Mo. App. 399 (1910).
5   *MacKenzie v. Trustees of Presbytery of Jersey City*, 67 N.J. Eq. 652 (1905); see generally *Northern Trust v. Continental Ill.*, 43 Ill. App. 3d 169 (1976).

trust has a general charitable intent unless the terms of the trust provide otherwise.[6]

The cy pres doctrine is a principle of equity governed by state statute and applied by courts as a saving device to charitable trusts. The doctrine directs that the application of the trust assets to charitable purposes conforms as closely with the donor's objective as possible when the donor's precise intention cannot be effectuated. In *Bd. of Trustees of Univ. of N.C. v. Heirs of Prince*,[7] the North Carolina Supreme Court cited the statute that set forth the rules for applying the cy pres doctrine in that state:

> If a trust for charity is or becomes illegal, or impossible or imprac-
> ticable of fulfillment . . . and if the settler, or testator, manifested a
> general intention to devote the property to charity, any judge of the
> superior court may . . . order an administration of the trust . . . as
> nearly as possible to fulfill the manifested general charitable inten-
> tion of the settler or testator.[8]

The drafter of such a trust may wish to draw the trust's purpose clause as broadly as possible so that the creator's general intent can be realized. This may also prevent the trust from becoming obsolete. On the other hand, a purpose clause can be narrowly drawn to restrict the trust to the creator's specific intent, if such a result is desired. A provision allowing for the *amendment* of a trust could eliminate the necessity to resort to the cy pres doctrine when its stated purpose cannot be fulfilled or is unclear.

---

6 See Restatement (Third) of Trusts § 67, cmt. b; Reporter's Notes, cmt. b; Uniform Trust Code § 413(a) (2010); *In re Elizabeth J.K.L. Lucas Charitable Gift*, 125 Haw. 351, 359 (Ct. App. 2011).

7 *Bd. of Trustees of Univ. of N.C. v. Heirs of Prince*, 311 N.C. 644 (1984).

8 N.C. Gen. Stat. § 36A-53(a), repealed in 2006; see also *Morris v. E.A. Morris Char- itable Foundation*, 589 S.E. 2d 414 (N.C. App. 2003) [noting that N.C. Gen. Stat. § 36A-53(a) "applies only when three conditions have been met: (1) the testator manifested a general charitable intent; (2) the trust has become illegal, impossible, or impracticable; (3) the testator has not provided for an alternative disposition if the trust fails"] [quoting *Trustees of L.C. Wagner Trust v. Barium Springs Home for Children*, 401 S.E.2d 807, 813 (N.C. App.), *aff'd in part, rev'd in part on other grounds*, 409 S.E.2d 913 (N.C. 1991)].

The Equitable Deviation Doctrine

A doctrine closely related to cy pres is the doctrine of equitable deviation. The cy pres doctrine applies when someone seeks to modify a creator's specific charitable purpose, while the equitable deviation applies when someone desires to make changes in the manner in which a charitable trust is carried out.[9]

The equitable deviation doctrine has been effectively used by trustees of charitable trusts in several instances.[10] This is quite complex, and the assistance of an experienced attorney is strongly suggested when this type of problem arises.

The Corporate Form

A charitable (or public) trust should be distinguished from a nonprofit or charitable corporation. A trust is governed by *common law* as well as statutory rules for trusts, whereas a corporation is purely a creature of statute. The rules relating to a corporation's conduct will usually emanate from a state's not-for-profit corporation statutes, as interpreted by the courts of that jurisdiction.

A charitable corporation has been described as one "organized for the purposes, among other things, of promoting the welfare of mankind at large, or of a community, or of some class forming part of it indefinite as to members and individuals and is one created for or devoted to charitable purposes."[11]

The not-for-profit corporation is created by complying with the law of the state of incorporation. Generally, the process requires the filing of *articles of incorporation* setting forth the name of the corporation, its duration, purpose, registered office, registered agent, and directors' and incorporators' names and addresses, as well as a provision stating that, upon *liquidation*, any funds remaining after the *debts* have been satisfied must be turned over to a similar organization.

Once the entity is created, a state's not-for-profit corporation statutes generally require an organizational meeting or, in some instances, an action by the board in lieu of an actual meeting. At this point, many of the

---

9   *Niemann v. Vaughn Cmty. Church*, 154 Wash. 2d 365, 378 (2005); see also *Phillip s v. Bd. of Hosp. Trustees of Portland*, 41 Or. App.401 (1979); Iris J. Goodwin, "Donor Standing to Enforce Charitable Gifts: Civil Society vs. Donor Empowerment," *Vanderbilt Law Review* 58 (2005): 1093, 1131–1135 (discussing the narrowness of the cy pres doctrine).

10 *Cleveland Museum of Art v. O'Neill*, 129 N.E.2d 669 (Ohio 1955); *Harris v. Attorney General*, 324 A.2d 279 (Conn. 1974).

11 *Lynch v. Spilman*, 67 Cal. 2d 251 (1967).

formalities necessary to carry on the day-to-day work of the corporation will be addressed. It is typical to adopt a corporate seal, appoint officers, authorize bank accounts, and adopt bylaws. The bylaws govern the internal workings of the corporation and may be thought of as the embodiment of non-statutory administrative procedures applicable to the corporation in question.

Tax-Exempt Nonprofit Corporations

A nonprofit corporation will probably want to obtain tax-exempt status, both to avoid paying income tax on money received for its charitable purposes and to encourage donations to the institution by making contributions tax-deductible.[12]

To obtain tax-exempt status, the incorporator should file IRS Form 1023, Application for Recognition of Exemption Under Section 501(c)(3) of the Internal Revenue Code or Form 1023-EZ (the streamlined version).[13] These forms are used by organizations claiming exemptions under Internal Revenue Code (IRC) § 501(c)(3) as charitable, religious, scientific, or educational organizations. The organization must also file an application for an Employer

---

12 The aggregate amount of such deductions is governed by certain percentage limitations, and artists who donate their own work can deduct only the cost of materials used to create the work. A number of tax issues arise when property, rather than money, is donated, ranging from problems donating anything less than an undivided interest (e.g., a future interest or a restricted gift) to valuation disputes. The IRS has established valuation guidelines, as well as special panels to review the deductions taken by the donor. These art advisory panels are often inconsistent. See *Calder v. C.I.R.*, 85 T.C. 713 (1985) (After Alexander Calder's death, the art advisory panel valued a collection of 1,292 gouache paintings for estate tax purposes at $949,750 but claimed that when 1,226 of those same gouaches were gifted only six weeks after Calder's death, they were worth $2.3 million for gift tax purposes). See also Patricia Cohen, "MoMA Gains Treasure That Met Also Coveted," *New York Times*, November 28, 2012, available at http://www.nytimes .com/2012/11/28/arts/design/moma-gains-treasure-that-metropolitan-museum -of-art-also-coveted.html (After death of art dealer Ileana Sonnabend, the IRS appraised *Canyon*, by Robert Rauschenberg, at $65 million, although the artwork cannot legally be sold because it includes a taxidermied bald eagle).

13 IRS Form 1023, Application for Recognition of Exemption Under Section 501(c)(3) of the Internal Revenue Code available at https://www.irs.gov/uac/about-form-1023. Only certain organizations are permitted to use Form 1023-EZ. One requirement is that total assets are less than $250,000. To determine eligibility, complete the worksheet in the instructions for the form available at https://www .irs.gov/pub/irs-pdf/i1023ez.pdf.

Identification Number, Form SS-4,[14] as well as a power of attorney authorizing one or more individuals to act on the organization's behalf.[15]

In addition to submitting the application, an organization claiming an exemption under § 501(c)(3) must show that its creating document permits it to operate only in a manner that will further its exempt purpose and contains an adequate provision for the distribution of its assets upon *dissolution*.[16] Such distribution must be solely for an exempt purpose. If the filing is completed within twenty-seven months from the end of the month in which the organization was created, the advance ruling will be retroactive to the date of creation.[17] In the event the application is filed after the twenty-seven-month period, tax-exempt status will be conferred only prospectively from the date of the advance ruling.[18]

An exemption from state and municipal tax laws is usually conferred automatically when the federal procedure is followed, although some states and municipalities may require an independent evaluation, so it is necessary to consult the state and city tax statutes of the jurisdiction in which the organization is located. Special care should be taken when dealing with leased property. Property leased from a private owner by a federally tax-exempt organization may not be exempt from local property tax.[19]

---

14 IRS Form SS-4, Application for Employer Identification Number (EIN), available at https://www.irs.gov/pub/irs-pdf/fss4.pdf.

15 IRS Form 2848, Power of Attorney and Declaration of Representative, available at https://www.irs.gov/pub/irs-pdf/f2848.pdf.

16 Treas. Reg. 1.501(c)(3)-1; IRS Publication 557 (Rev. January 2017), Cat. No. 46573C, *Tax-Exempt Status for Your Organization*, available at https://www.irs.gov/pub/irs-pdf/p557.pdf.

17 Treas. Reg. § 1.508–1(a) requires that a new organization must file the notice required by I.R.C. § 508 on Form 1023 within fifteen months of the end of the month it was organized. However, Treas. Reg. §§ 301.9100–2 provides an automatic twelve-month extension of the fifteen-month filing requirement. IRS Exempt Organizations Determinations Manual, IRM 7.25.1 (Sep. 26, 2014), available at https://www.irs.gov/irm/part7/irm_07-025-001.html. See also IRS, "Form 1023: Purpose of Questions About Organization Applying More than 27 Months After Date of Formation," available at https://www.irs.gov/charities-non-profits /form-1023-purpose-of-questions-about-organization-applying-more-than-27 -months-after-date-of-formation.

18 *Id.*

19 See *Lincoln Street v. Town of Springfield*, 159 Vt. 181 (1992); but see *Twin Valley Cmty. Serv., Inc. v. Town of Randolph*, 170 Vt. 648, 649 (2000) (property leased

If the taxing authorities believe that an institution is not complying with the law for tax-exempt entities, an investigation may be launched that could culminate in revocation of a prior ruling. Tax-exempt entities should, therefore, be cautious about engaging in politics, lobbying, or other activities that might jeopardize their favorable tax position.

State laws differ, so it is important to check with the attorney general before commencing any public fund-raising projects. In most states, the attorney general will require periodic reports to be filed before a charity can publicly solicit contributions.[20] The organization will have to contact the local office of the state attorney general to determine whether it is required to register as a public charity soliciting contributions.

Although the vast majority of tax-exempt organizations are legitimate, there are many that abuse their status.[21] Among the more prevalent abuses are excessive executive compensation, competitive advantages given insiders, "sweetheart" *contracts* with executives or their businesses, and excessive fund-raising charges.[22]

Many donors have become cautious about the recipients of their charitable donations. Donors may visit the website for the Better Business Bureau's Wise Giving Alliance[23] to determine whether a particular charity adheres to the ethical guidelines promulgated by the Bureau. Other avenues for evaluating charities are Charity Navigator,[24] GuideStar,[25] and CharityWatch.[26] It is

---

from a private owner could be exempt from local property tax because the private owner was also a nonprofit corporation and the two entities shared a single mission); *Vermont Studio Center, Inc. v. Town of Johnson*, 5 A.3d 904 (Vt. 2010) (artist residency program was not entitled to public use exemption from local taxes).

20 See, e.g., Or. Rev. Stat. § 128.802.

21 See, e.g., Ronald Chester, "Improving Enforcement Mechanisms in the Charitable Sector: Can Increased Disclosure of Information be Utilized Effectively," *New England Law Review* 40 (2006): 447 (despite recent media attention, legislators have been slow to enact reform legislation); Mark Side, "The Guardians Guarding Themselves: A Comparative Perspective on Nonprofit Self-Regulation" *Chicago-Kent Law Review* 80 (2005): 803 (cautions on risks of stricter accountability standards affects nonprofit autonomy and freedom).

22 See *U.S. News & World Report*, November 6, 1978, at 45.

23 BBB Wise Giving Alliance, www.give.org.

24 Charity Navigator, https://www.charitynavigator.org/.

25 GuideStar, https://www.guidestar.org.

26 CharityWatch, previously American Institute of Philanthropy, https://www.charitywatch.org/.

important that nonprofit directors and trustees are aware of how their organizations are rated on these websites and to seek accreditation from the Better Business Bureau.[27]

INTERNAL STRUCTURE OF CHARITABLE TRUSTS AND CHARITABLE CORPORATIONS

Both types of organizations (charitable trusts and charitable corporations) can function as either membership or nonmembership organizations. The requirements for membership should be spelled out in the creating instrument. Members may have powers analogous to *shareholders* in a business corporation or beneficiaries of a private trust, although they may not receive dividends if the institution opts for tax-exempt status. Alternatively, membership may merely entitle an individual to attend special shows or allow free entrance to a museum normally charging an admission. The particular attributes of membership vary from institution to institution.

The organizing group should determine whether or not a membership is desired and, if so, the role it wishes members to play in running the institution. This decision is not irrevocable in the case of a not-for-profit corporation, as it can amend its articles to add or delete any provision as long as the change is not inconsistent with its purpose or the law. Where the desire is to delete the organization's membership, a vote of that body will generally be required. In the case of a trust, amendments may be more difficult. In either event, state law should be consulted by an experienced attorney for specific *authority*.

Theoretically, each form of nonprofit organization requires a different internal political structure. A charitable trust will have a governing board of individuals usually referred to as trustees. These individuals, who may

---

27 This accreditation covers twenty different areas: board oversight, board size, board meetings, board compensation, conflicts of interest, effective policies, effectiveness reports, program expenses, fund-raising expenses, accumulation of funds, audit reports, detailed expense breakdowns, accurate expense reporting, budget plans, accuracy of fund-raising and information materials, annual reports, website disclosures, donor privacy, cause-related marketing disclosures, and complaints. See Better Business Bureau Wise Giving Alliance, "How We Accredit Charities," available at http://www.give.org/for-charities/How-We-Accredit-Charities/.

or may not be paid for their services, are responsible for institutional policy decisions.

A director is usually appointed to run the organization. This individual is generally a paid professional who will conduct the ongoing operations of the organization and report to the trustees. If policy decisions must be made, the director should obtain prior authority from the board to do so, although a director's unauthorized acts may subsequently be ratified.

The job of director requires a great deal of political and managerial skill. A director must be able to balance a budget, deal with the public and staff, and convince the trustees of what is best for the organization, all for a relatively low salary.[28] The director may be assisted by professional staff that is most commonly hired by the director with the advice and consent of the trustees.

A charitable corporation is traditionally run by a *board of directors* that is required by statute to manage the corporation's business and affairs. This group appoints officers who are responsible for the day-to-day operations of the organization. Corporations usually have as their officers a president, vice-president, secretary, and treasurer, although when an organization is run in the corporate form, it typically has the same internal structure as a charitable trust.

TRUSTEES AND DIRECTORS

For all practical purposes, the charitable trust and charitable corporation have the same goals. Regardless of which legal form the institution adopts, it will be controlled by either a board of trustees or directors. As a practical matter, the trustee of a charitable trust and the director of a nonprofit corporation may have identical roles in a nonprofit organization.[29]

---

28 Goldberger, "Doesn't Anybody Want This Job?" *New York Times*, June 26, 1994, at § 2, p. 1; Nicholas Penny, "Do Museum Directors Need Curatorial Experience?" *Apollo*, April 24, 2017, available at https://www.apollo-magazine.com/do-museum -directors-need-curatorial-experience/. However, salaries in the museum world are increasing. Alanna Martinez, "Revealing Stats on Museum Salaries May Make You Reconsider That Arts Degree," *Observer*, June 29, 2017, available at http://observer.com/2017/06/revealing-stats-on-museum-salaries-may-make- you-reconsider-that-arts-degree/.

29 Evelyn Brody, "Charity Governance: What's Trust Law Got to Do with It?" *Chicago- Kent Law Review* 80 (2005): 641 ("The fiduciary standards for trustees of

A board member should not be chosen as a "decoration" for the institution's letterhead for, if it appears that the selection of a particular trustee/director was a poor choice, an inoffensive removal might present some difficulty.[30] On the other hand, an organization cannot function efficiently when it consists of ineffectual or nonproductive members; for this reason, it has been suggested to place a provision in the bylaws mandating an automatic rotation of board members.[31]

LIABILITY OF TRUSTEES AND DIRECTORS

Perhaps the most important distinction between trustees and directors relates to the duties and liabilities the law imposes on the persons in control of each institution.[32] These duties are not uniform throughout the United States; rather, each jurisdiction determines whether trust law or corporation law will be applied to define the individuals responsible for running the entity. Thus, the stricter trust standard may be used as a measure of nonprofit corporate directors' activities; similarly, the less demanding corporate standard may be all that a trustee of a charitable trust is required to meet.

The standards to which trustees were held traditionally were somewhat stricter than those applied to corporate directors, but the current trend is to make the standards the same.[33]

---

charitable trusts and for directors of corporate charities are more similar than commonly believed." Drafters of trust instruments and corporate documents can achieve nearly the same results. The modern trust standard "less frequently operates more 'strictly' than the corporate standard.").

30   *Id.*

31   *Id.*

32   Compare *Assembly of America, Inc. v. Cafesjian,* 772 F. Supp. 2d 20 (D. D.C. 2011) (trustees held not to have violated fiduciary duties or good faith and fair dealing duties) with *In re Charles M. Blair Family Trust,* 183 P.3d 61 (2008 MT 144) (trustees violated fiduciary duties).

33   See Brody, *supra* note 95 (the modern trust standard "less frequently operates more 'strictly' than the corporate standard."); Thomas Lee Hazen & Lisa Love Hazen, "Punctilios and Nonprofit Corporate Governance—A Comprehensive Look at Nonprofit Directors' Fiduciary Duties," *University of Pennsylvania Journal of Business Law* 14 (2012): 347 ("While some more recent decisions continue the trust analogy, the general view today in the context of nonprofit corporations is to refer to principles of corporate rather than trust law.").

In *Stern v. Lucy Webb Hayes Nat'l Training School for Deaconesses and Missionaries*,[34] a hospital was established for the express charitable purpose of helping the poor and sick of the Washington, DC, area. The hospital, and later a school, was incorporated as a charitable corporation under the laws of Washington, DC. The corporate bylaws established and provided for three basic committees of the trustees that were responsible for the financial management of the hospital. During the course of approximately ten years, no required committee meetings were held.

Thus, the fiscal management of the hospital was left solely in the hands of two people who became almost autonomous in their power and control of the hospital's funds. This resulted in the trustees merely rubber-stamping the actions of those two individuals. The effect of this was to wreak havoc with the investments and budgetary functions of the institution and cause higher patient costs. Finally, in 1971, both men left the hospital's staff, and one of the trustees began an examination of the hospital's affairs. A lawsuit was commenced against the trustees for their alleged breaches of duty.

Judge Gesell, in *Stern*, noted that the law, as it relates to charitable corporations, does not fit neatly into the established common law categories of corporation or trust. He stated, however, that the modern trend is to apply corporate rather than trust principles in determining the liability of directors of charitable corporations because of the entities' close correlation to corporations in both form and substance.

If the organization you are involved with believes that it is experiencing problems with its trustees or directors, it should enlist the aid of an experienced attorney to assist in evaluating the situation and dealing with it appropriately.

CO-OPS

Cooperative corporations, or co-ops, are organizations created for the benefit of its members. A co-op is actually a form of partnership that can be structured as a trust or nonprofit corporation. When the organization is a co-op, an agreement between the participants must be drafted stating the obligations of each participant and the role each plays in the organization. For more

---

34 *Stern v. Lucy Webb Hayes Nat'l Training School for Deaconesses and Missionaries*, 381 F. Supp. 1003 (D.D.C. 1974).

information about co-ops and how to start one, see www.rd.usda.gov/files/
CIR45-14.pdf. Many states have statutes that define the rights and obligations
of the members of a co-op. You should check with an experienced attorney
when creating a co-op so that the organization complies with the laws of your
state. It would also be appropriate for you to discuss the benefits of having the
co-op structured as a nonprofit corporation or public trust, since having the
co-op organized as a business entity provides it with additional protection.
The members of a co-op that is structured as a business entity may not be
liable for the wrongful acts, omissions, or contracts of other members unless
they are authorized or approved.

CHAPTER 2

Nonprofit Organization Checklist

As discussed in the previous chapter, there are two forms available for the nonprofit organization. These forms are public trusts and the nonprofit corporation. A co-op can be created in either of these forms, though the participants should have a written agreement defining their participation. The structure of your organization will depend upon a number of considerations. Creating either of these forms is a rather simple process, but to do it right and enjoy all the advantages, it is highly recommended that you consult a competent lawyer. Of course, a lawyer's time costs money, but you can save some money if you come properly prepared. The following are some of the points you should be prepared to discuss with your lawyer.

ACCOUNTANT

Other than yourself, the most important person with whom your attorney will work is your *accountant*. The accountant will provide valuable input on the organization's financial structure, funding, capitalization, tax-exempt status, and other issues. Even we consulted with respected accountants to determine the accuracy of the tax information in this book.

BUSINESS NAME

Regardless of its form, every organization will have a name. Contact your attorney ahead of time with the proposed name of the organization. A quick inquiry to the corporation commissioner or secretary of state will establish whether the proposed name is available. Many corporation division offices have online services that could enable you to begin the process yourself. You or your attorney can reserve your chosen name until you are ready to use it. You will also have to consider whether the organization will have a special mark or logo that needs *trademark* protection. For a discussion of trademarks, see chapter 7.

STRUCTURE

It is also important to determine which form your organization will adopt since each available structure has benefits and drawbacks. The forms to consider and their pros and cons are discussed below and in chapter 1.

Cooperative Corporations

If it is determined that you will conduct your organization as a co-op, it is essential that you have a formal written agreement prepared by a skilled attorney. The more time you and the other prospective participants spend on being well prepared by discussing these details in advance of meeting with a lawyer, the less such a meeting is likely to cost you.

Following are the eight basic items of a co-op agreement that you should consider.

1. Name

As noted, every organization will have a name. Some co-ops simply use the surnames of the *principal* participants. The choice, in that case, is nothing more than the order of the names—which depends on various factors from prestige to the way the names sound in a particular order. If the organization's name does not include the participants' full names, it will be necessary to file the proposed name with the appropriate agency. Care should be taken to choose a name that is distinctive and not already in use. If the name is not distinctive, others can use it. If the name is already in use, you could be liable for trade name or trademark infringement.

2. Description of the Co-op

In describing the activity, the participants should agree on the basic scope of the activity—its requirements in regard to capital and labor, each party's individual contributions of capital and labor, and perhaps some plans regarding future growth.

3. Capital

After determining how much capital each participant will contribute, the participants must decide when it will be contributed, how to value the property contributed, and whether a participant can contribute or withdraw any property at a later date.

4. Duration

Sometimes co-ops are organized for a fixed amount of time or are automatically dissolved on certain conditions, such as the completion of a project.

5. Distribution of Funds

You can make whatever arrangement you want for distribution of funds. Although ordinarily a participant is not paid, it is possible to give an active participant a salary. Not all the earnings of the co-op need to be distributed by year's end as salary. You must work with both an experienced attorney and accountant to be sure that the co-op you create as a nonprofit organization complies with the tax law or the organization will lose its tax-exempt status. This is quite technical, and proper organizational structure and operations are very important.

6. Management

The power in the co-op can be divided many ways. All participants can be given the same voice, or some may be given more than others. A few participants might be allowed to manage the business entirely, with the remaining participants being given a vote only on specifically designated issues.

Besides voting, three other areas of management should be covered. First is the question of who can sign *checks*, place orders, or enter into contracts on behalf of the co-op. Under state laws, any participant may do these things so long as they occur in the usual course of business. Since such a broad delegation of authority can lead to confusion, it might be best to delegate this authority more narrowly. Second, it is a good idea to determine a regular date for co-op meetings. Finally, some consideration should be given to the possibility of a disagreement arising among the participants that leads to a deadlock. One way to avoid this is to distribute the voting power so as to make a deadlock impossible. In a two-person co-op, however, this would mean that one participant would be in absolute control. That might be unacceptable to the other participant. If power is divided equally among an even number of participants, as is often the case, the agreement should stipulate a neutral party or mediator who could settle any dispute and thereby avoid a dissolution of the co-op.

7. Prohibited Acts

By law, each participant owes the co-op certain duties by virtue of being an agent of the co-op. First is the duty of diligence. This means the participant must exercise reasonable care in acting as a participant. Second is a duty of obedience. The participant must obey the rules of the co-op and, most importantly, must not exceed the authority that the co-op has entrusted in him or her. Finally, there is a duty of loyalty.

A participant may not, without approval of the other participants, compete with the co-op in another organization. A participant also may not seize upon an opportunity that would be of value to the co-op without first telling the co-op about it and allowing the co-op to pursue it, if the co-op so desires. A list of prohibited acts should be made a part of the participant agreement, elaborating and expanding on these fundamental duties.

8. Dissolution and Liquidation

Dissolution identifies the legal end of the organization but need not affect its ability to continue if the participant agreement has provided for the continuation of the organization after a dissolution. Nonetheless, a dissolution will affect the arrangement because the participant who withdraws or is expelled will no longer be available.

Details as to how the organization will continue to operate should be decided before dissolution. At the time of dissolution, it may be impossible to negotiate. After a participant leaves, the co-op may need to be *reorganized* and recapitalized. Again, provisions for this should be worked out in advance if possible.

Since a nonprofit co-op may be created in the form of a nonprofit corporation or public trust, the agreement must comply with the law with respect to these organizational structures as well. If the co-op is structured as a partnership, then the partnership rules would apply, and the members should have a detailed agreement spelling out their rights and obligations. An experienced business attorney should be consulted so that the agreement contains all of the appropriate items such as those discussed above.

Not-for-Profit Corporations

Corporations are hypothetical, legal persons and, as such, are responsible for their own acts and contracts. Thus, if a visitor to a museum slips on a banana peel, if a Boy Scout leader's car negligently injures a pedestrian, or if the food served at a church social causes food poisoning, the corporation, and not its members, will be liable (assuming the proper formalities have been adhered to).

NOTE: Any individual personally responsible for a wrongful act will also be liable.

Officers and Structure

State statutes generally require a corporation to have some chief operating officer, such as a president or manager. In addition, state statutes may require other administrative officers, such as a secretary. The corporate bylaws should have a separate description for specialized officers. Many nonprofit organizations have executive directors who are responsible for the day-to-day operations of the organization. It is important to spell out the role of the executive director and determine whether that person or the president is the chief executive officer of the organization. It is also important to specify which of those individuals will be able to make the decision if a dispute arises between them. Individuals considering a position as an executive director should not be overwhelmed by the legal challenges that may arise and should realize the extraordinary rewards and benefits they are likely to obtain from serving in that role.

Capitalization

At this point, the attorney works closely with your accountant. Issues to be resolved include:

- What will be the initial capitalization or funding of the corporation?
- Will founding members make loans to the organization?
- Will grants be obtained?
- What value will be placed on assets that are contributed to the organization?
- Will contributors be entitled to treat the donations as charitable for tax purposes?

Governing Board

An initial decision must be made as to who will be on the board of directors of a corporation and how many initial directors there will be. You must also decide whether members will have the right to elect members of the board or, if there are no members, how the board will be determined. For example, it could be set up so that each year one member is reevaluated by the remaining members. That is, the remaining members can reappoint the person or appoint a replacement.

IN PLAIN ENGLISH

It is a good idea for there to be an odd number of directors in order to avoid the potential for a voting deadlock, and the IRS strongly recommends at least three directors if the organization is to qualify for tax-exempt status —and it will more carefully scrutinize organizations with fewer than three directors. Religious organizations may have as few as one director if it is a tenet of that religion.

Housekeeping

Your attorney will need to know several other details. For instance, the number of employees the organization anticipates for the coming twelve-month period must be stated on the application for a federal taxpayer ID number. You must also decide whether the organization's tax year will end on December 31 or on another date.

The following preliminary decisions must also be made: the amount of, if any, salaries for its officers or managers must be authorized; the date for the annual meeting set; a registered agent selected (generally, your attorney will assume this role); and a bank for your organization's use determined.

Employee Benefits

Be prepared to consider employee benefit plans, such as life and health insurance, pension, or other retirement plans, as well as other fringe benefits such as medical, dental, etc. Even if you do not plan to implement such programs when the corporation is created, it is nonetheless a good idea to consider whether such programs may be instituted in the future.

Tax-Exempt Status

As mentioned in chapter 1, a nonprofit corporation must apply to the Internal Revenue Service for tax-exempt status if it wishes to avoid having to pay taxes. Some states also require the organization to apply for state tax-exempt status as well. These issues will be discussed more fully in chapter 3. Further, many states also require nonprofit organizations to file with the state attorney general in order to engage in fund-raising activities. It is important for you to have your attorney determine what your state's requirements are, and it is essential for you to comply with those requirements.

Public Trusts

As discussed in chapter 1, the second type of nonprofit organization is the public trust. Rather than having the organization run by a board of directors, a public trust is run by its trustees. Essentially, the rules for appointing trustees and replacing them are the same as with nonprofit corporations. That is, public trusts may have members who may be entitled to vote, or the trustees in nonmembership trusts can serve for fixed periods, or can be reconsidered for continued service annually, bi-annually, etc. Here too it is important for the creator of the trust to work with an experienced attorney in drafting the organizational documents. Similarly, the creator of the trust will have to determine the availability of the name selected and comply with the law of the state where the trust is to be created. Devoting some time and thought to the issues identified in this chapter before meeting with the attorney selected to assist in creating the organization will be beneficial in saving a great deal of time and expense.

As you can see, there is much to discuss at the first meeting with your lawyer. A little time and thought prior to that meeting will prove to be a worthwhile investment.

CHAPTER 3

Applying for Tax-Exempt Status

A nonprofit organization that desires to obtain tax-exempt status must comply with both federal and state tax laws. The federal statute that addresses tax exemptions is section 501(c) of the Internal Revenue Code. Since accurate recordkeeping is essential when dealing with tax issues, the organization should enlist the aid of an experienced accountant or tax professional as soon as possible.

In addition to exemption from federal income tax, organizations that comply with the rules and obtain tax-exempt status may also be entitled to obtain the right to have less expensive postage available. Those organizations may also be entitled to apply for grants from the government and from other charitable organizations. In fact, there are a host of benefits available to many nonprofit tax-exempt organizations.

FEDERAL TAX EXEMPTION

The federal law that deals with exempt organizations is section 501(c). There are twelve possibilities for a nonprofit to select. In order to determine the most appropriate and comply with the law's requirements, the organization's representatives must evaluate its mission, source of funding, and a number of other factors required by the law.

501(c)(1): Tax-Exempt by Act of Congress

501(c)(1) is available to organizations that are created by an act of Congress. This would include such organization as the Smithsonian Institution, the National Gallery of Art, the United States Post Office, and the Veterans

Administration. In fact, any organization created by Congress to benefit the group Congress identified will likely be exempt from taxation under this section. The attorney general of the United States generally represents this kind of organization, though, many of them have in-house attorneys as well. It is highly unlikely that determining this type of organization's status and taxability would ever be an issue.

501(c)(2): Holding Companies for Other Nonprofits

This type of organization is created for the purpose of holding property, such as land and buildings, for the purpose of generating revenue from that property and turning that revenue over to another tax-exempt organization. It is used, for example, in situations where a church creates a nonprofit organization that owns a rental house it obtained through a donation. The revenue generated by the rental house would be turned over to the church. This type of arrangement is used for the purpose of segregating liability. That is, if someone were injured on the rental property and filed a lawsuit against it, the church would not be exposed to the potential liability for the injury.

This arrangement might also be used in situations where a nonprofit may be concerned about whether the revenue-generating property could jeopardize its tax-exempt status and, therefore, in order to avoid that situation from occurring, it might wish to create another nonprofit organization and have that organization apply for an exemption under 501(c)(2). If the newly created organization runs into problems, only it would wind up with tax liability but the principal organization would not.

When the Metropolitan Museum of Art in New York *licensed* the use of its ancient fabric design collection to the Springmaid sheet company, it received significant *royalties* from that arrangement. In fact, the royalties were so large that the museum feared that it might jeopardize its tax-exempt status. This would have been a good situation for the museum to create a new entity and have that entity elect to be taxed under section 501(c)(2) of the Internal Revenue Code.

501(c)(3): Charitable Organizations

This is likely the most popular section of the tax-exempt law. It applies to organizations created and "operated exclusively for religious, charitable, scientific, testing for public safety, literary, or educational purposes, or to foster national or international amateur sports competition . . . or for the prevention of cruelty to children or animals." This section is used by the vast majority of nonprofit organizations created in the United States.

An organization electing 501(c)(3) status cannot pay a portion of its profits to any individual. This does not prevent the organization from paying salaries to employees or paying commissions to fund-raisers so long as those commissions are reasonable for the money they raise. The organization must comply with the law regarding withholding tax for employees and fund-raisers, and the individuals who receive that money will be taxed on it as well.

Some cooperative organizations, or co-ops, have tried to function as tax-exempt entities in an effort to reduce overhead costs. To qualify as a tax-exempt organization under section 501(c)(3), an organization must be created and operated exclusively for charitable, educational, or scientific purposes.[1] Tax regulations state that museums and similar organizations are examples of exempt educational organizations.[2]

In Rev. Rul. 71–395,[3] the IRS took the position that a cooperative that did not charge admission but sold the works of its members and remitted a portion of the proceeds of the sale to the individual who created the work was not entitled to tax-exempt status, citing § 1.501(c)(3) of the regulations. The IRS apparently viewed the economic benefit to the members as sufficient to deprive the organization of its exempt status.

Subsequently, in Rev. Rul. 76–152,[4] the IRS affirmed and clarified its position. There, a group of patrons had formed an organization to promote community understanding of recent trends. The organization's sole activity was to display—and possibly sell—contemporary art in its gallery. Works selected for display were consigned by the artists, who set the prices but did not have any other control over the organization. The organization retained a 10 percent commission on sales of the works, much less than the amount charged by commercial galleries and insufficient to cover operating costs, which were mainly paid for by contributions to the organization.

The IRS took the position that the organization was not entitled to tax-exempt status as an educational organization because it served the private

---

1   See generally John D. Colombo, "In Search of Private Benefit," *Illinois Public Law and Legal Theory Research Papers Series*, no. 06-02 (March 6, 2006), available at https://ssrn.com/abstract=888811.

2   26 CFR 1.501(c)(3).

3   Rev. Rul. 71–395, 1971–2 C.B. 228 (IRS 1971).

4   Rev. Rul. 76–152, 1976–1 C.B. 151 (IRS 1976).

interests of the artists, who received 90 percent of the proceeds of sale from the works they consigned. The IRS distinguished the facts in Rev. Rul. 66–178,[5] where an organization had fostered and developed the arts by holding an art exhibit at which the works of unknown but promising artists were gratuitously displayed. Admission was charged, and a catalog was available for purchase, but none of the works were offered for sale.

In *Goldsboro Art League, Inc. v. Commissioner,*[6] the court held that two galleries displaying works for sale were tax-exempt under IRC § 501(c)(3). The galleries selected works through art juries based on their unconventional styles rather than on salability. Eighty percent of the proceeds of the sale were remitted to the artists whose work was sold, while the remaining 20 percent was retained by the organization to defray its expenses. The court noted that the primary function of those galleries was educational, and thus, their sales activities were incidental. The court held:

> In the instant case, since there are no other art museums or galleries in the area, petitioner has found difficulty attracting artists to exhibit their work without the incentive of the Art Gallery and Art Market. Petitioner has a jury to select which works will be displayed, and we find it significant that the works are chosen not for their salability but for their representation of modern trends. Exhibiting an artist's more daring works in a part of the country where there are no nearby art museums or galleries illustrates that petitioner's purpose is primarily to educate rather than to sell.
>
> Moreover, petitioner's activities with respect to the Art Market and Art Gallery must be viewed in connection with petitioner's other activities. The clear impression that we get from the record is one of petitioner's dedication to teach the public, through a variety of means, to appreciate art. We find that petitioner's sales activities are incidental to its other activities and serve the same overall objective of art education. This is not a case where the other activities are adjunct to petitioner's sales, but, rather, where petitioner's sales activities are secondary and incidental to furthering its exempt purpose.

---

5   Rev. Rul. 66–178, 1966–1 C.B. 138 (IRS 1966).
6   *Goldsboro Art League, Inc. v. Commissioner,* 75 T.C. 337 (T.C. 1980).

We are convinced, moreover, that petitioner is not operating these galleries for a profit. Petitioner retains only approximately 20 percent of the gross receipts from the sales and uses this amount to defray its expenses. A review of petitioner's books for 3 years shows that petitioner has either made no profit or, at most, a negligible one, for these years.

Finally, we reject respondent's contention that petitioner is operated for the private benefit of individuals. Firstly, we find that petitioner's purpose in operating these two galleries is art education for the benefit of the public. Secondly, the private benefit prohibited under section 501(c)(3) relates to a benefit to "designated individuals, the creator or his family, shareholders of the organization, or persons controlled, directly or indirectly, by such private interests." Sec. 1.501(c)(3)-(d)(1)(ii), Income Tax Regs. The artists exhibited in these two galleries had their works selected by a jury which these artists did not control. Similarly, the proscription against private inurement to the benefit of any shareholder or individual does not apply to unrelated third parties. Of the more than 100 artists exhibited in the two galleries, only 2 members of petitioner have exhibited their works in these galleries and neither of these members is on petitioner's board of directors.

The court in *Cleveland Creative Arts Guild v. Commissioner*[7] examined the activities of another nonprofit arts organization located in a rural area of Tennessee. The Guild, located thirty miles from the nearest gallery or museum, was similarly formed to "enhance the cultural life of the community" primarily through the operation and maintenance of art studios and classrooms. The Guild, however, sponsored seasonal art festivals and craft shows that resulted in a number of sales of works by local artists. After considering the holding in *Goldsboro*, the court found the sales activity incidental to the organization's exempt purposes.

The court first noted that the Guild conducted only seasonal, short-term sales events, while *Goldsboro* involved year-round exhibitions. Further, only about 28 percent of the exhibitors at the festival were members of the Guild,

---

7   *Cleveland Creative Arts Guild v. Commissioner*, 50 T.C. Memo (CCH) 272 (T.C. 985).

the selection committee used minimal qualifying criteria to admit works for sale, and only a 10 percent commission was retained. The sales activities were challenged in large part because advertisements for some of the festivals placed a strong commercial emphasis on the activity, but the court considered this factor inconsequential.[8]

In Priv. Ltr. Rul. 8634001,[9] another art organization dedicated to education and community awareness obtained a favorable ruling on rental and sales activity. The organization retained a 40 percent commission on works sold, a rate more typical of commercial galleries than of nonprofit organizations. Nevertheless, the IRS found that the sales and rental activity made up only a small part of the organization's art-related activities, which included sponsoring rotating exhibits, organizing trips to museums, assisting in musical and theatrical productions, and conducting seminars, lectures, workshops, and competitions.

As to some extent in *Goldsboro*, the selection of works was loosely directed toward new and progressive styles, whereas the only other gallery in the community selected works based entirely on commercial salability. All other nearby galleries were sixty to one hundred miles away. The IRS noted that the organization's rental of works to local offices resulted in greater public exposure to local artists in furtherance of the organization's goal.

It also found that *consignment* activity per se is not fatal to a nonprofit's tax-exempt status, citing Rev. Rul. 80106,[10] which upheld the tax-exempt status of a thrift shop that sold items left on consignment, as well as donated items, to support its charitable purposes. The thrift shop had met the requirements that consignment fees be negotiated as part of an arm's length transaction resulting in a reasonable percentage of the sales price and that expenditures for acquisition of inventory on consignment were, likewise, not unreasonable.

More recently, in Private Letter Ruling 201516066,[11] an artist cooperative that operated an art gallery was found not to qualify as a tax-exempt organization, though the gallery also engaged in educational and charitable activities, including providing one-day art workshops, hosting an annual 5K and

---

8   See also Jessica Pena and Alexander L.T. Reid, "A Call for Reform of the Operational Test for Unrelated Commercial Activities in Charities," *New York University Law Review* 76 (2001): 1855, 1872–1874.

9   PLR 8634001 (IRS Aug. 31, 1986).

10 Rev. Rul. 80–106, 1980–1 C.B. 113 (IRS 1980).

11 PLR 201516066 (Jan. 21, 2015).

fun run, awarding scholarships, and providing community art/artist talks and school/youth tours of the gallery. The court held:

> Providing a display and retail space for member artists and allowing each member artist to set the sales price, select the works for sale, and receive a commission promotes the private interests of the artist members. Any education of the public by display of the artwork is secondary to the promotion of the artists by operation of the co-op.

The IRS concluded that the co-op operated primarily for the private purposes of its members rather than for the public and thus did not qualify for tax-exempt status.

It is therefore clear that nonprofit organizations that provide incidental benefits for their members may obtain tax-exempt status under section 501(c)(3) so long as the organization is created primarily for the benefit of the public. If, on the other hand, the organization's primary benefit is for its members, it will not qualify under this section of the code.

A 501(c)(3) organization may not carry on propaganda activities or attempt to influence legislation. Nor can it support or oppose any candidate for office. In other words, the organization is prohibited from engaging in political activity. On May 4, 2017, President Donald Trump signed an executive order permitting churches and other religious organizations the right to make political statements that would not jeopardize the organization's tax-exempt status. It is clear that this issue will ultimately wind up in court.

The organizations that rely on this section of the Internal Revenue Code include virtually every organization created for the benefit of the public and for a charitable purpose. It is likely that the vast majority of nonprofit organizations that you are familiar with are relying on this section in order to obtain tax-exempt status. Under section 501(c)(3), the organization must fill out Form 1023, which can be obtained online from www.irs.gov.

When a nonprofit organization is created and tax-exempt status is desired, the organization must provide an accounting of its financial activity as of the date of the application. This means that organizations that have had little to no financial activity will likely not have much to disclose and the application should be straightforward. If, on the other hand, the organization's founders have been engaging in extensive activities before tax-exempt status is sought, then the accounting disclosures will be more significant. In this type of situation, it is important to work with an experienced accountant who can assist with those disclosures.

Customarily, the organization's founders will use their best efforts to fill out the application. Since the information requested is technical and since the items can be significant when reviewed by an IRS agent, it is strongly recommended that an experienced attorney assist the organization by reviewing the application and providing recommendations before it is filed with the IRS.

Once the organization receives its tax-exempt status, it will need to continue following the rules in order to maintain it. Here, too, the organization should work with experienced lawyers and accountants in order to be sure that none of its activities jeopardize its ongoing tax-exempt status.

Organizations under Section 501(c)(3) may be considered either public charities or, in some cases, private operating foundations. This is a very technical area of the tax law, and it is essential for your organization to work with experienced professionals in order to determine which of these characterizations will apply to it. The accounting requirements for private operating foundations are extraordinarily technical and much more demanding than the rules that apply to public charities. For this reason, most nonprofits try to avoid being characterized as private operating foundations, and you should have an experienced accountant or tax lawyer assist you in determining your organization's status and what it can do to comply with the law.

501(c)(4): Social Welfare Organizations

The 501(c)(4) tax exemption was created for organizations that are created exclusively for the promotion of social welfare. This would include, for example, local airports, community associations dealing with housing, parking, newspapers, and related local activities, organizations created for the purpose of preserving local traditions and architecture, and organizations created to assist in relieving unemployment such as, for example, local employment groups. This section of the code is available for those organizations that are generally created for the purpose of providing local community benefits and activities.

If your organization intends to apply for tax-exempt status under this section, it would be appropriate to have an experienced lawyer and accountant review the application before it is filed with the IRS in order to be sure that the right section is relied on and that the application complies with the law.

When applying for tax-exempt status under this section, Form 1024-A should be used. That form can be obtained from the IRS website, www.irs.gov.

This section also prohibits the organization from providing benefits to individuals other than as salaries for employees or as payment for fund-raising activities in the same manner as section 501(c)(3). It is important to realize that even though the organization is exempt from federal tax, the employees receiving salaries and the fund-raisers who are paid for their work will be required to pay tax on the income they receive. Similarly, the organization must also comply with the law by withholding payroll taxes in the same manner as any other employer.

501(c)(5): Labor, Agricultural, and Horticultural Organizations

This section is available for labor unions and nonprofit agricultural and horticultural organizations. In order to obtain tax-exempt status under this section, the organization must complete Form 1024, which is available from the IRS website, www.irs.gov.

Again, it is important to realize that even though the organization is exempt from federal tax, the employees receiving salaries and the fund-raisers who are paid for their work will be required to pay tax on the income they receive. Similarly, the organization must also comply with the law by withholding payroll taxes in the same manner as any other employer.

If your organization intends to apply for tax-exempt status under this section, it would be appropriate to have an experienced lawyer and accountant review the application before it is filed with the IRS in order to be sure that the right section is relied upon and that the application complies with the law.

501(c)(6): Business Leagues

Section 501(c)(6) is available for organizations created as business leagues such as the Rotary Club, chambers of commerce, real-estate boards, boards of trade such as the Chicago Board of Trade, and professional football leagues like the NFL. In order to obtain tax-exempt status under this section, the organization must complete Form 1024, which is available from the IRS website, www.irs.gov.

This section also prohibits the organization from providing benefits to individuals other than as salaries for employees or as payment for fund-raising activities in the same manner as section 501(c)(3). It is important to realize that even though the organization is exempt from federal tax, the employees receiving salaries and the fund-raisers who are paid for their work will be required to pay tax on the income they receive. Similarly, the organization must also comply with the law by withholding payroll taxes in the same manner as any other employer.

If your organization intends to apply for tax-exempt status under this section, it would be appropriate to have an experienced lawyer and accountant review the application before it is filed with the IRS in order to be sure that the right section is relied on and that the application complies with the law.

501(c)(7): Social and Recreational Clubs

Section 501(c)(7) is available for organizations that are created for pleasure and recreation. This includes, for example, hunting and fishing clubs, country clubs, hobby and dinner clubs, college fraternities and sororities, and homeowners' associations whose primary function is to maintain recreational facilities. In order to obtain tax-exempt status under this section, the organization must complete Form 1024, which is available from the IRS website, www.irs.gov.

This section also prohibits the organization from providing benefits to individuals other than as salaries for employees or as payment for fund-raising activities in the same manner as section 501(c)(3). It is important to realize that even though the organization is exempt from federal tax, the employees receiving salaries and the fund-raisers who are paid for their work will be required to pay tax on the income they receive. Similarly, the organization must also comply with the law by withholding payroll taxes in the same manner as any other employer.

If your organization intends to apply for tax-exempt status under this section, it would be appropriate to have an experienced lawyer and accountant review the application before it is filed with the IRS in order to be sure that the right section is relied on and that the application complies with the law.

501(c)(8): Fraternities

Fraternal beneficiary societies, orders, or associations operating under the lodge system such as the Knights of Columbus, the Knights of Pythias, and the Elks Club are covered in this section. In order to obtain tax-exempt status under this section, the organization must complete Form 1024, which is available from the IRS website, www.irs.gov. This type of organization is permitted to provide its members and their dependents with life, sickness, accident, and other insurance-like benefits.

Again, it is important to realize that even though the organization is exempt from federal tax, the employees receiving salaries and the fund-raisers who are paid for their work will be required to pay tax on the income they receive. Similarly, the organization must also comply with the law by withholding payroll taxes in the same manner as any other employer.

Here, if your organization intends to apply for tax-exempt status under this section, it would be appropriate to have an experienced lawyer and accountant review the application before it is filed with the IRS in order to be sure that the right section is relied on and that the application complies with the law.

501(c)(9): Voluntary Employees' Beneficiary Associations

Section 501(c)(9) is available for organizations that desire to provide insurance-like benefits for life, accident, and sickness to the members in a manner similar to that which is available under section 501(c)(8). This section is available for employment groups rather than fraternal organizations. In order to obtain tax-exempt status under this section, the organization must complete Form 1024, which is available from the IRS website, www.irs.gov.

This section also prohibits the organization from providing benefits to individuals other than as salaries for employees or as payment for fund-raising activities in the same manner as section 501(c)(3). It is important to realize that even though the organization is exempt from federal tax, the employees receiving salaries and the fund-raisers who are paid for their work will be required to pay tax on the income they receive. Similarly, the organization must also comply with the law by withholding payroll taxes in the same manner as any other employer.

If your organization intends to apply for tax-exempt status under this section, it would be appropriate to have an experienced lawyer and accountant review the application before it is filed with the IRS in order to be sure that the right section is relied on and that the application complies with the law.

501(c)(10): Domestic Fraternal Societies

This section is available for fraternal-style organizations, like the Shriners and the Order of the Eastern Star, which are similar to those that rely on 501(c)(8), but these organizations do not provide insurance-like benefits.

Instead, these organizations must be created for the purpose of donating to other nonprofits. This type of organization would be created for fund-raising activities by a fraternal organization when that fraternal organization wishes to have the money raised by a 501(c)(10) organization donated to it or to another nonprofit. In order to obtain tax-exempt status under this section, the organization must complete Form 1024, which is available from the IRS website, www.irs.gov.

This section also prohibits the organization from providing benefits to individuals other than as salaries for employees or as payment for fund-raising activities in the same manner as section 501(c)(3). It is important to realize that even though the organization is exempt from federal tax, the employees receiving salaries and the fund-raisers who are paid for their work will be required to pay tax on the income they receive. Similarly, the organization must also comply with the law by withholding payroll taxes in the same manner as any other employer.

If your organization intends to apply for tax-exempt status under this section, it would be appropriate to have an experienced lawyer and accountant review the application before it is filed with the IRS in order to be sure that the right section is relied on and that the application complies with the law.

501(c)(11): Teachers' Retirement Fund Associations

Exemption under section 501(c)(11) is available for local teacher retirement funds. Funds may only be obtained for this type of nonprofit from public taxation, assessments on the teaching salaries of members, and investment profits. In order to obtain tax-exempt status under this section, the organization must complete Form 1024, which is available from the IRS website, www.irs.gov.

This section also prohibits the organization from providing benefits to individuals other than as salaries for employees and retirement benefits to members. It is important to realize that even though the organization is exempt from federal tax, the employees receiving salaries or members receiving pension benefits will be required to pay tax on the income they receive. Similarly, the organization must also comply with the law by withholding payroll taxes in the same manner as any other employer.

If your organization intends to apply for tax-exempt status under this section, it would be appropriate to have an experienced lawyer and accountant review the application before it is filed with the IRS in order to be sure that the right section is relied on and that the application complies with the law.

501(c)(12): Benevolent Life Insurance Companies, Mutual Ditch or Irrigation Companies, Cooperative Telephone Companies, and Cooperative Electric Companies

Section 501(c)(12) is available for organizations that are local life insurance organizations, mutual irrigation companies, and cooperative telephone companies, and only if 85 percent of the income is collected from the members to pay expenses. This is a very limited form of nonprofit status that is only available for a small group of nonprofits. In order to obtain tax-exempt status under this section, the organization must complete Form 1024, which is available from the IRS website, www.irs.gov.

This section also prohibits the organization from providing benefits to individuals other than as salaries for employees or as payment for fund-raising activities in the same manner as section 501(c)(3). It is important to realize that even though the organization is exempt from federal tax, the employees receiving salaries and the fund-raisers who are paid for their work will be required to pay tax on the income they receive. Similarly, the organization must also comply with the law by withholding payroll taxes in the same manner as any other employer.

If your organization intends to apply for tax-exempt status under this section, it would be appropriate to have an experienced lawyer and accountant review the application before it is filed with the IRS in order to be sure that the right section is relied on and that the application complies with the law.

Since federal tax-exempt status is very important for nonprofit organizations, and since the application can be difficult and the requirements for applying are very technical, it is important for the organization to obtain the services of an experienced accountant and attorney before filing an application. In addition, the organization must continue to comply with the law in order to retain its federal exemption. For this reason, it is strongly recommended that the organization continue to work with experienced professionals so that none of its activities will jeopardize its federal status.

CHAPTER 4

Developing Your Fund-raising Plan and Fund-raising

A fund-raising plan is essential to a nonprofit organization. This chapter discusses some of the issues every nonprofit should consider when developing the fund-raising plan and the legal requirements, pitfalls, and opportunities of fund-raising as a nonprofit. Since fund-raising is a vast and complex subject that continuously changes, it could be considered in a multivolume text. We will discuss some of the key issues which nonprofits should consider here, but in order to be sure that you are taking advantage of every fund-raising opportunity, you may wish to consult with a fund-raising expert, and you should also read other books that address nonprofit fund-raising. For an excellent discussion of this subject with respect to New York nonprofits, see *Managing the Future: A Leader's Guide*, written and edited by Susan Crawford. The purpose of this book is not to educate the reader on how to raise funds; rather, this book is intended to identify many of the legal issues which may arise during fund-raising activities.

In order for a nonprofit to be able to fulfill its mission, it must obtain funds. It is, therefore, essential for a nonprofit to have an appropriate fund-raising plan from the day it begins operation and throughout its ongoing activities.

Some nonprofits hire experts to assist in developing the plan, and the experts are paid for the work they perform either in advance of their activities or as a percentage of what they are able to earn for the nonprofit. It is essential for the organization to have an appropriate contract with any fund-raising professional it deals with. This contract should be prepared by an experienced attorney. The lawyer should cover the key issues of the relationship including compensation, responsibility, authority, termination, and a myriad of other issues that an experienced attorney will likely point out.

Customarily, the fund-raising plan will determine the most appropriate source of funds and the best way to obtain those funds. Generally, the fund-raising plan will begin with a brainstorming meeting between the interested nonprofit and, if an expert is involved, the expert as well. At the brainstorming session, the parties will present ideas and recommendations for individuals and organizations that might be willing to contribute to the nonprofit. In addition, other fund-raising opportunities should be discussed. These should include, among other things, government organizations such as the National Endowment for the Arts and Humanities, state organizations such as state arts and humanities committees or commissions, and private organizations such as the Ford Foundation, Rockefeller Foundation, etc. In fact, there is a catalog of organizations that donate money to nonprofit organizations. See foundationcenter.org and www.cfda.gov. It would be a good idea for someone to take *minutes* of the meeting and for the parties to agree that a discussion at the meeting should be kept confidential so that the material developed will remain within that organization.

All recommendations should be evaluated and, if implementation is appropriate, then it is necessary to have the plan properly approved by the organization. In order to take advantage of these opportunities, someone must prepare an appropriate proposal complying with the rules of the organization to which a request is made. There are specialists who can assist in preparing those proposals, though the cost of hiring a specialist can be significant and there are no guarantees that the proposal will be successful. If the organization's members can develop proposals on their own, there can be substantial savings.

Other fund-raising activities include donations that provide the donor with tax benefits if structured properly. The donation can be cash, marketable securities, or merchandise. If marketable securities are used, then the donor may be permitted to deduct the fair market value of the security when donated, even though it was acquired for significantly less money. The nonprofit may then retain those securities until it actually needs the cash or sell the securities for their then–fair market value. Of course, the nonprofit will need to work with a licensed securities dealer in order to comply with the securities laws. It should be noted that if the securities are not listed on a national exchange or publicly traded, they will likely be difficult to sell since there is rarely a market for securities that are not publicly traded, and a nonprofit should be sensitive to this issue when accepting a donation of securities.

If tangible property is to be donated, then the donor must obtain an appropriate appraisal with the value of the property; this appraisal must comply with IRS Form 8283 if the donor wishes to obtain a tax deduction for that donation. When the tangible property is donated to a nonprofit and that tangible property is intended to, and does, help the nonprofit fulfill its charitable function, then the deduction that the donor can obtain is higher than donations of property that are unrelated to the charitable activity. For example, if a person donates land to a church so that it can expand its parking facility, then the percentage of the charitable deduction will be greater than if the donation consisted of tables and chairs that the church did not need. In this situation, the church would need to dispose of the furniture in order to obtain cash, which it could use. The percentage deduction the donor of the furniture would receive would be a lower percentage than that which the donor of the land could obtain.

When intangibles, such as *patents*, copyrights, trademarks, and other forms of *intellectual property* or rights are donated, there is a similar rule. The donors of intangible items will need to obtain appraisals, comply with the tax laws by using IRS Form 8283, and determine whether the intangible item is for the organization's charitable purpose, in which case even the percentage of the fair market value that can be deducted will be higher, or whether the intangible property is not related to the organization's charitable function, in which event the percentage deduction will be lower. If the intangible is generating income for the donor—as, for example, when a copyright is licensed to a user for a royalty payment—then the donor might be better off arranging for a portion of the income to be donated to the charity. This can be accomplished by having the cash royalty formally assigned to the nonprofit in a written agreement, or it can be accomplished informally when the donor determines that a cash donation would be appropriate. If this type of arrangement is contemplated, then it would be a good idea for the donor to consult an experienced accountant or tax preparer in order to comply with the tax laws and obtain the maximum benefits from the donation.

CHARITABLE AUCTIONS

Other fund-raising activities include parties, charity auctions, and charity balls. Charity auctions have become extremely popular. Customarily, the person or persons who chair this function obtain donations from members, supporters, or others in the community of merchandise, vacation packages, home dinners, use of the donor's vacation home, services such as free accounting services for a limited period, and the like. These items are then auctioned, either in a silent auction where the item is identified on a sheet of paper and the participants write down their bid, or in a conventional auction, where the participants engage in open bidding. The donor is permitted to deduct a percentage of the fair market value of the item to be donated, and the successful bidder is permitted to deduct the difference between the value of the item obtained and the higher amount paid for it. If an item was created by the donor, then the donor is only permitted to take a charitable deduction for the cost of materials involved and not its fair market value. If services are involved, the donor is not permitted to take a tax deduction for the fair market value of those services, either. All the donor is allowed to deduct is the actual value of out-of-pocket expenses paid for in providing those services.

It is important for the organization to keep accurate records for these events since there can be significant problems if, for example, the successful bidder deducts the full amount paid even though the item obtained is worth 75 percent of that price. In this case, the only legitimate deduction would be 25 percent, not 100 percent. In addition, since the item is not being used for the charity's mission, then the amount that the person donating the item may deduct is not 100 percent of its value but rather a lesser percentage than if the item were used for the charitable mission.

Auctions themselves have a number of legal issues which should be considered. That is, when an item is purchased at an auction, the buyer should understand that the item is being sold as is. The organization should make this clear when the auction begins and in any auction catalog used. In addition, the individuals participating in an auction should realize that the bid is the offer and that the auctioneer is merely soliciting offers that the auctioneer may accept. Once the auctioneer accepts a bid, a binding contract is made, and the bidder is obligated to honor that contract. The organization may enforce the contract if the bidder refuses to pay. Auction practices and legal issues are quite technical. They are beyond the scope of this text, but those who are interested in obtaining more information about them may wish to consult *Art Law in a Nutshell, Vol. 6*, published by the West Publishing Group.

PRECIOUS METAL COLLECTION

Another clever fund-raising idea involves the use of precious metals. Here, the organization advises its members or supporters that it is commencing a fund-raising activity whereby supporters are urged to check their jewelry boxes, drawers, and other storage places in their homes and offices in order to find items of precious metal that had been purchased in the past and is no longer functional or desirable. For example, broken gold chains, single earrings, broken rings, and the like. These items that are no longer desired may be donated to the charity for its benefit. The charity can then have the items appraised by companies that purchase precious metals, and the charity can receive cash for the donated precious metals. The donor is permitted to deduct the amount the charity receives for the precious metal from the donor's taxes, and the charity obtains the cash benefit. In this situation, donors are obtaining tax deductions for items that are virtually useless to the donor and that were purchased years ago, likely at prices far less than the current fair market value of the precious metal, and the charity is able to obtain a significant cash benefit from the donation. This fund-raising activity can be extremely lucrative for everyone involved. In fact, it is not only available for discarded parts of jewelry, but it can also be used for coins, such as dimes and quarters that were made of silver at one time; flatware that may no longer be in vogue; and other types of precious metals that the donor no longer desires to retain. If coins are involved, the organization should determine whether the precious metal value or the numismatic value is higher, and the organization should attempt to obtain the highest return for that item. Section 331 of Title 18 of the United States Code prohibits fraudulently altering or defacing coins coined at the mints of the United States if you represent to others that the coin is something other than the altered coin that it is. It does not prohibit the sale of precious metal coins, nor does it appear to prohibit having them melted down. Similarly, if the flatware, hollowware, or other precious metal items are involved, the organization should determine whether the meltdown value is equal to or less than the value of the artistic view of the item, and the higher return should be obtained.

The only limitation is that the activity must be able to attract attention, cause participants to be willing to donate to the charity, and the activity must comply with the tax law. Nonprofit organizations are continuously developing new methods for generating funds so that they can continue to provide the public benefits they desire. PBS, for example, periodically has fund-raising programs where donors are given gifts such as recordings, books, prints, and the like in exchange for their donations. The Boy Scouts of America provided donors with plaques and badges in exchange for their donations, and religious organizations such as churches and synagogues provide their donors with afterlife benefits for their donations.

Many nonprofits encourage donations of money or property through an individual's estate plan. Thus, the individual may donate money or property through a will or an afterlife trust. In this event, the document used must comply with the law for afterlife donations. That is, virtually every state requires that wills unambiguously define the donation and that they comply with the law of the state where the donor resides when the will is signed. If money or property is to be disposed of through either a will or a trust, then an experienced attorney should be consulted to be sure that the donation is what the donor intends and that it complies with the laws of the donor's residence as well. Customarily, this means that a will must be witnessed by at least two individuals, and in many states, it must also be notarized. State law should also be consulted to determine the requirements for trusts that are used as will substitutes.

If the donation to a nonprofit cannot be realized because the objective is impossible, then the law in the vast majority of states is that the closest objective should be used. This is known as the cy pres doctrine. If, for example, the donor states in the will that $100,000 should be donated to a historical society for the purpose of creating a new building but by the time the donation is made the cost of a new building would far exceed the $100,000, then the court in which the will is probated may allow the money to be used by the organization to either improve or expand its current building. Likewise, if a gift is made to a charity that no longer exists, the cy pres doctrine will allow the court where the will is probated to give the gift to another organization that has the closest purpose to the original organization.

Since the vast majority of taxpayers pay taxes on a calendar year, it is customary for nonprofits to solicit donations at the end of each year. This is because the individual will be able to take a deduction for the amount donated that year even if the money is donated on the very last day of the year. That is, the donor will receive the full deduction for the year even though the donor will have had the benefit of that money for every day of the year except the last. If a donor sends a check to a charity on New Year's Eve, then the donor will be permitted to take a tax deduction for the amount sent even though the charity will not receive that check or be able to cash it until the following year. Many donors take advantage of this process.

All of an organization's fund-raising activities must comply with the law including both tax and business law. That is, the organization should not misrepresent its activities or the benefits that can be achieved by the organization. The organization's activities should be accurately described, and they must comply with all appropriate laws, such as not providing excessive alcoholic beverages at a function, or any alcoholic beverages to underage individuals, etc. In addition, the fund-raising activities must also comply with the tax law. If a benefit is given to the donor, such as a gift or a party, then the amount that may be deducted must be reduced by the value of the gift or benefit received by the donor.

BORROWING FROM BANKS

Some organizations may find that they need more funding than is available from grants or donations. In that event, the organization may be forced to borrow money from financial institutions. Before a financial institution lends money to a nonprofit, the financial institution will customarily require a nonprofit to prepare a financial statement. If the financial institution believes that the nonprofit organization's assets are not adequate to secure the loan, then the financial institution will require guarantees from individuals or other organizations so that the financial institution can be sure the loan is repaid. In situations such as this, it is important for the nonprofit to work with an experienced business lawyer so that all parties involved are aware of the risks and benefits in the arrangement.

TAX SHELTERS

Some nonprofits have come up with schemes that may be highly questionable. For example, some museums were involved in highly questionable tax shelters whereby individuals purchased an entire run of limited edition prints or editioned sculptures for some cash and a large promissory note. The artwork was donated to pre-identified museums, and the donors claimed huge tax deductions. The IRS challenged these programs as abusive and improper. This resulted in having the deductions disallowed, and the organizations involved were sanctioned. This subject will be discussed more fully in chapter 14 as well.

Nonprofits should avoid becoming involved in questionable activities since they are very risky for the individuals involved and result in negative publicity for the organization as well. If something appears to be too good to be true, like highly leveraged tax shelters, it likely is not true.

CHAPTER 5

Liability of Members and Organizational Liability

Nonprofit organizations are created for the purpose of benefiting society. Unfortunately, some organizations have experienced significant problems because they did not establish appropriate safeguards to protect the public from unscrupulous individuals who take advantage of the opportunity provided by an organization to achieve inappropriate and, in many cases, unlawful objectives. In this chapter, we will discuss some of the more egregious examples of this type of problem. The chapter will also cover situations in which the organization itself may exceed the bounds of acceptable conduct.

ORGANIZATIONAL LIABILITY FOR THE WRONGFUL ACTS OF INDIVIDUALS

Individuals will be liable for their own wrongful acts and for omissions to act when those omissions result in injury to others. In addition, if the individual commits the act or omission within the scope of a nonprofit's activity, the organization may be liable. Further, if the organization approves the activity, or does not take steps to correct it, the organization will be responsible for the wrongdoer's conduct and significant liability can result. In fact, in *Kerry Lewis v. Boy Scouts of America*, decided in 2010, the Boy Scouts were held liable for $18.5 million. The damage awards in these cases are significant.

In recent years there have been a number of situations in which individuals have engaged in unlawful activities that resulted in significant organizational liability. A very unfortunate example of this occurred in 1997. In *Lourim v. Swensen*, a Boy Scout leader was sued for sexually assaulting a child in his Boy Scout troop. Unfortunately, the leader was a pedophile who had a questionable past, and the troop provided him the opportunity to sexually abuse children. The individual was sued, and because he had problems in the past, which it was claimed should have been identified by the local Scout Council, the council was held liable as well. In fact, because the Boy Scouts of America did not then have an appropriate program to protect their members from pedophiles such as this, it was also held liable.

Regrettably, this is not the only instance of this kind of problem. In fact, in *T. R. v. BSA*, which was decided in 2008, there was a similar problem. In this case, the plaintiff sued both the City of the Dalles and the Cascade Pacific Council because of the wrongful activities of a Boy Scout leader named James Donald Tannehill. The message was clearly conveyed to the Boy Scouts that appropriate safeguards are essential if the scouting movement wishes to continue functioning, and the Boy Scouts got that message.

Once the organization realized the problem, it took steps to provide a safe environment for all of its members. Today, the Boy Scouts of America has one of the best programs to protect the youth involved in its organization. No child is allowed to be with an adult unless there are two adults present. In addition, every adult is required to take a youth protection course before registering as an adult leader and before regularly renewing that registration. Other safeguards such as requiring restrooms to be segregated for use by adults and youth have been incorporated into the program. In fact, the Boy Scouts of America now allows girls to participate in the program, and the organization has begun developing additional rules to provide the safest environment possible for all of the youths and adults involved in the program.

Organizations such as the Boy Scouts, the Church of Jesus Christ of Latter-Day Saints, the Catholic Church, Jewish synagogues, and schools have been involved in a number of high-profile cases. In fact, there are a number of cases in which the damage awards were so significant that the organizations' existence has been put in jeopardy. In 2004, the Roman Catholic Archdiocese of Portland, Oregon, was forced to file *bankruptcy* because of the problems caused by pedophile priests. In fact, the archdiocese wound up being liable for over $53 million in *damages*. The amounts involved in these suits are often staggering and can result in the loss of important charitable organizations that were created for the purpose of benefiting society.

ISSUES TO CONSIDER

Clergy malpractice has occurred throughout the United States, and it is important for organizations to establish safeguards to prevent its reoccurrence. In fact, virtually every religious denomination has experienced some problems. When an orthodox rabbi used his position to seduce young women in his synagogue, the organization forced him to resign and relocate. Unfortunately, the remediation occurred after the fact and, as a result, the youngsters involved experienced serious traumas. In August 2018, a prominent Catholic cardinal was forced to resign from his position because it was alleged that he sexually abused minors and adults for decades. Despite the fact that the religious organizations did resolve the situation, financially there is nothing that can be done to undo this type of wrong. Safeguards are essential.

Even law schools have experienced problems. Some time ago, a law professor who became a dean at a prominent California law school was found to have used his position to obtain sexual favors from students in exchange for grades. Here too, the school took steps to remediate the problem, but regrettably, they occurred after the fact. Politicians have also misused their prestige to obtain sexual favors. In fact, it is now well known that many of our prominent presidents have misused their positions to obtain sexual favors and other improper returns.

It is clear that nonprofits must take steps to provide safe environments for their members and for those with whom they interact. The Boy Scouts have invested a great deal of time and resources in creating a safe environment for everyone involved in their program. The Catholic Church, the LDS church, and other organizations that have experienced problems have also integrated safeguards into their programs.

AGENCY

Nonprofit organizations are responsible for the acts and omissions of their employees, volunteers, members, and others who participate in its activities and may be responsible for many of the wrongful acts of their *independent contractors* as well. The law in this area is well established.

Authority

The nonprofit organization as principal will be liable to third parties for its agent's breach of contract only if the agent is acting within the scope of the agent's authority. Employees and volunteers are agents of their employers. Members and others who participate in the activities may also be agents of the nonprofit organization if they are acting on behalf of the nonprofit organization or with the nonprofit organization's authority. The law recognizes three different types of *agency* authority—actual, apparent, and inherent.

Actual authority is what the nonprofit organization intentionally confers upon the agent either by written or oral agreement. This authority may vary considerably. At one extreme, the agreement might include a power of attorney that grants the agent absolute authority to contract on behalf of the nonprofit organization. This is not the customary relationship between agent and nonprofit organization. Generally, the nonprofit organization gives the agent the authority to negotiate contracts but reserves the right to accept or refuse the contract. Sometimes, the nonprofit organization may limit the agent's authority to negotiating contracts for specific events only, such as securing an event space or procuring a grant. The agent's authority may also be confined to a particular geographical area, such as North America.

The agent's actual authority to act on behalf of the nonprofit organization need not always be expressed explicitly—sometimes it may be implied from circumstances. Implied actual authority is what the nonprofit organization, as principal, intentionally or inadvertently allows the agent to believe he or she possesses. If, for example, the agreement with the agent expressly limits the agent's authority to negotiation with California restaurants but the nonprofit organization has customarily allowed the agent to negotiate worldwide, then the agent probably does have implied actual authority to negotiate with any restaurant in the world. In this example, the agent may also have apparent authority to act.

Apparent authority is authority the nonprofit organization has not actually granted to the agent but that the nonprofit organization indicates to a third party has been granted to the agent. Thus, if the nonprofit organization leads a particular event space coordinator to believe that the agent is authorized to negotiate on the nonprofit organization's behalf, even if that coordinator is outside the scope of the agency contract, the nonprofit organization will be responsible for the agent's negotiations with that particular event space coordinator. It should be emphasized that apparent authority exists only in dealings with the third party to whom the agent's authority has been stated. A fourth party cannot allege the agent's apparent authority because of hearing about it from the third party.

Finally, an agent may have *inherent authority* to act. This type of authority encompasses all acts and duties that are customarily permitted to an agent while carrying out an agreed-upon responsibility. The scope of an agent's inherent authority depends upon whether a person is a *general agent* or a *special agent*. The distinction between these two types of agents is based on the agent's status, especially in regard to the duration of the agent's relationship with the nonprofit organization.

A general agent is authorized to act in a series of transactions involving continuous service. A special agent, on the other hand, is authorized to act in a single transaction only, or possibly in a short series of transactions not involving continuous service. The general agent is usually considered to have inherent authority to act on behalf of the principal in all matters connected with the job the agent has been hired to do. The special agent's inherent authority, on the other hand, is limited to specific acts dictated by the principal's instructions or necessarily implied from the act to be done. Agents that are retained for a single project would be considered special agents. The agent's inherent authority, therefore, would probably not extend beyond those acts actually or apparently authorized. Should the agent be in the continuous employment of the nonprofit organization—and therefore a general agent— the inherent authority would encompass all acts customarily associated with the nonprofit organization's agents.

Ratification

Ratification is an important concept when dealing with the acts of an agent. The term describes affirmation or confirmation by a principal of a previously unauthorized act by an agent. By ratifying, the principal affirms the unauthorized act and is legally bound by it as if it had been initially authorized. Thus, although the nonprofit organization will be liable for any of the agent's acts for which the agent has actual, apparent, or inherent authority, the principal will not be liable for unauthorized acts unless they are ratified.

Ratification may be express or implied from any act, words, or course of conduct that tend to show the principal's intent to ratify. Even silence may constitute ratification. If, for example, a nonprofit organization has full knowledge of a contract executed without authority by an agent and accepts the benefits of the contract, the nonprofit organization may have ratified the act and is therefore bound to the contract.

Disclosure

The agent alone will be liable to a third party for breach of contract if the agent did not have authority or if the act was not ratified. Where the act was authorized or ratified, the agent, as well as the nonprofit organization, may be liable depending upon whether the nonprofit organization (and thus the agency relationship) was fully disclosed, partially disclosed, or not disclosed. If the agency relationship was *fully disclosed*, generally the nonprofit organization alone will be a party to the contract and is thus liable for its breach. As a general rule, the agent will be liable as well, if the nonprofit organization was partially disclosed or undisclosed. The nonprofit organization is *partially disclosed* if the agent reveals that he or she is acting as an agent but does not say on whose behalf, or if the nonprofit organization is named, but there is no indication of an agency relationship. The nonprofit organization is *undisclosed* when the agent does not name the nonprofit organization or indicate the agency relationship, but instead appears to the third party to be acting alone. If both the agent and nonprofit organization are liable for the same breach, the third party cannot sue them both but must instead elect to sue one or the other.

Employees and Volunteers

The liability of a nonprofit organization for an agent's torts, or wrongful acts, is determined, in part, by the nature of the agent's employment or volunteer activities—that is, by whether the agent is legally considered to be an independent contractor or a servant. The term *servant*, in the legal sense, means an employee or volunteer over whom an employer has more control than the employer has over an independent contractor. If the nonprofit organization retains only the right to control or approve the end result of the agent's activities and leaves the means to the agent's discretion, the agent is probably an independent contractor. If the nonprofit organization retains the right of control and approval over most of someone's activities and decisions, the law will probably regard that person as a servant, whether or not the nonprofit organization actually exercises the right of control or approval. Consultants are almost always independent contractors, though other people hired by a nonprofit organization (such as secretaries and professional staff) would more likely be considered servants. Many nonprofit organizations have volunteers, members, and donors. These individuals might be characterized as servants or independent contractors depending on the level of control the nonprofit organization has over their activities.

The nonprofit organization is liable for the servant's torts, or wrongful acts, that were within the scope of employment. For example, if a Boy Scout leader injures a youth while engaged in Scouting activities, the nonprofit organization will likely be liable—even though the nonprofit organization did not authorize or ratify the bad behavior. The nonprofit organization will generally not be liable for the torts of an independent contractor, but there are exceptions. First, the principal will be liable for any torts of the independent contractor that involve nondelegable duties. These are duties that are so important to the public welfare that the principal is legally responsible for their proper performance even if that performance is delegated to an independent contractor. For example, a nonprofit organization would be liable for not paying payroll withholding taxes even if the nonprofit organization delegated responsibility to its accountant to see that taxes were paid. Similarly, a nonprofit organization that publishes defamatory literature will be liable even if a private detective was hired to check out the accuracy of the facts.

Fraud and deceit are other circumstances in which the nonprofit organization will be liable for the acts of an agent if the nonprofit organization has authorized the agent to make misrepresentations to a third party. Likewise, a nonprofit organization could be liable for not exercising due care in hiring or retaining an agent. For example, if the nonprofit organization continues to employ an agent known to respond violently, the nonprofit organization may be liable to others hurt by the agent. The other circumstance in which principals can be liable for the acts of an agent—ultrahazardous activities, such as the use of explosives—rarely concern nonprofit organizations.

Termination of Agency

The authority of the agent to act on behalf of the nonprofit organization ends with the termination of the relationship. By law, the relationship automatically terminates

- upon the death or loss of capacity of either the agent or the nonprofit organization;
- when the goal of the agency becomes impossible to achieve;
- once the purpose of the relationship has been fulfilled; or
- when the time period for which the agency was created has lapsed.

The agency can generally be terminated voluntarily if the nonprofit organization revokes or if the agent renounces the agency relationship. The parties are generally free to revoke or renounce at any time, regardless of whether the agency is governed by a contract since the agency relationship is consensual. However, if a contract is involved, termination of the agency may result in liability for its breach. If, for example, the contract calls for the agency to last for one year, either party is free to terminate prior to that time—but not without incurring liability for damages.

The only exception to the rule of voluntary termination is an agency relationship that involves *a power coupled with an interest*. In this situation, neither party may terminate prior to the expiration of the interest. A power coupled with an interest exists when the agent has a vested interest in the thing or property involved in the agreement. For example, a grant writer might have a power coupled with an interest if the nonprofit organization has contracted with the grant writer for a commission based on the success of the grant proposal. The agent's power to negotiate or execute contracts for that work would be coupled with an ownership interest, and the agent's power would be irrevocable. When an agent is compensated simply for acting as an agent, as is the case when an agent receives a commission for negotiating a donation, there is no power coupled with an interest, since the agent does not have an interest in the donation itself. A mere interest in the proceeds from the sale is not sufficient to make the power irrevocable. The concept of a power coupled with an interest is extremely complex, and a lawyer should be consulted if an irrevocable agency is desired or involved.

When the agency is terminated, the nonprofit organization must give *actual notice* to third parties who have dealt with the agent and *reasonable notice* to third parties who have knowledge of the agency but who have not actually dealt with the agent. This is assuming the agent is a general agent, such as one who has been hired to represent the nonprofit organization on an ongoing basis. Reasonable notice means reasonable efforts to notify these third parties, whether or not the efforts succeed and the third parties actually receive notice of the termination. The nonprofit organization is not required to give notice to third parties that have neither dealt with the general agent nor know of the relationship. If the nonprofit organization is required to give notice but fails to do so, the nonprofit organization remains liable for the acts of the agent even though that agent's authority has, in fact, been terminated. The nonprofit organization is not required to give notice of termination of a special agency, a situation in which the agent has merely been hired for a single project or to accomplish a single goal. Third parties who deal with a special agent do so at their own risk.

LIABILITY WAIVERS

Many nonprofits require their members and participants to sign agreements whereby the individual waives any claims against the organization. These documents are frequently drafted so as to claim to insulate the organization, its officers, and others involved with it from liability for any act or omission. The attorneys who prepare these documents attempt to cover every possible situation, but it is likely that they would be considered overly broad and "unconscionable" if they are used to insulate an organization or its staff from liability for intentional wrongful acts.

If your organization is considering the use of an agreement such as this, it should consult with an experienced attorney who can advise on the enforceability of liability waivers in your state and provide you with a contract that is more likely to be enforceable in the event it is ever needed. It is better for a nonprofit organization to have agreements with its members and other participants that comply with the laws in effect in the states in which it functions rather than to have its agreements struck down when enforcement is necessary.

CONCLUSION

The lesson to be learned from these and the numerous other cases that involve individuals who engage in unsavory activities and expose their organizations to significant liability for those wrongful acts is that safeguards must be clearly established when the organization is created. Those safeguards must also be continued throughout the organization's ongoing activities, and the organization must periodically update those safeguards. In order to avoid having your organization become the next headline for a case involving a wrongdoer, you and the others involved in your organization must continuously evaluate its activities and upgrade the safeguards that protect everyone involved with the organization.

CHAPTER 6

Contracts

Contracts are an essential part of virtually every organization, for-profit and nonprofit alike. Clearly, the entire field of contract law cannot be covered here but, by becoming aware of some of the ramifications of contract law, you will see where you need to be cautious.

CONTRACT BASICS

A contract is a legally binding promise or set of promises. The law requires that the parties to a contract perform the promises they have made to each other. In the event of nonperformance—usually called a breach—the law provides remedies to the injured party. For the purposes of this discussion, it will be assumed that the contract is between two people, though it frequently involves nonprofit organizations as well. It should be noted that when nonprofit organizations are involved, there are additional considerations, such as whether the person acting on behalf of the nonprofit has appropriate authority, how that authority must be evidenced, and, regardless of authority, whether that individual's act will be deemed within the appropriate scope of the nonprofit's activity. For more on the topic of authority, see chapter 5. These issues complicate the analysis. You should discuss these issues with your organization's attorney.

The three basic elements of every contract are the *offer*, the *acceptance*, and the *consideration*. To illustrate these elements, suppose a salesperson shows a customer a copy machine at an office supply store and suggests that he or she buy it (the offer). The customer says he or she likes it and wants it (the acceptance). They agree on a price (the consideration). That is the basic framework, but a great many variations can be played on that theme.

TYPES OF CONTRACTS

Contracts may be express or implied. They may be oral or written. There are generally at least two types of contracts that must be in writing if they are to be legally enforceable:

1. any contract that, by its terms, cannot be completed in less than one year, and
2. any contract that involves the sale of goods for over $500.

Express Contracts

An express contract is one in which all the details are spelled out. It can be either oral or written. If you are going to the trouble of expressing contractual terms, you should put your understanding in writing. For example, you might make a contract with a retail store for six dozen gallons of apple cider to be delivered to you on October 1, at a price of $1.75 per gallon, to be paid within thirty days of receipt. This scenario is fairly straightforward. If either party fails to live up to any material part of the contract, a breach has occurred. The other party may withhold performance of his or her obligation until receiving assurance that the breaching party will perform. In the event no such assurance is forthcoming, the aggrieved party may have a cause of *action* and sue for breach of contract.

If the apple cider is delivered on October 15, but you had advertised the availability of the special apple cider at your charitable function during the week of October 1, time was an important consideration, and you would not be required to accept the late shipment. If time is not a material consideration, then, even with the slight delay, this probably would be considered substantial performance, and you would have to accept the delivery.

Implied Contracts

Implied contracts are usually not reduced to writing and need not be very complicated. An example might be if you call a supplier to order five boxes of computer paper without making any express statement that you will pay for the paper. The promise to pay is implied in the order and is enforceable when the paper is delivered.

With implied contracts, however, things can often become a lot stickier. Supposing an individual arranges for a religious choral group to perform at the individual's party and the choral group spends a great deal of time rehearsing and performing for that person. The individual requesting the service enjoys the music, invites numerous friends, and is overheard saying that the presentations were fantastic. Is there an implied contract to pay for that service in this arrangement? That depends on whether your organization customarily provides this kind of free service, particularly when it must spend significant resources in providing it.

UNDERSTANDING CONTRACT PRINCIPLES

In order to understand the principles of offer, acceptance, and consideration, we will examine them in the context of several potential situations for hypothetical organization president Pat Smith. Smith is an automobile dealer who has an impressive collection of vintage cars in mint condition. Let us look at the following situations and see whether an enforceable contract comes into existence.

- At a cocktail party, Jones expresses an interest in Smith's cars. "It looks like the market value of your cars keeps going up," Jones tells Smith. "I'm going to buy one while I can still afford it."

  Is this a contract? If so, what are the terms of the offer—the particular car, the specific price? No, this is not really an offer that Smith can accept. It is nothing more than an opinion or a vague expression of intent.
- Brown offers to pay $14,000 for one of Smith's cars that she saw in an auto show several weeks ago. At the show, it was listed at $14,500, but Smith agrees to accept the lower price.

  Is this an enforceable contract? Yes! Brown has offered, in unambiguous terms, to pay a specific amount for a specific car, and Smith has accepted the offer. A binding contract exists.
- One day, Jones shows up at Smith's car lot and sees a particular car for which he offers $14,500. Smith accepts and promises to transfer the title the following week, at which time Jones will pay for it. An hour later, Brown shows up. She likes the same car and offers Smith $16,000 for it.

  Can Smith accept the later offer? No—a contract exists with Jones. An offer was made and accepted. The fact that the object has not yet been delivered or paid for does not make the contract any less binding.

- Green discusses certain renovations he would like Smith to perform on a particular car Smith has just acquired. He offers to pay $16,000 for the car if the final product is satisfactory to him. Green approves preliminary sketches, and Smith completes the work. But when Green arrives to pick up his car, he refuses to accept it because it does not satisfy him.

Is there a contract in this case? Green is making the offer in this case, but the offer is conditional upon his satisfaction with the completed work. Smith can only accept the offer by producing something that meets Green's subjective standards—a risky proposition. There is no enforceable contract for payment until such time as Green indicates that the completed work is satisfactory.

If Green comes to Smith's car lot and says that the car is satisfactory but then, when Smith delivers it, says he has changed his mind, it is too late. The contract became binding at the moment he indicated the work to be satisfactory. If he then refuses to accept it, he would be breaching his contract.

PROVING AN AGREEMENT

Contracts are enforceable only if they can be proven. All the hypothetical examples mentioned could have been oral contracts, but a great amount of detail is often lost in the course of remembering a conversation. The best practice, of course, is to get it in writing. The function of a written contract is not only that of proof, but also to make very clear the understanding of the parties regarding the agreement and the terms of the contract.

Some organizations prefer to do business strictly on the basis of a handshake, particularly with individuals and business with whom they regularly deal. The assumption seems to be that the best relations are those based upon mutual trust alone. Although there may be some validity to this, organizations really should put all agreements in writing. Far too many trusting people have suffered adverse consequences because of their reliance upon the sanctity of oral contracts.

Under even the best of relationships, it is still possible that one or both parties might forget the terms of an oral agreement. It is also possible that both parties might have quite different perceptions about the precise terms of the agreement reached. When the agreement is put into writing, however, there is much less doubt as to the terms of the arrangement. Thus, a written contract generally functions as a safeguard against subsequent misunderstandings or forgetful minds.

Perhaps the principal problem with oral contracts lies in the fact that they cannot always be proven or enforced. Proof of oral contracts typically centers around the conflicting testimony of the parties involved. If one of the parties is not able to establish by a preponderance of evidence (more likely than not) that his or her version of the contract is the correct one, then the oral contract may be considered nonexistent—as though it had never been made. The same result might occur if the parties cannot remember the precise terms of the agreement.

WHEN WRITTEN CONTRACTS ARE NECESSARY

Even if an oral contract is established, it may not always be enforceable. As already noted, there are some agreements that must be in writing in order to be legally enforceable.

An early law that was designed to prevent fraud and perjury, known as the *Statute of Frauds*, provides that any contract that, by its terms, cannot be fully performed within one year, must be in writing. This rule is narrowly interpreted, so if there is any possibility, no matter how remote, that the contract could be fully performed within one year, the contract need not be reduced to writing.

For example, if a benefactor agrees to write and donate one book each year to a school's library for a period of five years in exchange for his name being on the building, the contract would have to be in writing. By the very terms of the agreement, there is no way the contract could be performed within one year. If, on the other hand, the contract called for the benefactor to write and donate five books within a period of five years, the contract would not have to be in writing under the Statute of Frauds. It is possible, though perhaps not probable, that the benefactor could write and donate all five books within the first year and his name could certainly be put on the building at the beginning of the arrangement. The fact that the benefactor does not actually complete performance of the contract within one year is immaterial. So long as complete performance within one year is within the realm of possibility, the contract need not be in writing to be enforceable.

The Statute of Frauds further provides that any contract for the sale of goods valued at $500 or more is not enforceable unless it has been put into writing and signed by the party against whom enforcement is being sought. The fact that a contract for a price in excess of $500 is not in writing does not void the agreement or render it illegal. The parties are free to perform the oral arrangement, but if one party refuses to perform, the other will be unable to legally enforce the agreement.

The law defines *goods* as all things that are movable at the time the contract is made, except for the money used as payment. The real question becomes whether a particular contract involves the sale of goods for a price of $500 or more. Although the answer would generally seem to be fairly clear, ambiguities may arise.

In addition, some states have identified specific contracts that are enforceable only if in writing regardless of the other rules which would otherwise apply. For example, Oregon state law prescribes that a contract for landscape work, regardless of its duration or price, must be in writing.

Essentials to Put in Writing

A contract should be written in simple language that both parties can understand and should spell out the terms of the agreement.

A contract should include the following:

- the date of the agreement;
- identification of the parties (i.e., the buyer and seller in the case of sale of goods or services);
- a description of the goods or services sold;
- the price or other consideration; and
- the signatures of the parties involved.

To supplement these basics, an agreement should spell out whatever other terms might be applicable, such as pricing arrangements, payment schedules, insurance coverage, and consignment details. Many transactions are important enough that additional clauses covering certain contingencies should be added as well.

Finally, it should be noted that a written document that leaves out essential terms of the contract presents many of the same problems of proof and ambiguity as an oral contract.

IN PLAIN ENGLISH

The terms of the contract should be well-conceived, clearly drafted, conspicuous (i.e., not in tiny print that no one can read), and in plain English, so everyone can understand them.

No-Cost Written Agreements

At this point, nonprofit organizations might object, asserting that they do not have the time, energy, or patience to draft contracts. After all, their mission is to provide social benefits, not to formulate written contracts steeped in legal jargon.

Fortunately, the organization will not always be required to do this, since the other party may be willing to draft a satisfactory contract. However, be wary of signing any form contracts—they will almost invariably be one-sided, with all terms in favor of whoever paid to have them drafted.

As a second alternative, the organization could employ an attorney to draft contracts. However, this might be cost-effective only for substantial transactions. With respect to smaller transactions, the legal fees may be much larger than the benefits derived from having a written contract.

The Uniform Commercial Code (UCC), which is a body of commercial law adopted in every state within the United States except Louisiana (though it has adopted legislation that is comparable to the UCC), provides organizations with a third and, perhaps the best, alternative. While the UCC applies only to the sale of goods, in situations where it applies, businesses need not draft contracts or rely on anyone else (a supplier, retailer, or attorney) to do so.

Confirming Memorandum

The UCC provides that, where both parties are merchants and one party sends to the other written confirmation of an oral contract within a reasonable time after that contract was made and the recipient does not object to the *confirming memorandum* within ten days of its receipt, the contract will be deemed enforceable.

A merchant is defined as any person who normally deals in goods of the kind sold or who, because of occupation, represents himself or herself as having knowledge or skill peculiar to the practices or goods involved in the transaction. Most nonprofit organizations will be considered merchants.

It should be emphasized that the sole effect of the confirming memorandum is that neither party can use the Statute of Frauds as a defense, assuming that the recipient fails to object within ten days after receipt. The party sending the confirming memorandum must still prove that an oral contract was made prior to or at the same time as the written confirmation. (However, once such proof is offered, neither party can raise the Statute of Frauds to avoid enforcement of the agreement.)

The advantage of the confirming memorandum over a written contract lies in the fact that the confirming memorandum can be used without the active participation of the other contracting party. It would suffice, for example, to simply state: "This memorandum is to confirm our oral agreement." Since you would then still have to prove the terms of that agreement, it would be useful to provide a bit more detail in the confirming memorandum, such as the subject of the contract, the date it was made, and the price or other consideration to be paid. Thus, you might draft something like the following:

> This memorandum is to confirm our oral agreement made on July 3, 2020, pursuant to which Supplier agreed to deliver to Purchaser on or before September 19, 2020, five boxes of business cards for the purchase price of $600.

The advantages of providing some detail in the confirming memorandum are twofold. First, in the event of a dispute, you could introduce the memorandum as proof of the terms of the oral agreement. Second, the recipient of the memorandum will be precluded from offering any proof regarding the terms of the oral contract that contradicts the terms contained in the memorandum. The recipient or, for that matter, the party sending the memorandum, can introduce proof only regarding the terms of the oral contract that are consistent with the terms, if any, found in the memorandum.

Thus, the Purchaser in the example would be precluded from claiming that the contract called for delivery of ten boxes of business cards because the quantity was stated in the written memo and not objected to. On the other hand, the Purchaser would be permitted to testify that the oral contract required the Supplier to engrave the business cards in a specific way since this testimony would not be inconsistent with the terms stated in the memorandum.

IN PLAIN ENGLISH

If drafting a complete written contract proves too burdensome or too costly, the organization should submit a memorandum in confirmation of the oral contract. This at least surpasses the initial barrier raised by the Statute of Frauds. Moreover, by recounting the terms in the memorandum, the organization is in a much better position to prove the oral contract at a later date.

ADDITIONAL TERMS

One party to a contract can prevent the other from adding or inventing terms that are not spelled out in the confirming memorandum by ending the memorandum with a clause requiring all other provisions to be contained in a written and signed document. Such a clause might read as follows:

> This is the entire agreement between the parties and no modification, alteration, or additional terms shall be enforceable unless in writing and signed by both parties.

If you use such a clause, be sure there are no additional agreed-to terms that have not been included in the written document. A court will generally be confined to the four corners of the document when trying to determine what was agreed to between the parties. This means that nothing more than what is on the paper containing the agreement will be allowed as evidence.

An exception to this rule is that a court may allow oral evidence for the purpose of interpreting ambiguities or explaining the meaning of certain technical terms. The court may also permit the other parties to introduce evidence of past practices in connection with the contract in question, in connection with other agreements between the parties, or even in connection with contracts between other parties.

Organizations should not rely on oral contracts alone since they offer little protection in the event of a dispute. The best protection is afforded by a written contract. It is a truism that oral contracts are not worth the paper they are written on.

CONTRACTING ONLINE

In 2000, the *Electronic Signatures in Global and National Commerce Act (E-Sign Act)* became effective. This act was intended, among other things, to encourage online commerce and provide the parties who take advantage of it with the ability to contract in cyberspace.

Where a contract is required to be in writing, parties can decide to contract electronically by affirmatively agreeing to do so. When an organization dealing with a party is required to provide a contract or notice in writing, that organization must both seek the party's consent to receipt of an electronic document and verify that the document can be accessed and retained by the party. For example, the organization must notify the party of the hardware and software requirements for accessing the document.

Once a party consents to electronic receipt of documents, the party must notify the organization of any change in email address. If the party desires to withdraw his or her consent to electronic receipt, the location where documents can be sent must be disclosed to the organization as well.

Online contracting is available only when there is a method for preserving electronic contracts and other relevant data electronically. This will eliminate the need for warehousing hard copies of the documents for online contracting. No special technology must be used for online contracting, and the parties are free to establish their own vehicle for accomplishing the act's requirements. Electronically signed documents can be encrypted if the parties agree. There are a number of companies such as DocuSign and Adobe that can assist the parties with online contracts.

CONSUMER PROTECTION LAWS

The federal government and many states have enacted legislation designed to give consumers the opportunity to change their minds and cancel unwanted sales. The federal law generally applies to any sale, loan, or rental of consumer goods or services over a certain amount. This applies only when the seller or the seller's representative personally solicits the sale and the buyer's agreement, or offer to purchase, is made at a place other than the seller's place of business. The seller's place of business is defined as the main or permanent branch office or local address of the seller.

These laws protect the consumer by offering a *cooling-off period* within which to notify the seller of the consumer's intention to cancel the purchase. The consumer may receive a return of all money paid and rescind any contract signed without further obligation. In effect, the consumer is given a period of time, typically up to midnight of the third business day following the sale, during which to determine whether he or she really wants to go through with the transaction. These laws also protect nonprofit organizations as consumers.

The seller's principal obligation under these regulations is to disclose to the potential consumer that such a cooling-off period exists and that it is the consumer's right to take advantage of that escape clause and cancel the sale if desired. The form and content of this disclosure requirement are spelled out in the federal regulations.

To comply with the statute, a seller must furnish the buyer with a fully completed receipt or copy of any agreement pertaining to the sale at the time the sale is made or the agreement is signed. The receipt or agreement must be in the same language that was principally used in the oral sales presentation. For example, if the presentation was made in Spanish, the receipt or agreement must also be in Spanish. The receipt or agreement must also include the seller's name and address, time and date of sale, and a statement on the first page that contains the following language:

> The buyer may cancel this transaction at any time prior to midnight of the third business day after the date of this transaction. See the attached notice-of-cancellation form for an explanation of this right.

The notice-of-cancellation form must detail the buyer's rights and obligations in the event the buyer chooses to cancel the sale.

In addition to the federal regulation, many states have enacted similar consumer protection statutes that provide for a cooling-off period and contain a similar disclosure requirement. It is strongly advised that if your organization engages in consumer sales, as for example, from trade shows, craft shows, farmer's markets, or other locations not in a permanently established location, you confer with an attorney who can advise you of the legal requirements in your particular state.

MAIL-ORDER SALES

A popular method of selling is through mail-order services or catalog sales through snail mail or online. Here too, the federal government has established certain guidelines aimed at protecting the consuming public. When a seller solicits a sale online, through the mail or through a mail-order catalog, the seller must reasonably expect to be able to ship any ordered merchandise to the buyer within the time stated in the solicitation. If no time period is stated, the merchandise must be shipped within thirty days after receiving a properly completed order. If the seller is unable to ship the merchandise within the specified time limit, the seller must offer the buyer the option of either consenting to a delay in shipping or of canceling the order and receiving a prompt refund. The seller is also required to inform the buyer of any anticipated delays in shipping and to explain why the shipping deadline cannot be met. Many nonprofits provide merchandise through online websites and catalogs. These offerings would be subject to this legislation.

CHAPTER 7

Trademarks

Branding has become a part of the lexicon of important terms today. In fact, virtually every organization strives to develop its brand and the awareness that results from this process. One of the most important aspects of branding is the establishment of a means of identifying a product or service by use of a name, symbol, logo, device, or combination of these items, commonly known as trademarks or *service marks*.

A trademark is used to define marks that are affixed to goods. Service marks are used to define marks that are used in connection with services. Both are commonly referred to simply as *trademarks* or just *marks*. There are also marks that are used for purposes of certification. These are known as certification marks. Prominent examples of these would be UL and Energy Star. There are, as of the date of this writing, thirty-four international classifications for goods and twelve classifications for services.

Nonprofit organizations all have names which are protectable, and many have logos which are protectable as well. The fleur-de-lis used by the Boy Scouts of America, the clasping hands of the Boys & Girls Club, and the cross of the Red Cross are a few prominent examples. Many nonprofits license the use of their trademarks and logos. This subject will be discussed further in chapter 10.

Although modern trademark law has broadened the protection available for trademark owners, its historical antecedents date back to medieval England. In those days, certain craft guilds often required members to place their individual marks on the products they produced, so that, in the event a product proved defective, the guild could trace its origins to a particular craftsman and impose appropriate sanctions. Thus, the use of marks enabled the guild to maintain the integrity of its name. Moreover, merchants would often affix marks to their products for purposes of identification. Should the product be stolen or misplaced, the merchant could prove ownership by reason of the mark.

The use of marks for purposes of identification would no doubt have worked quite well in an ideal society where all the citizens led principled and moral lives. But such was not the case. It is not particularly surprising that unscrupulous merchants quickly realized that there was easy money to be made from the use of another's mark or one confusingly similar. The shoddy merchants could more readily sell their products by affixing to them the marks belonging to quality manufacturers.

It was in response to this problem of consumer fraud that the first trademark laws developed. Initially, the emphasis was on prevention of one person passing off products as that of another. In contrast, modern American law focuses upon whether one mark is sufficiently similar to another to cause confusion in the minds of the buying public. The emphasis has, therefore, shifted from the subjective intent of a dishonest manufacturer or merchant passing off goods as those of another to the objective determination of consumer confusion.

Despite this shift, the essential purpose of trademarks and trademark laws has changed little since the days of the craft guilds. Trademarks still function primarily as a means of identifying the source of a particular product. Trademark laws are also designed to enable the trademark proprietor to develop *goodwill* for the product as well as to prevent another party from exploiting that goodwill—regardless of whether that exploitation is intentional or innocent.

Nonprofit organization staff members may be able to search the US Patent and Trademark Office website (www.uspto.gov) in order to determine whether the nonprofit's trademarks are very similar to registered trademarks or marks that are pending registration. Determining the availability of a registration may be quite technical and it is important to work with experienced trademark practitioners in order to avoid significant problems. Unlike copyright registration, trademark registration generally requires experienced legal assistance. There are several websites that claim to be helpful with trademarks and offer registration assistance for a flat fee. Regrettably, the vast majority of these sites charge more than trademark lawyers, and they often do not provide the promised assistance necessary to successfully register the mark. In fact, many organizations have been forced to pay experienced intellectual property lawyers to complete the registration process unsuccessfully started by one of these online sites.

DEFINITION

A simplification of the federal definition of a trademark is:

> any word, name, symbol, device, or any combination thereof, adopted and used by a person, or which a person has a bona fide intention to use in commerce and subsequently does use, which identifies and distinguishes his or her goods or services, including a unique product, from those manufactured or sold by others, and indicates the source of those goods or services, even if that source is unknown.

A trademark owner may be a licensee, broker, or distributor. The term *use in commerce* means the bona fide use of a mark in the ordinary course of trade—not a use made merely to reserve a right in the mark. Reservation of a mark prior to its use can be achieved by filing an intent-to-use application with the US Patent and Trademark Office (PTO).

The key concept of trademark law is that the trademark must be distinguishable. In order to secure trademark protection, one must develop a distinctive mark. The most distinctive trademarks are those that are purely arbitrary or fanciful (i.e., those that have no meaning or connotation other than identifying the source of a particular product). For example, the trademark *Kodak* to identify a brand of cameras is purely arbitrary. Less distinctive are trademarks that have another meaning, such as the trademark *Shell* to identify gasoline. Although such trademarks as Shell are not purely arbitrary, they are nevertheless afforded substantial protection since the other meaning bears no resemblance to the product identified.

PROHIBITED TRADEMARKS

Generic and descriptive names are not considered distinctive enough to be granted trademark status. A generic word merely identifies the product for what it is. Thus, the use of the name *Beer* to identify a brand of beer is generic and would not be accepted as a trademark. Similarly, a descriptive name only characterizes the attributes or qualities of the product. For example, using the name *Raisin Bran* to identify a cereal is merely descriptive of the product's ingredients and might have difficulty gaining trademark status.

Generic words are never afforded trademark protection. Descriptive trademarks, however, may be protected in limited circumstances. A descriptive mark may be protected if the proprietor of the mark can prove that it has acquired a secondary meaning. Secondary meaning will exist when the public no longer connects the words of the trademark with the literal, dictionary meaning, but rather with a unique product. For example, the descriptive term *TV Guide* also has a secondary meaning as the (registered) trademark of a particular publication that contains television program listings and topical articles about the industry.

Some trademarks, even though they are considered distinctive, are nevertheless prohibited by statute or public policy. Obscene or scandalous trademarks are generally denied trademark protection. Thus, when a band attempted to register The Slants as its name because the performers were Asian, the application was denied because it was deemed disparaging. The applicant ultimately appealed the denial and had the rule declared unconstitutional as a violation of the First Amendment.

A similar problem arose when a group of Native Americans challenged the use of the word Washington Redskins by a football team. Initially, the team's registration was in jeopardy, but as a result of the Supreme Court ruling in the Slants case, the issue is now moot, and the team is back using Washington Redskins as a federally registered trademark.

Trademarks that are deemed deceptive and misleading, such as the mark Idaho Potatoes to identify potatoes produced in some area other than Idaho, are also denied protection.

CERTIFICATION MARKS

As previously noted, certification marks are used by organizations to certify certain qualities of products or services. For example, bar associations only permit individuals who have completed the educational and exam requirements to indicate they are licensed to practice law in the association's territory. The attorney is permitted to use the certification mark authorized by the association. Similarly, CPAs, doctors, and other licensed professionals are permitted to use the certification marks of their professional associations when they have complied with the appropriate rules as well.

It is important to note that an organization may not use the same mark as its name and as a certification mark. Thus, the Good Housekeeping organization's certification mark is its Seal of Approval. The trademark for the organization is the GH or Good Housekeeping.

PROTECTING A TRADEMARK

In order to secure trademark protection, it is not sufficient merely to adopt a distinctive mark. The trademark must be used in the ordinary course of trade or used in commerce. The use requirement is fundamental to trademark law and is necessary for common law protection, as well as federal and state registration.

Common law is the body of law developed from court decisions rather than from state or federal statutes. Federal or state registration of a trademark has certain advantages but is not necessary. Common law protection will suffice and has the benefit of not requiring any interaction with governmental agencies.

A trademark is deemed to be used when it has been placed in any manner on the product, its containers or displays associated with it, or on any of the tags or labels affixed to the product. Thus, it is not always necessary that the trademark actually be physically affixed to the goods. As long as the trademark is associated with the product at the point of sale and in such a way that the product can be readily identified as coming from a particular manufacturer or source, the trademark may be protected. Examples include the Girl Scout logo on Girl Scout Cookies or museum reproductions that bear the logo of the museum. It should be noted, however, that the mere listing of a trademark in a catalog, the ordering of labels bearing the trademark, the use of the trademark on invoices, or the exhibition of trademarked goods at a trade show alone may not be sufficient in and of themselves to constitute use, since the use of the trademark was not associated with the point of sale.

While some nonprofits customarily engage in limited commercial activity and the marks they use would be deemed trademarks, it is more common for nonprofits to be involved with and provide services that would be identified by service marks.

IN PLAIN ENGLISH

To ensure trademark protection, the trademark proprietor is well advised to physically affix the trademark to the product. In this way, the product is certain to bear the trademark when it is sold. Proper use of a service mark is accomplished by identifying the service by the mark in advertising, signs, brochures, and the like.

Confusingly Similar

Common law protects the trademark proprietor against someone else subsequently using a trademark that is confusingly similar. This raises the question of when trademarks are considered confusingly similar. Generally, trademarks will be confusing if they are similar in sound or appearance, particularly if the trademarks are affixed to similar products or if products are marketed throughout the same or similar geographic areas.

On the other hand, if two products bearing similar trademarks are not related or are marketed in different geographic areas, there may not be any infringement. Thus, an organization that distributes products solely in the Northwest could probably adopt and use a trademark already used by an organization distributing its product solely in the state of Maine, provided the mark of the Northwest organization does not adversely affect the value of the trademark used by the Maine organization.

Moreover, a Northwest animal shelter could probably adopt and use a trademark used by a Northwest fine art museum. In these situations, there may be no infringement since it is not likely that the use of the mark by the animal shelter would confuse fine-art patrons. Here again, appropriation of another's trademark may be wrongful if the use, even by a noncompeting business, would dilute the value of the mark to the original owner. (Remedies for trademark infringement will be discussed later in this chapter.)

FEDERAL REGISTRATION

The trademark proprietor can procure greater protection under federal or state statutes than under the common law. The federal statute governing trademarks is known as the Lanham Act of 1946. It is not the function of the Lanham Act to grant trademark rights since those are secured by the common-law principles discussed above but, rather, to provide a central clearinghouse for existing trademarks via registrations.

In 1989, the Trademark Law Revision Act of 1988 (TLRA) became effective and made substantive changes to the previous trademark laws. In addition, the trademark law was amended in 1996 to add a federal *antidilution* provision. Though the Lanham Act provides much of the skeleton of trademark law, these amendments add the needed detail to make trademark law a more complete body of law. Unfortunately, the Supreme Court weakened the antidilution provision in 2005, and, as a result, legislation has been introduced in Congress to clarify and likely strengthen this form of protection.

Prior to enactment of the TLRA, a mark could be registered only upon actual use in interstate commerce. This requirement was satisfied when an applicant sold a few units of the product bearing the trademark in an interstate transaction. A mark could essentially be reserved for later use by making a token use at the time of application. The minimum token use requirement allowed the registering of trademarks that might never be used and possibly prevented other proprietors from legitimately using the mark. This judicially sanctioned practice also clogged the federal register with unused marks.

Under the TLRA, token use is no longer permitted. Actual use of the mark is required in order for a trademark to be registered. In addition, the revised law allows for the filing of an application for a trademark based on a bona fide intention to use that mark in the future. This reserves and protects a mark for a limited time and to a limited extent prior to its being used in commerce. If the mark is not actually used within a certain time period, the trademark registration will be denied.

There are two official registers for trademarks: the Principal Register and the Supplemental Register. Marks registered on the Principal Register enjoy all of the benefits of the trademark law. Marks registered on the Supplemental Register do not enjoy all of those benefits. The following sections on how to register a trademark apply to the Principal Register. (A separate section included later in this chapter describes what the Supplemental Register covers and how it may be used.)

Applications Based on Actual Use

The use requirement is met if the mark is protected as a common-law trademark. Once the proprietor has established a mark's actual use in commerce, the mark can be registered by filing an application with the PTO. This process entails filling out an application, sending in a drawing of the mark, including specimens of the mark used in commerce, and paying the required fee. (The filing fee is constantly changing, though there is a reduced fee for those who file online and agree to prosecute the entire registration through an online procedure. For current information, see www.uspto.gov.)

If the examining officer at the PTO accepts the application, the trademark will appear shortly thereafter in the *Official Gazette of Trademarks*. Anyone who believes that he or she would be injured by the issuance of the registration has thirty days to file a written notice stating the reasons for opposition. If nobody objects or if the objections are found to be without merit, a certificate of registration will be issued.

Applications Based on Intent-to-Use

Under the TLRA, a right to a particular mark can be preserved for future use through an intent-to-use provision. This does not remove the requirement of actual use in commerce, which is still necessary for registration of the mark.

Protection of a mark for future use can be accomplished by filing an application based on the applicant's bona fide intent to use the mark in commerce. An intent-to-use registration should not be requested merely for the purpose of attempting to reserve a mark. The statute does not explicitly define bona fide intent, but the good faith of the applicant will be determined from the circumstances surrounding the application and the applicant's conduct with respect to the mark. The history behind the statute's enactment suggests that the applicant's conduct concerning the intent-to-use mark will be measured against standards accepted in the trade or business.

Opposition

If the intent-to-use application satisfies the requirements of the PTO regulations, it will receive approval for publication in the *Official Gazette*. Upon such publication, a thirty-day period for opposition to registration of the mark begins to run. This period is similar to that accorded applications for registration of marks that are in actual use. Those applications that go unopposed receive a notice of allowance. The date the notice is issued is very important because the reservation of the mark is limited to a period of six months from the date of allowance, during which time actual use of the mark in commerce must begin, or the trademark application will lapse.

Extensions

If an applicant fails to commence using the mark in commerce within the allowable six-month period, it is possible to obtain an extension for another six months. This extension is automatic upon application and payment of the fee only if submitted before the original six-month period expires. Four additional six-month extensions are also possible but require, in addition to the application and fee submission before expiration of the then current six-month period, approval by the PTO upon a showing of good cause why such extension should be granted. In no event shall the period between the date of allowance and the commencement of use of the mark in commerce be permitted to exceed thirty-six months.

In making a request for an extension, the applicant must include the following:

- a verified statement of continued bona fide intent to use the mark in commerce;
- the specification as to which classification(s) of goods and services the intent continues to apply; and
- the required fee.

Application forms are available from the PTO website at www.uspto.gov.

Statement of Use

Once actual use of the mark in commerce has occurred, the applicant must file a verified statement of use. If everything is in order, the mark will be registered for the goods or services that the statement of use indicates. The Commissioner for Trademarks shall notify an applicant as to whether a statement of use has been accepted or refused. An applicant will be allowed to amend the statement of use if the mark was not used on all the goods initially identified.

Constructive Use

An important concept found in the Lanham Act and improved by later amendments is that of constructive use. This concept, which has been called the cornerstone of the intent-to-use method, also applies to use-based applications. When an application to register a mark is filed under the doctrine of constructive use, filing constitutes use of the mark as of the filing date. Thus, when the application to register is filed, a right of priority to exclusive use of the mark is created throughout the United States. This is true only if the mark is filed for registration on the Principal Register. The constructive use doctrine does not apply to domestic (or foreign) applications on the Supplemental Register.

This doctrine gives applicants a strong incentive to file for registration as early as possible. The constructive use statute provides priority filing protection and, thereby, prevents others from acquiring the mark by simply using it before the intent-to-use applicant does. Constructive use greatly reduces disputes as to which party has priority, thus saving costs and limiting uncertainty in infringement or opposition proceedings.

Exceptions

Exceptions to the priority right of use are marks used prior to the applicant's filing date, intent-to-use applications filed prior to the applicant's filing date, and use-based applications registered prior to the applicant's filing date. Applications for registration filed by foreign applicants are also excepted if the foreign application was filed prior to the constructive use application.

Assignments

The current law generally prohibits assignment of intent-to-use applications, thereby preventing applications for marks being filed by individuals for the sole purpose of selling them. However, an intent-to-use application may be assigned to the applicant's business.

Benefits of Registration

Registering your mark provides you many benefits. First, registration enables a proprietor to use the "®" symbol or the phrase "registered trademark" in conjunction with the mark. This may well deter others from using the mark. Proprietors of marks that have not been registered are prohibited from using the above symbols with their marks. Commonly, "TM" for trademark or "SM" for service mark is used in conjunction with an unregistered mark during the application period. These designations have no official status, but they do provide notice to others that the user is claiming a property right in the mark.

Second, registration on the Principal Register is evidence of the validity of the registration, the registrant's ownership of the mark, and the exclusive right to use the mark on identified goods in commerce.

Finally, a registered trademark that has been in continuous use for a period of five consecutive years may become incontestable. By registering the trademark, the proprietor may secure rights superior to those of a prior but unregistered user, but only if the original user does not object to the registrant's use within five years.

Duration

Under the trademark law, registration remains in effect for a period of ten years. It may be renewed in additional ten-year increments by filing an application for renewal during the six months prior to the expiration of the existing ten-year term.

Supplemental Register

Supplemental Register applications may be made directly if the applicant is sure that registration on the Principal Register is unlikely or in response to the PTO's final refusal to register the mark on the Principal Register. This registration provides protection for individuals capable of distinguishing their marks from those of others but whose marks do not comply with the requirements for registration on the Principal Register. Marks for the Supplemental Register are not published for, or subject to, opposition. They are, however, published as registered in the *Official Gazette*. If a person believes that he or she will be damaged by the registration of another's mark on the Supplemental Register, that person may, at any time, petition for cancellation of the registration.

Applications filed on the Supplemental Register cannot be based on intent-to-use and do not enjoy the benefits of constructive use. Under the Lanham Act, an application filed on the Supplemental Register had to be in lawful use for a year prior to the filing of the application. For a mark to be eligible for registration on the Supplemental Register under the 1989 amendment, the domestic applicant's mark merely must be in lawful use in commerce, meaning a bona fide use in the ordinary course of trade.

Loss of Protection

A use or intent to use is a prerequisite to trademark protection. It should be noted that some forms of use might result in the loss of a trademark. A number of well-known trademarks such as Aspirin, Thermos, and Escalator have been lost as a result of improper usage. Trademark protection is lost because the mark is used in some capacity other than as an adjective modifying a noun. When a trademark is used as a noun or a verb, it no longer functions to identify the source of the product but rather becomes the name of the product itself. At that point, the mark becomes generic and is not subject to protection.

Abandonment of a mark will also result in loss of protection. A trademark is deemed abandoned when it has not been used for two years and there is no intent to resume its use. Token use will not be sufficient to avoid abandonment. To avoid abandonment, the proprietor does not have to use the mark in interstate commerce in the ordinary course of trade or business, but the mark should be used in intrastate commerce.

INFRINGEMENT

A trademark that is in use and has been infringed upon allows the trademark proprietor to sue the infringing party either for monetary damages or for an injunction prohibiting the infringing use, or sometimes for both. Monetary damages may be measured either by the plaintiff's losses resulting from the infringement or by the defendant's profits. In certain exceptional circumstances where the defendant's conduct is willful and flagrant, the plaintiff might also be entitled to exemplary damages equal to three times the actual damages and/or attorney's fees.

The relevant sections under the Lanham Act provide for remedies for infringement on marks that actually are in use. This effectively precludes an intent-to-use applicant from suing for infringement because use has not been made of the mark. The law permits anyone who feels that he or she will be damaged by acts that are likely to cause confusion, mistake, or deception as to the origin, sponsorship, or approval of the complainant's goods or services with those of another to sue for unfair competition. Under the act, all remedies available for infringement actions are also available for actions of unfair competition.

Antidilution

In 1996, the federal trademark law was amended to provide special protection to famous marks. The statute does not define *famous mark*, though case law has adopted much of the legislative history that suggests a famous mark is a mark that has been around for a long time and enjoys extensive notoriety.

In the past, it was possible to appropriate a mark for use on goods or services that do not compete with those of the mark's owner, so long as there was no likelihood of confusion. As a result, it was possible, for example, to call a dog food "Cadillac," intending to suggest that it was the elite form of canine fare, despite the fact that the automobile manufacturer of Cadillacs did not have anything to do with the dog food. The likely intent of the dog food company was to suggest that it was the "Cadillac" of dog foods and thus the top of the line. Under the 1996 amendment, this type of use would probably not be permitted since the dog food manufacturer's use of the mark "Cadillac" would likely be considered a dilution of the General Motors trademark.

While antidilution statutes had been in effect in several states, they were not universal. The federal statute now provides protection, at least for famous marks. The remedies available for violations of the antidilution statute are comparable to those that are provided for trademark infringements, though where the mark that is causing the dilution is not identical, it may be necessary to prove actual confusion. As a result of the Supreme Court's interpretation of the federal antidilution statute as requiring actual confusion and the feeling by many that the law has been undermined, legislation was passed by Congress that clarifies and strengthens the antidilution protection for famous marks.

INTERNATIONAL PROTECTION

As of the date of this writing, there is no multinational treaty to which the United States belongs that provides international trademark protection. The European Union has established a pan-European trademark registration for its member nations, but the United States is not a party to that treaty.

In 2003, the United States became a party to the Madrid System, which is the closest that this country has come to providing its citizens with international trademark protection. Under the Madrid System, Americans can apply for trademark protection in seventy-eight countries as of the date of this writing by filing the appropriate application and paying the required fees to the US Patent and Trademark Office. It is, thus, no longer necessary for US companies to hire specialists in every country in which trademark registration is desired. Under this new arrangement, the application filed with the PTO can identify the member countries in which registration is sought and the class of goods or services to be covered. The cost savings for using this process is significant, and the convenience will provide US organizations with a more efficient method of obtaining foreign trademark registrations in the Madrid System member nations. It should be noted that the countries party to the Madrid System continue to increase. The fees required for registration are set by each country, in its own currency, and, as a result, are constantly in flux. In order to determine the actual fee at any time, an applicant should check the online registry, which contains a fee meter based on the number of countries, the classes in which a mark is to be registered, and the countries' currency exchange rates. For a current listing of participating countries, as well as the fees charged and application process, see http://www.wipo.int/madrid.

STATE REGISTRATION

Trademarks can also be registered under state law. The trademark proprietor may file, with the appropriate state officer, a trademark application, along with documentation similar to that required by the Lanham Act. State law protection of a trademark does not extend beyond the borders of the state. The number of specimens of the mark needed to complete registration may vary from state to state, and the registration fee may also be different. Protection under state law can be broader than that found under federal laws. Remedies available under state law are also very likely to be different from those found under the federal statute. If a conflict arises between federal and state trademark law, it is important to remember that under the supremacy clause of the US Constitution, federal law will supersede state law.

USING AN ATTORNEY

Registration can be quite beneficial to an organization that has invested time, money, and energy in developing a reputation for quality services. Procuring trademark protection on either the state or federal level may require a considerable amount of time and skill. In this regard, an attorney may prove invaluable. An attorney can, first of all, determine if the benefits to be derived from registration justify the expenses. The total cost of trademark registration usually runs about $1,500, not counting any artist's fees for drawings. Second, an attorney can research trademark databases to determine if there are any conflicting marks. Finally, an attorney can complete the application and deal with any problems that may occur while it is being processed for registration.

  If you are interested in contacting attorneys who specialize in trademark work, you can consult your state bar association for some recommendations.

CONCLUSION

Since nonprofits have names and reputations that are used by others to identify the organization, and since nonprofits often derive extreme benefits from their activities, it is important to determine an appropriate method to protect the organization from others who may be misidentified as either the organization or authorized by it. For this, and many other reasons, it is important for nonprofits to protect their names and logos.

CHAPTER 8

Copyrights

It is quite common for nonprofit organizations to use literature, computer software, videotapes, artwork, and similar material created by others. This material may be protected by copyright law, and its unauthorized use may subject the user to liability for copyright infringement. There are, however, some situations in which you may be able to use another's work without obtaining permission. The guidelines for this use are found in the federal copyright law.

Some nonprofit organizations develop their own copyrightable brochures, advertising copy, catalogs, posters, and the like. Since nonprofit organizations tend to take a proprietary view of their creations, they may wish to prevent others from using their work without permission. Again, copyright law provides the vehicle by which these works may be protected. This chapter discusses some significant portions of the copyright law and their possible application to your organization.

The Copyright Office website (www.copyright.gov) is very user-friendly and, unlike the Trademark Office website discussed in chapter 7, is available for nonprofits to use on their own. The Copyright Office website contains a number of well-written articles explaining much of the law of copyright in clear, understandable terms so that nonprofits can use this site with little or no legal assistance. The website contains a database for looking up previous copyright registrations, and registrations can even be applied for online.

COPYRIGHT LAW FOUNDATION

Copyright law in the United States has its foundation in the Constitution, which provides in Article I, Section 8, that "Congress shall have the power to promote the progress of science and useful arts, by securing for limited time to authors and inventors the exclusive right to their respective writings and discoveries." The first Congress exercised this power and enacted a copyright law. The legislation was periodically revised, but no major changes were made in the law from 1909 until the Copyright Revision Act of 1976 became effective on January 1, 1978.

Prior to enactment of the 1976 law, unpublished works were protected by common law copyright governed by state laws. This protection could vary considerably from state to state. Federal protection under the 1909 act began by protecting a published work to which a copyright notice was attached. The Copyright Revision Act of 1976 preempts the field of copyright law—in other words, it is now the only legislation governing copyright. This law was significantly amended once again in 1989 when the United States became a party to the international copyright treaty known as the Berne Convention.

PUBLICATION

Publication, within the context of copyright law, is a technical term that applies to all copyrightable material. Under the old law, it meant an unrestricted public display. Today, publication is defined as the distribution of copies of a work to the public by sale or other transfer of ownership, or by rental, lease, or loan.

COPYRIGHTABLE MATERIAL

An author, from the point of view of copyright law, is a creator—be it a photographer, sculptor, writer, computer programmer, or musician. An author is granted copyright protection to original works of authorship fixed in any tangible medium of expression.

IN PLAIN ENGLISH

There have been debates over what constitutes a writing, but it is now clear that the term *author* includes the creator of computer software programs.

The 1976 act expressly exempts from copyright protection any idea, procedure, process, system, method of operation, concept, principle, or discovery. In short, a copyright extends only to the expression of creations of the mind, not to the ideas themselves. Frequently, no clear line of division between an idea and its expression exists. For now, it is sufficient to note that a pure idea, such as a plan to create an innovative advertising program, cannot be copyrighted—no matter how original or creative that idea is.

The law and the courts generally avoid using copyright law to arbitrate the public's taste. Thus, a work can be copyrighted even if it makes no pretense to aesthetic or academic merit. The only requirements are that a work be original and show some creativity.

Originality—as distinguished from uniqueness—requires that a work be created independently. Originality, however, does not require that it be the only one of its kind. For example, cartographers who independently create identical maps are each entitled to copyright protection. Because their works often look similar to untrained observers, many cartographers will include a minor intentional error on a map so that if the identical error appears on another map alleged to have been independently created, this minor error will provide obvious evidence of copying.

SCOPE OF PROTECTION

A copyright is actually a collection of five exclusive rights. First is the right to reproduce a work by any means. The scope of this right can be hard to define, especially when it involves works such as software, microfilm, or videotape. Under the Copyright Act of 1976, someone may reproduce protected works without permission only if such reproduction involves either a fair or an exempted use as defined by the act (explained later in this chapter).

Second is the right to prepare *derivative works* based on a copyrighted work. A derivative work is one that transforms or adapts the subject matter of one or more preexisting works.

Third is the right to distribute copies to the public for sale or lease. However, once a person sells a copyrighted work or permits uncontrolled distribution, the right to control further uses of that work usually ends. This is known as the *first sale doctrine*. It is superseded in a situation where the work is merely in the possession of someone else temporarily by virtue of bailment, rental, lease, license, or loan. In these instances, the copyright owner retains the right to control the further sale or other disposition of the work. Moreover, the first sale doctrine does not apply if the copyright owner has a contract with the purchaser restricting the purchaser's freedom to use the work, as is the case with many software programs. In such a case, if the purchaser exceeds the restrictions, he or she may incur liability. In this situation, however, the copyright owner's remedy will be governed by contract law rather than by copyright law.

One should distinguish between the sale of a work and the sale of the copyright in that work. If nothing is said about the copyright when the work is sold by the copyright owner, the seller retains the copyright. Since the purchaser of the work may not be aware of this, a seller may wish to call it to the purchaser's attention, either in the sales memorandum or on the work itself. If a license is granted, it should be in writing and should be very specific in the scope of rights being granted. For example, a person who has purchased a license to videotapes of a lecture may not generally market the copyrighted instruction manual used in conjunction with the lecture. The drafter of the license should be clear in defining the boundaries of permissible uses.

Fourth is the right to perform the work publicly, such as to broadcast a film on television or to show it in a lecture room or meeting room.

Fifth is the right to display the work publicly. Once the copyright owner has sold a copy of the work, however, the purchaser has the right to display that copy but is generally still prohibited from reproducing it.

These rights are divisible. This means they can be transferred in whole or in part. If the copyright owner takes no special action upon selling the work, he or she is presumed to have retained all rights. If desired, the copyright owner may explicitly transfer any one or more of these rights.

OWNERSHIP

As a general rule, the creator of a work owns the copyright. The person who owns the copyright also automatically owns the exclusive rights. Under the old law, when a work was sold, ownership of a common law (prepublication) copyright passed to the purchaser unless the creator reserved the copyright in a written agreement. In other words, there was a presumption in the law that a sale included the work itself plus all rights in that work.

The Copyright Act of 1976, as amended, reversed the presumption that the sale of a work carries the copyright with it. Today, unless there is a written agreement to the contrary, the creator retains the copyright when the work is sold.

Joint Works

The creators of a *joint work* are co-owners of the copyright in the work. A joint work is defined as a work prepared by two or more authors with the intention that their contributions be merged into inseparable or interdependent parts of a unitary whole. Thus, whatever profit one creator makes from the use of the work must be shared equally with the others, unless they have a written agreement that states otherwise.

The key point is the intent that the parts be absorbed or combined into an integrated unit at the time the work is created. Although such an intent must exist at the time the work is created, not at a later date, the authors do not necessarily have to work together, work during the same period, or even know each other. However, the joint works definition does not include the situation where an artist creates a work such as a piano solo, without intending that the work involve another artist, and later commissions lyrics. If there is no intention to create a unitary or indivisible work, each creator may own the copyright to that creator's individual contribution.

In *Ashton-Tate Corp. v. Ross*, the Ninth Circuit Court of Appeals held that joint authorship was not established by the mere contribution of ideas and guidance for the user interface of a computer spreadsheet. Joint authorship requires each author to make an independently copyrightable contribution.

Works Made for Hire

Works considered to be *works made for hire* are an important exception to the general rule that a person owns the copyright in a work he or she has created. If a work was created by an employee on the job, the law considers the product a work made for hire, and the employer will own the copyright. However, the parties can avoid the application of this rule with a well-written contract. If the employment contract states that creating the copyrightable material in question is not part of the scope of employment, the employee retains the copyright, and the creation is not a work made for hire.

A work made for hire is defined as a work made by an employee within the scope of his or her employment. The principle is based on the following grounds:

- The work is produced on behalf of and under the direction of the employer.
- The employee is paid for the work.

- The employer, having paid all the costs and bearing all the risks of loss, should reap any gain.

Courts may also consider the amount of an employer's artistic advice before, during, and after the work was created.

Independent Contractors

Some courts developed a doctrine whereby an independent contractor was considered to be a special employee for copyright purposes when a commissioning party had the right to exercise control over the work. This resulted in the commissioning party, rather than the independent contractor, owning the copyright. In 1989, the US Supreme Court, in *Community for Creative Non-Violence v. Reid*, held that unless the party creating the work is an actual employee as that term is defined in the law, the copyright will belong to the creator rather than to the commissioning party. The court left open the question of whether the work could be considered a joint work by virtue of the party's intent.

If the creator is an independent contractor, the works will only be considered works for hire when:

- the parties have signed a written agreement to that effect and
- the work is specially ordered or commissioned as a contribution to a *collective work*, a supplementary work (one that introduces, revises, comments upon, or assists a work by another), a compilation, an instructional text, answer material for a test or the test itself, an atlas, motion picture, or an audiovisual work.

Thus, unless there is a contractual agreement to the contrary, the independent contractor owns the copyright. It has been held in some jurisdictions that, in order to be valid, the written contract must predate the performance of the work.

Volunteers present a challenge for copyright purposes. If the volunteer is more like an employee, then that individual would likely be considered an employee for copyright purposes. If, on the other hand, the volunteer does not act as an employee and merely acts independently, the rule for independent contractors would apply. Since the role of volunteer is ambiguous, it is important for a nonprofit organization to clarify the volunteer's situation in a well-written contract covering, among other things, copyright ownership in material created by the volunteer for the organization's use.

Derivative Works

In the case of a derivative work, the contributing author owns only what that person contributed. A derivative work is defined as:

> a work based upon one or more preexisting works, such as translation, fictionalization, motion picture version, sound recording, art reproduction, abridgment, condensation, or any other form in which a work may be recast, transformed, or adapted, or a work consisting of editorial revisions, annotations, elaborations, or other modifications which, as a whole, represent an original work of authorship.

Thus, any work based completely or substantially upon a preexisting work, if it satisfies the originality requirement and is not itself an infringing work, will be separately copyrightable. The distinction between a derivative work and a joint work lies in the intent of each contributor at the time the contribution is created. If the work is created with the intention that the contributions be merged into inseparable or interdependent parts of a unitary whole, then the merger creates a joint work. If such intention occurs only after the work has been created, then the merger results in a derivative or collective work.

Collective Works

A collective work is defined as:

> a work, such as a periodical issue, anthology, or encyclopedia, in which a number of contributions, constituting separate and independent works in themselves, are assembled into a collective whole.

The originality involved in a collective work is the collection and assembling of preexisting works that may themselves be copyrightable, without any changes in such material. This assemblage of works is copyrightable.

COPYRIGHT PROTECTION FOR UTILITARIAN OBJECTS

Because copyright law was originally intended to protect literary works, earlier versions of the law omitted protection for three-dimensional designs. These designs were not given copyright protection until 1870.

The Copyright Act of 1909 did not contain any protection for utilitarian objects, but the regulations adopted to interpret the law extended copyright protection to the artistic elements of a utilitarian piece. The regulation stated that the aesthetic, but not mechanical or utilitarian, aspects of the item would be protected.

Despite the lack of specific legislation, some protection is available for manufacturers of utilitarian objects. The copyright law may be relied on to a limited extent. For example, if an individual draws a copyrightable picture and obtains copyright protection for that design, then the copyrighted picture could be used or incorporated into any utilitarian item and be protected. Similarly, architectural drawings are entitled to copyright protection.

NOTICE REQUIREMENT

The requirement that original works and all copies have a copyright notice affixed to them on publication is basic to both the Copyright Act of 1909 and the Copyright Revision Act of 1976. The notice consists of the international symbol "©" or the word "copyright" or its abbreviation "Copr.," the name of the author (in the case of works for hire, this is usually the employer), and the year of first publication. For example:

Copyright 2004 by John Doe

or

© John Doe, 2004

The order of the words is unimportant.

Under the Copyright Act of 1909, a publication without notice caused the work to fall into the public domain. Once the rights were lost, they could not be retrieved. It was publication with notice that created a federal copyright under this law.

Under the Copyright Revision Act of 1976, a federal copyright is created as soon as an original work is made in tangible form. Until 1989, however, the proper notice had to be attached at publication if you wished to retain a copyright after publication. However, a savings clause provided methods for saving a copyright when notice was omitted.

Due to the 1989 amendment to the 1976 act, notice is not required on works created or first published after March 1, 1989. Although notice is not required, notice should still be used to make others aware of your rights. One who copies a work, believing it to be in the public domain because there is no notice, may be considered an innocent infringer. In this situation, the author whose work is copied will likely not recover significant damages. In fact, the court might even allow the copier to continue using the work.

APPLICATION PROCESS

To register a copyright, you must file an application form with the Copyright Register, Library of Congress, Washington, DC 20559. The forms can be downloaded and completed at the Copyright Office's website at www.copyright.gov. Online registration is preferred, and the Copyright Office provides economic benefits for its use. That is to say, online registration is cheaper and more efficient than paper registration. You must also deposit two of the "best copies" of the work by conventional mail if the deposit cannot be accomplished online.

You may be able to upload a text or image as part of the registration process; however, if the text or image is published in hard copy, then the hard copy will be considered the "best copy" and should be mailed to the Copyright Office as part of the registration.

Remember, if you have a copyright notice on your work, or if your work was published after March 1, 1989, even without a notice, you already have a copyright. Finally, you must pay the appropriate filing fee. For the actual fee in effect at this time see www.copyright.gov. Under the Copyright Revision Act of 1976, as amended, registration is necessary only:

- as a prerequisite to commencing an infringement action;
- when the copyright owner wishes to take advantage of the savings provision of Section 405; or
- if the Register of Copyrights demands registration of published works bearing a copyright notice (which is not likely to happen unless you have been in correspondence with that office).

The law separates registration from the deposit requirements. Under the 1909 Act, registration involved filing a copyright application, paying a $6 fee, and depositing two copies of the work itself or two photographs of the original. However, fine prints came within the requirements of actual copies, making it necessary to deposit two actual prints. Congress recognized the economic hardship this caused artists and the fact that many of them intentionally failed to take advantage of copyright protection because of the burdensome deposit requirement and therefore modified it. Now, the Register of Copyrights is allowed to exempt certain categories from the deposit requirement or provide for alternative forms of deposit. This has been done in the case of computer software, films, videotapes, and other items.

IN PLAIN ENGLISH

Under the present law, you should deposit two of the best copies of the work with the Library of Congress within three months of publication. If the objects are bulky, fragile, or valuable, photographs may be deposited instead of the actual work. The same photograph privilege applies to fine prints in editions of 300 or fewer. Filing the application need not be done at the time of deposit. When you feel depositing two copies is a hardship, you may apply for a waiver of the two-copy deposit requirement.

DELAYING REGISTRATION

Although you can delay registration, there are at least two reasons why you should deposit the work and register the copyright (i.e., file the application) within three months of publication. First, the copyright law prohibits the awarding of attorney's fees and statutory damages for infringements that occur before registration, unless registration took place within three months of publication. Second, if you deposit the required two copies of the work within three months but postpone sending the registration form and fee, the Copyright Office will require two more copies of the work when you eventually do send in the form and money. Finally, if the two copies are not deposited within the requisite three-month period, the Register of Copyrights may demand them. If the copies are not submitted within three months after demand, the person upon whom the demand was made may be subject to a fine for each unsubmitted work. In addition, such person or persons may be required to pay the Library of Congress an amount equal to the retail cost of the work. If no retail cost has been established, the costs incurred by the Library of Congress in acquiring the work, provided such costs are reasonable, will be substituted. The copyright proprietor who willfully and repeatedly refuses to comply with such a demand may be liable for additional fines.

PERIOD OF PROTECTION

The Copyright Act of 1909 granted copyright protection to a work for a twenty-eight-year period that could be renewed for one additional twenty-eight-year period. Under the revised law, a work created on or after January 1, 1978, has copyright protection from the instant it is fixed in tangible form until seventy years after the creator's death. If the work was created jointly, the copyright expires seventy years after the last author dies. There are no renewals for copyrights created under the 1976 act. Copyrights granted under the 1909 act that were in effect on January 1, 1978, automatically received an extension to create a term of ninety-five years from the date the copyright was first obtained. It is important to note that this automatic extension applies only to copyrights that were in effect on January 1, 1978. Thus, if the copyright on a work had lapsed prior to January 1, 1978, the copyright would not have been revived unless the work was first published in a foreign country and that copyright was still in effect in the country of origin and that country is a treaty partner with the United States. In that event, the US copyright can be revived. This area of law is quite complex and very confusing. If your nonprofit is involved in a situation where the date of protection is unclear or where a question of whether the copyright was established overseas and may still be in effect overseas, you should consult with an experienced copyright attorney. In all cases, copyright terms end on December 31 of the given year.

The copyright period of life plus seventy years applies only to works created by human beings using their own names. In other cases, for example, a nonprofit that obtains a copyright in accordance with the doctrine of works made for hire, or for works created anonymously or pseudonymously, the period of protection is either 120 years from creation or 95 years from first publication, whichever expires first.

INFRINGEMENT

The federal courts have exclusive jurisdiction over copyright infringement *litigation*. Under both the 1909 and 1976 acts, the trial judge has wide discretion in setting damages. Under the 1909 act, a judge could award either actual damages (plaintiff's out-of-pocket losses or defendant's profit) or statutory damages. Under the 1976 act, as amended in 1989, a judge may also award actual damages and the range of statutory damages is greater: as little as $200 for innocent infringement, between $750 and $30,000 for the typical case, and up to $150,000 for willful infringement. Both acts allow the awarding of reasonable attorney's fees to the prevailing party. Both acts also provide for injunctions against continued infringement and, in some cases, impoundment. The statute of limitations for both acts allows a plaintiff three years to file a lawsuit after the infringement occurs. This time frame refers to the date the infringement was committed, not the date the infringement was discovered.

In the case of willful infringement for commercial gain, criminal sanctions may also be imposed. The law was amended in 1982 to provide more severe penalties for those who unlawfully reproduce and sell sound recordings, motion pictures, audiovisual works, or phonorecords. Under these provisions, a criminal infringer may be imprisoned and/or fined.

Fair Use

Not every copying of a protected work is an infringement. There are two basic types of noninfringing use—*fair use* and exempted use.

The Copyright Act of 1976 recognizes that copies of a protected work for purposes such as criticism, comment, news reporting, teaching (including multiple copies for classroom use), scholarship, or research can be considered fair use and, therefore, not an infringement. However, this is not a complete list, nor is it intended as a definition of fair use.

In addition, the act cites four criteria to be considered in determining whether a particular use is or is not fair:

1. the purpose and character of the use, including whether it is for commercial use or nonprofit educational purposes;
2. the nature of the copyrighted work;
3. the amount and substantiality of the portion used in relation to the copyrighted work as a whole; and
4. the effect of the use upon the potential market for, or value of, the copyrighted work.

The act does not rank these four criteria, nor does it exclude other factors in determining the question of fair use. In effect, all that the act does is leave the doctrine of fair use to be developed by the courts.

The US Supreme Court has interpreted the scope of the fair use doctrine in connection with motion pictures. In *Universal Studios, et al. v. Sony Corporation, et al.*, decided in 1984, the plaintiff movie producers claimed that the defendant, Sony Corporation, was enabling consumers to violate the plaintiff's copyright by selling a machine that could make off-the-air copies of the plaintiff's copyrighted works. This activity, it was alleged, should subject the defendants to liability for copyright infringement as both facilitator and conspirator. The Supreme Court rejected this contention and held that the copying of copyrighted works in one's own home for noncommercial purposes was fair use, at least when applied to audiovisual works. The majority of the justices expressly refrained from considering the applicability of this doctrine to any other forms of copyrighted works.

In *American Geophysical Union v. Texaco, Inc.*, the US Court of Appeals for the Second Circuit held that making even one copy of a copyrighted professional journal for purposes of retaining an article in one's file for reference purposes was an infringement. The court pointed out that if the employees of the Texaco research lab desired additional copies of articles in the copyrighted journals, reprints could have been purchased. The making of an unauthorized copy deprived the copyright owner of a sale and was, therefore, an infringement.

It has also been held that the mere fact that permission to quote from a copyrighted work has been requested and denied does not necessarily mean that a use will be infringing. In *Maxtone-Graham v. Burtchaell*, the defendant, a Catholic priest, requested permission to quote from the plaintiff's book of interviews with women who were, as the title suggests, *Pregnant by Mistake*. Since the priest's intended use of the quoted material was to support his pro-life publication, permission was denied. He, nevertheless, used the excerpts. In the resulting litigation, the court held that the use was fair since the priest's unauthorized use of the copyrighted material was a productive use and the plaintiff was not necessarily deprived of sales. It is, therefore, still relatively unclear how broad or narrow the scope of the fair use doctrine really is.

Exemptions

In many instances, the ambiguities of the fair use doctrine are resolved by statutory exemptions. The exempted uses apply to situations where the public interest in making a copy outweighs the potential harm to the copyright pro-prietor. For example, the library and archives exemption allows libraries and archives to reproduce and distribute a single copy of a work provided that certain requirements are met. However, this exemption in no way affects the applicability of fair use, nor does it apply where such copying is prohibited in contractual arrangements agreed to by the library or archive when it acquired the work.

INTERNATIONAL PROTECTION

The United States is a party to three multinational copyright treaties. The Buenos Aires Convention, in effect in the Southern Hemisphere, provides international protection within member countries provided the words "all rights reserved" are added to the copyright notice. Those words must appear in the official language of the country in which the copyright is initially pro-tected (i.e., Spanish, English, or Portuguese). The United States is also a party to the Universal Copyright Convention, which requires a copyright owner to comply with the copyright laws of the copyright owner's country, provided that country is also a party to the Universal Copyright Convention. It also requires the copyright owner to use the international copyright symbol "©" as part of the copyright notice.

As previously noted, the oldest multinational copyright treaty is the Berne Copyright Convention, though the United States did not become a party to it until 1989. This treaty mandates the relaxation of copyright formalities and requires greater protection be afforded copyright owners. For a list of the countries that are parties to these treaties and have reciprocal rights with the United States, see www.copyright.gov.

The protection afforded copyright owners under these treaties is auto-matic so long as the aforementioned minimal compliance standards are met. In this respect, international protection of copyrights is usually more avail-able than international protection of other forms of intellectual property.

If you desire more information, visit the Copyright Office's website at www .copyright.gov or write to the Copyright Office, Library of Congress, Wash-ington, DC, 20559, and ask for a free copyright information packet.

CONCLUSION

It is clear that nonprofit organizations create, own, use, and enjoy many items that may be protected by copyright. It is important for you to be familiar with the law so that you can avoid violating it and so that your organization can take advantage of it.

CHAPTER 9

Advertising

Many nonprofit organizations promote their activities and engage in significant advertising even though they are not engaged in a business for profit. The purpose of advertising is to call attention to the organization's activities rather than just to earn a profit.

There is a host of different issues that arise in the context of advertising. When preparing an advertising program, it is essential for you to take care not to violate the rights of other businesses or individuals. Care should be taken to work with an attorney skilled in advertising law in order to be assured of having an effective program that will enable you to sell your product or service without exposing your organization to potential liability. A poorly planned advertising program is likely to be more harmful than none at all. This chapter covers several important legal considerations that may arise when planning an advertising program.

GOVERNMENT REGULATION

To begin with, an organization may always tout the qualities of its products or services, but those representations must be true. If there are any misrepresentations contained in ads or promotions, the state or federal government may file a lawsuit to redress this wrong.

Most states have consumer protection laws that, among other things, impose fines and other legal sanctions on organizations that engage in misleading advertising. The state attorney general can cause an offending advertisement to be withdrawn and may even require corrective advertising. Similarly, the *Federal Trade Commission (FTC)* is involved in policing businesses that are engaged in interstate commerce. If your organization's activities extend beyond your state boundaries and either touch or affect another state, then the

Federal Trade Commission has jurisdiction over your organization. This is also true if you advertise over the web. Indeed, advertising online may subject your advertising to regulation throughout the world, and the laws of other countries may be quite different than those in the United States.

If the product or service that your organization provides has any medicinal benefits, then it must first be approved by the Food and Drug Administration (FDA). The approval process is quite technical and will require you to work closely with an expert specializing in this area of practice. Failure to comply with the requirements of the Food and Drug Administration could subject you to fines and, in some instances, imprisonment.

COMPARATIVE ADVERTISING

It has become quite common for organizations to tout the merits of their products and services by comparing them with those of their competitors. This form of comparative advertising is permissible in the United States provided that the statements made are true. Other countries, for example South Africa, have different rules with respect to advertising. But an organization advertising in the United States would be permitted to use the name of a competitor and describe the competitor's products in an advertisement, even though the comparison will likely point out the competing product's or service's inferiority. This is true as long as there is no likelihood that a consumer would believe the advertiser is also selling the competing product or service and as long as the statements made are accurate.

Example: In a leading case, it was held permissible to use the names of famous perfumes in an advertisement that stated that those who like the famous perfume will also like the advertiser's less expensive product. The court felt that there was no possibility of a consumer being confused into believing that the expensive perfume manufacturer was advertising for the cheaper knockoff scent. In addition, since the perfume smelled the same, the statements made were felt to be accurate.

A closely related situation arises when one makes disparaging remarks about the product of another. In this situation, the one who intentionally or negligently makes untrue disparaging remarks about the product or service of another business may be held legally accountable to the injured party. It should be noted that for a disparaging remark to be actionable, it must be both untrue and believable by a reasonable person. If the statement made was so outlandish as to be unbelievable, it is unlikely the owner whose product was disparaged will be able to prove any injury. Thus, if a car manufacturer claimed its competitor's vehicle was so poorly constructed that it literally fell apart within the first week of use, the likelihood is that this gross exaggeration would not be believed and, therefore, would not be actionable.

Environmental nonprofits frequently make disparaging remarks about products deemed environmentally harmful such as plastic, petroleum, genetically modified organisms, and the like. This could give rise to liability if the statements made are untrue and injurious. If the intention is to call attention to the environmentally unfriendly product or process, then care must be taken to be sure that every statement made is accurate or both the individual and the organization that the individual is affiliated with may incur significant liability.

PUBLICITY AND PRIVACY

An organization may use a celebrity to endorse its product, provided the celebrity consents to the endorsement. If not, the organization may be liable to the celebrity for violating his or her right of publicity. This right is granted by the majority of states in the United States to those who commercially exploit their names, voices, or images, such as sports figures, actors, or singers. The use of a look-alike for commercial purposes may also be actionable. Thus, when manufacturers used look-alikes for Jackie Onassis, Woody Allen, and the rap group the Fat Boys, liability was imposed.

People who have not achieved notoriety because of their commercial activities may have a right to privacy and, thus, may have a claim if their names or likenesses are used in an advertisement without their permission. This applies even to employees, volunteers, and members. They must grant permission for their names, voices, or likenesses to be used for advertising purposes.

If an individual's photograph is not the focal point of the ad, but rather is merely an incidental part, such as a head in a crowd or a member of an audience, then an individual's permission may not be essential for the photograph to be used commercially.

Even though you may not be required to have permission from an individual before using his or her photograph, it is a good idea to get a signed photo release whenever possible. The release should be worded in such a way as to give your organization permission to use the name and likeness or, where relevant, the person's voice, for any and all purposes, including advertising your organization. This will protect you if, for example, the individual ultimately becomes popular and you wish to use the photos you obtained at an earlier date before the individual became a celebrity.

UNAUTHORIZED USE OF TRADEMARK

An advertiser may be permitted to use the name or logo of another organization in its ad as long as there is no likelihood that the average viewer would believe that the ad was sponsored by the organization whose name or logo you are using. For example, it would be permissible for you to have an ad for a baseball team contain a photo of individuals incidentally holding a distinctively shaped Coca-Cola bottle, as long as it is clear from the advertisement that the soft drink manufacturer is not sponsoring the ad.

Nonprofit organizations such as the Metropolitan Museum of New York, colleges, law schools, and even the Boy Scouts of America frequently license the use of their trademarks. When they do, they must impose quality control standards for that use or the license would be deemed a "naked license." If this occurs, then, unfortunately, the organization could wind up losing all rights to its trademark. An experienced trademark lawyer should be consulted when preparing a trademark license.

GEOGRAPHIC LOCATIONS

Geographic locations may also be used in advertisements without obtaining the owner's consent. It would be permissible for an organization to advertise its product by having someone stand in front of a famous building, such as the Empire State Building or the Space Needle. Similarly, an automobile advertisement may show its vehicle streaking through a metropolitan area and passing several famous businesses.

This is so because items of utility are not copyrightable. Buildings, parks, and other landmarks may incidentally be used in advertising programs without the owner's permission. (However, it was held that a building that was architecturally unique, identifiable, and famous could enjoy the protection of the *trade dress* laws when it was featured prominently on a poster.)

TRADE DRESS

A form of advertising that has been given special protection is package design. While it is true that the copyright laws do not protect functional items, such as product packaging, the courts have developed a form of protection known as trade dress. This means that the design elements of a particular packaging design are protectable as long as they are not otherwise functional, i.e., a hanger or a lid. The trade dress form of protection may be automatic and has been extended beyond traditional packaging.

Example: A leading case involved Blue Mountain Greeting Card Company. It had developed a distinct and very identifiable line of greeting cards. The cards had become quite well known and commercially successful. The Hallmark Greeting Card Company realized this fact and designed a line of cards that were not identical to those of Blue Mountain but, in essence, appropriated the Blue Mountain look and feel. Consumers seeing the Hallmark cards would reasonably believe that they were merely an extension by Blue Mountain of its popular line. For this reason, the court held Hallmark liable for infringing Blue Mountain's trade dress in the cards.

The US Supreme Court, in 1992, endorsed the expansion of the trade dress doctrine in *Two Pesos v. Taco Cabana*. In this case, the court stated that the nonfunctional aspects of a business might be protectable trade dress provided they are distinctive and identifiable. A restaurant's architectural features, décor, and menu may be protected so long as they have a distinctive look and feel, are not functional, and have achieved notoriety. Thus, it is likely that the bare aluminum and pine interior of a Chipotle would be considered protectable trade dress. The trade dress doctrine has been used to prevent copying of a business's distinctive theme, a food company's packaging, and a jewelry manufacturer's earring backers.

In 2000, the US Supreme Court clarified the trade dress doctrine by providing that product design trade dress can be established only by conducting an extensive survey of consumers in order to determine that they recognize the unique look and feel of the item involved. As of this writing, the court has not applied the same requirement to package design trade dress.

IN PLAIN ENGLISH

Many organizations have begun to register their trade dress. This is accomplished by registering the distinctive look and feel. By doing this, the proprietor gains the presumption of validity under federal trademark law (Lanham Act) and the presumption that the trade dress has been established. Examples of registered trade dress are the distinctive shape of a Coca-Cola bottle, the McDonald's golden arches, and the three stripes on Adidas running shoes.

Celebrity Trade Dress

Individuals can also have distinctive styles. For example, when an advertiser hired one of Bette Midler's backup singers to replicate Ms. Midler's distinctive vocal rendition of a song for a commercial, Ms. Midler sued and recovered for the knockoff. It was held that the intentional copying of the singer's famous, distinctive style and voice was a form of infringement and actionable. When, however, a manufacturer hired a group that looked and sounded like the group known as the Fat Boys, the federal court in New York held the manufacturer liable only for violating the celebrities' publicity rights. The court refused to impose liability for the unauthorized use of the Fat Boys' sound since the New York publicity statute extends protection merely to one's name, portrait, or picture and not to one's sound. The Bette Midler case relied on a California statute that, among other things, protects a celebrity's voice.

Many nonprofit organizations such as the Rock and Roll Hall of Fame have a distinctive trade dress that may be protectable.

INSURANCE

Many organizations have obtained insurance to cover the risk of advertising injury. The general business liability policy used by many insurance companies contains an advertising injury provision as well. If your organization engages in advertising activities, it would be appropriate to consider obtaining advertising injury insurance in order to be sure that your organization has appropriate coverage if a problem should occur. You should discuss the cost and benefits of this kind of insurance with an experienced insurance agent or broker.

If a problem arises in which you feel that your organization may be at risk, it would be appropriate to tender the claim to your insurance carrier to determine whether coverage of the problem is available. If, on the other hand, you feel that a person or entity is infringing your intellectual property, it would be appropriate to consult with an experienced intellectual property lawyer.

CONCLUSION

The benefits of advertising are clear; yet, if not done properly, the detriments can be significant. This is particularly true today with the advent of inexpensive online advertising. Care must be taken to comply with the laws of every jurisdiction into which an advertisement may be launched. By working with an experienced lawyer, you will reduce your organization's potential exposure.

CHAPTER 10

Licensing

Once you have protected your intellectual property through trademark, trade dress, patent, or copyright, you may want to exploit your creations and prevent others from interfering with your rights. For instance, you may convert pictures from your copyrighted catalog into posters and sell them. If another organization likes your work and wishes to duplicate it, you can exploit your own intellectual property by granting the other organization a license.

IN PLAIN ENGLISH

Licensing has become so important that entire trade shows devoted to this field have emerged. One of the most prominent is the Licensing Expo held every year at the Mandalay Bay Convention Center, in Las Vegas. For more information, check the website at www.licensingexpo.com.

In situations where copyrights are not available, an organization may nevertheless be able to obtain beneficial arrangements. When the Metropolitan Museum of New York was approached by the Springmaid sheet company for the purpose of obtaining rights to use ancient fabric designs in the museum's collection, the museum's attorney came up with a clever way to obtain economic benefits from ancient designs. The museum agreed to allow the sheet company access to the museum's archives and for the right to use the museum's name in exchange for a significant royalty. In fact, the money generated by this arrangement turned out to be so significant that the museum feared the possibility of losing its tax-exempt status. What the museum did was to exchange access and use of its name for money and the arrangement was formalized in a written contract.

GENERAL CONSIDERATION

A license to use your copyright, trademark, trade dress, or patent should be in writing. It should describe the scope of the user's permission, such as how long the license will last, whether the user can market copies throughout the world or only in specific locations, and whether the license allows exploitation of the entire intellectual property or only a portion of it (i.e., use of a copyrighted photo on T-shirts, but not on anything else). Care should be taken when defining these boundaries. If a US license permits sales or other exploitation of the licensed products or technology in, for example, Canada, then Canadian sales to a gift shop supplier that ships the goods to the United States may be within the scope of permitted use, resulting in the US licensees competing with Canadian licensees for sales within the United States. This situation is known as a *gray market*, which can be controlled by using care in drafting the license agreement.

Lawyers who specialize in intellectual property can be helpful in explaining the numerous possibilities available to you through the licensing process. They can be helpful in drafting a document that will afford you maximum protection while another person exploits your intellectual property. A skilled lawyer can also determine whether the licensing arrangement you are proposing could be subject to *franchising* laws (see *The Law (in Plain English)® for Small Business*, Fifth Edition, chapter 9).

NOTE: Skilled drafters will avoid ambiguity in language such as "American" when intending "the United States" since all countries in the North and South Americas may be considered American.

It is also important to record your license in the appropriate place—the Copyright Office or the office of the Commissioner of Patents and Trademarks—when such recording is available. An intellectual property lawyer should be able to assist you with this process.

LICENSING OPPORTUNITIES

A nonprofit organization may have numerous opportunities to obtain benefits from licensing items which are not otherwise protectable. For example, as discussed above, when the Springmaid sheet company wished to obtain the right to reproduce historical patterns in its collection, the right of access to that collection and the use of the museum's name were licensed. Similarly, when the National Gallery of Art and a number of prominent US museums agreed to an arrangement for a traveling exhibition of the King Tut exhibit, an extraordinary licensing arrangement was agreed to. In that situation, the museums were granted the right to reproduce pieces from the King Tut exhibition, which reproductions were available for sale in the US museums' gift shops. The contract provided that the profits from these sales would go to the Egyptian museum in Cairo for the purpose of remodeling that museum and upgrading its display areas. Sales of the reproductions exceeded $10 million, and that money was ultimately paid to the Egyptian museum. In this situation, the Egyptian museum was able to obtain a significant profit from allowing the reproduction of historical items in its collection. The agreement between the parties provided safeguards for the reproductions and allowed the reproductions to be identified as authentic copies of items in the Egyptian collection. In this situation, historical artifacts that are not protected by copyright, trademark, or other forms of intellectual property, have nevertheless been used for the purpose of generating revenue. The right to reproduce and the right of access had been cleverly leveraged into an economic benefit for the nonprofit.

LICENSING CONSIDERATIONS

Several issues should be considered before deciding whether to grant a license. While the factors that follow may influence your decision to license or not to license, by no means is it intended to be an exhaustive list.

Nature of the Work

First, the nature of the work, technology, and so on must be considered. If the property rights to be licensed are in a new technology that is susceptible to rapid change (i.e., a new development in the computer or electronic industry) or a product that is simply one of many alternatives on the market, then the value of the license to the potential licensee will be decreased. The licensee may then require that updated product enhancements be provided as part of the license agreement. On the other hand, if the product is a new development that exists without alternatives or if the trademark is a very strong one, as with the Red Cross or Salvation Army, the licensor is in a much stronger negotiating position to demand a higher price.

Sublicensing

Another issue to consider is whether or not the licensee will be permitted to sublicense. When permitted, the right to sublicense can affect the price paid for a license. In the area of music licensing such as with church music, sublicense rights are often part of the licensee organization's comprehensive mission. Sublicense provisions should be carefully drafted and tied directly to the terms of the original license agreement. All ownership of the licensor's rights should be retained by the licensor via specific provisions in the original license agreement. Provisions should be made for quality-control checks of the licensed property. All provisions in the original license agreement should be drafted to apply to any sublicense agreements negotiated by the licensee.

Patented Technology

Since many colleges and universities rely a great deal on licensing patented technology as part of their programs, it is important to consider this form of intellectual property licensing as well. When an organization is considering licensing a patented technology, the safety of the technology and potential for liability arising from its use should be evaluated. Licenses can be drafted with exculpatory clauses in which the licensee agrees to assume all liability arising from the use of the licensed technology.

Exculpatory clauses that deal with latent *design defects* (i.e., defects not readily discoverable), however, may not entirely insulate the licensor from liability. Careful testing of the technology to ensure the removal of defects will reduce the risk of such a situation occurring.

The exculpatory clause itself, by careful enumeration of what liabilities the licensee assumes, can also provide extra protection to the licensor. The exculpatory clause should be written by an attorney experienced in drafting this type of provision.

International Concerns

Care should also be taken to avoid allowing your intellectual property to be exploited in countries that do not honor US intellectual property laws, countries that have laws that are less protective than ours, or countries that have no intellectual property law at all. The US State Department has a watch list of countries that do not honor their intellectual property treaty obligations and of countries that have a poor record of enforcement with respect to intellectual property.

The advent of the Internet has presented a myriad of new challenges. Since material may be captured anywhere in the world, even in areas that may not be desirable, care should be taken in determining what is placed on the web and whether your license permits or prohibits web postings.

Naked License

If you are licensing your trademark, then it is essential for you to establish quality control standards and for you to enforce those quality control standards; otherwise, the license may be considered a "naked license," and in that event, your trademark can be invalidated. It is very important for you to work with an experienced intellectual property lawyer when licensing your trademark.

Method of Payment

Once the decision to license has been made, the price of the license must be negotiated. Payment for the license should be spelled out in the license document. You can demand a flat fee in exchange for permission to use your copyright material, trademark, or patent, or your organization may prefer to receive some portion of the income as a royalty. This payment can either be a fixed amount per item or a percentage, perhaps 5 percent, of the money received by the person exploiting the right. Care should be taken to specifically define the sum upon which the percentage will be based. Specify, for example, if it will be a percentage of the net or gross receipts from the sale of items covered by the license, and carefully define the term used.

Royalties

Payments based on sales are referred to as royalties. One should be very careful to define when they are due and payable and on what basis they are to be calculated. Unfortunately, numerous unscrupulous individuals have used creative accounting to reduce their obligations.

Example: In the case of *Buchwald v. Paramount Studios*, Art Buchwald established that he, and not Eddie Murphy, was responsible for the treatment that ultimately became the movie *Coming to America*. Pursuant to his contract with Paramount, Buchwald was to receive a share of net profits. As of the date of trial, the movie had grossed $350 million, but by the use of creative accounting, Paramount alleged a net loss of $18 million on the picture. The poorly drafted, one-sided contract deprived Buchwald of his fair share of the movie's earnings.

Currency

If international transactions are involved, be sure to specify which country's currency is to be used. The value of US dollars, Canadian dollars, and Australian dollars for example, typically differ. There is also a cost involved in currency conversion.

Accounting Report

It is also important to include in a licensing agreement a provision whereby your organization can verify the accuracy of the records showing what is due. This can be accomplished by requiring the person to whom the license is granted to have an accounting report preceding or accompanying any royalty checks. There should be an agreed-upon right to have an independent party *audit* the books in the event that you dispute the validity of the report.

Acknowledgment of Ownership

In order to retain the protection afforded by the patent, trademark, or copyright laws, you must require any person who uses your organization's creation to acknowledge its ownership and include the appropriate notice on the work. It is common to see a legend that states, for example, "Reproduced with permission of the Oregon Historical Society, the copyright owner."

Quality Control

Since the work marketed after your organization has granted a license will bear its name or trademark, it will usually be difficult, if not impossible, for consumers to distinguish between your organization's work and those works reproduced by the person to whom you have granted a license. For this reason, it is important for you to retain some degree of quality control over the licensed product. In fact, as noted above, trademark law requires quality control. It has been held that a naked license (one without quality control measures) is void. A provision in the license should, therefore, require the licensee to demonstrate the method by which the item will be reproduced and some means by which you can evaluate the quality of the final products.

Signature

In order for the license to be valid and enforceable, both parties should sign it. You should make it clear that the license is personal and may not be assigned or exploited by anybody but the person or entity to whom it is given unless your organization gives its written permission. If your organization is dealing with a business entity, then you should make it clear that a transfer of a large percentage ownership in that entity will be deemed an assignment even though the entity still retains the license. In this way, your organization will not be surprised by having the business entity to which it granted a license under new management. It is also wise to provide that the license is void and no longer in effect if any of its terms, including payment of royalties, are violated.

TRADE SECRETS

Another form of protection, known as trade secret law, allows exploitation of a particular innovation and may afford even greater protection than copyright (see chapter 8) or patent laws. A trade secret may be loosely defined as anything that has not been revealed and could give you a competitive advantage. The secret should cover something that you actually use in your organization and that you take some reasonable steps to protect. For example, lists of donors, suppliers, members, and fund-raising techniques may all be protectable trade secrets.

A trade secret may be lost if the owner fails to either identify it or take reasonable steps to protect it. Otherwise, the trade secret protection is perpetual. In fact, one of the most famous trade secrets is the recipe for Coca-Cola, which is more than a hundred years old. Attempts to misappropriate Coca-Cola company trade secrets are currently being prosecuted under both federal and state trade secret laws.

Trade Secret Protection

All that is necessary for something to be protectable as a trade secret is the following:

- it gives you a competitive advantage;
- it will, in fact, be treated as a secret by you; and
- it is not generally known in your industry or business.

The fundamental question of trade secret law is—what is protectable? The way you use knowledge and information, the specific portions of information you have grouped together, and the mere assembly of information itself may all be trade secrets even if everything you consider important for your secrets is publicly available information. For example, if there are numerous methods for producing a particular dye and you have selected one of them, the mere fact that you have selected this method may itself be a trade secret. The identity of your suppliers may be a trade secret, even if they are all listed in the yellow pages. The fact that you have done business with these people and found them to be reputable and responsive to you may make the list of their names a trade secret.

Many trade secrets will be embodied in some form of a document. One of the first things you should do is to mark any paper, photograph, or the like "confidential." You should also take steps to prevent demonstrations of your trade secret, such as manufacturing methods. Taking these steps will not create trade secret protection. However, the fact that an effort has been made to identify the materials and methods you consider secret will aid you in establishing that you treated them as a trade secret should litigation ever occur.

Protecting a Trade Secret

In this area, a little thought and cleverness will go a long way toward giving you the protection of the trade secret laws.

Physical Security

First, you should have some degree of physical security. It has been said that physical security is 90 percent common sense and 10 percent true protection. You should restrict access to the area in which the trade secret is used. Some precaution should be taken to prevent visitors from peering into the manufacturing area where the secret process, formula, or technique is employed. The credentials of delivery and service persons should be examined. Employee access to trade secret information should be on a need-to-know basis. Employees should not be granted automatic free access to the material you desire to keep as a trade secret. Extra care should be taken with laptops, PDAs, and the like, because if they are lost or stolen, a tremendous amount of data is at risk of disclosure.

Employee Access

As noted, documents, pictures, or sketches containing trade secrets should be clearly labeled. A procedure should be established for controlled employee access to the documents. For instance, one person could be responsible for granting access to them, and a sign-in/sign-out process could be instituted for those permitted access to the documents.

Fragmenting Information

If possible, the information that you consider to be a trade secret should be fragmented. This means no one employee should have possession of the entire secret. Thus, no one person will have sufficient information to hurt you.

Confidentiality Agreements

It is also a good idea to have employees sign a confidentiality or nondisclosure agreement when hired. An attorney who deals with intellectual property can prepare agreements for use within your business.

If it ever becomes important for you to reveal a secret to an outsider, such as when someone desires to purchase the right to exploit your innovation through a licensing arrangement, a different form of confidentiality agreement is in order. These agreements generally provide that in exchange for disclosure of the confidential trade secret information, the party receiving such information will keep it in confidence and will not use or disclose it without the express written permission of the person making the disclosure. Again, your intellectual property lawyer can prepare such an agreement for you.

Vague Labeling

Another method of protecting your trade secret is to engage in some vague labeling. For example, if your trade secret consists of a unique mixture for a glaze, then instead of having the components of the glaze bear their true names, you should label them "Ingredient A," "Ingredient B," "Ingredient C," etc. Then, if an employee quits or if a stranger happens into your office, all they will learn is that by mixing some portion of A with some portion of B, combined with some portion of C, the desired result will be achieved. This will not be very useful information. Similarly, if the trade secret is the temperature at which a glaze is fired, instead of actually marking the thermometer, you may wish to have the original temperature marks removed and replaced by colored zones.

IN PLAIN ENGLISH

If you are publishing in or contributing to industry or trade journals, take care not to reveal trade secrets. Occasionally, manufacturers or their employees inadvertently disclose valuable information in an attempt to impress their colleagues.

MISAPPROPRIATING TRADE SECRETS

In order to avoid the charge that you are stealing someone else's trade secret, you should question employees who come to work for you from a competitor. If there is any possibility of a new employee using the competitor's trade secret information, the new employee should meet with the former employer and get written permission to use the information while working for you.

Trade secrets have been deemed so important that in the mid-1990s, the US Congress passed a federal law making it a crime to misappropriate another's trade secret. It was felt that if the United States were to retain its technological competitive edge, the government must assist industry with this form of protection. Since its enactment, there have been several high-profile cases underscoring both the importance of trade secrets and the federal government's efforts in helping to protect them.

Trade secret laws may be the only protection available for your business secrets. Care should therefore be taken to restrict access to the information and to treat the information as truly secret. Contractual arrangements both with employees and outsiders are quite useful. These, coupled with your common sense in the day-to-day operation of your business, will go a long way toward protecting your intellectual property.

CHAPTER 11

The Internet

It has become commonplace for individuals and nonprofit organizations to establish a presence on the Internet. Elaborate websites have appeared with regularity for not only large multinational organizations but also for smaller nonprofits and individuals. The vast majority of nonprofit organizations have established websites.

Technology allows even the smallest nonprofit organizations to create elaborate interactive sites that attract a good deal of positive attention. Theories abound on what makes a website appealing. For some, interactive graphics are the key; others feel it is important to provide browsers with something of value to take with them, such as information or the opportunity to obtain souvenirs of the visit. Some music publishers provide samples of the music they handle, while visual artists may encourage visitors to download images displayed on their sites. Some nonprofit organizations offer memberships and ask for donations online. With these new technologies, nonprofit organizations are faced with additional concerns and considerations for their daily operations.

PROTECTING ORGANIZATION PROPERTY

The Internet's rapid growth has raised significant questions regarding the extent of legal and intellectual property protection. One of the earliest cases involved the Church of Scientology and raised the question of whether US copyright laws and state trade secret laws are enforceable online. In that case, several former church members were sued for posting copyrighted material on the Internet that they had received in confidence.

The court held that these traditional forms of intellectual property protection were, indeed, applicable to the Internet. In addition, it was held that the

Internet service provider (ISP) could also be exposed to liability for merely permitting the infringing material to appear on the web. As elsewhere, one who facilitates or aids in the commission of an infringing act may be liable as a contributory infringer. Congress later changed this situation for ISPs who do not have control over the content of the material posted.

The Church of Scientology also claimed that the wrongdoers misappropriated the church's trade secrets and sought an injunction to have the offending material removed from the website. The court rejected this argument, pointing out that once information is posted online, it is no longer secret, and the injunction was denied. However, if a protected trade secret is posted on a website in violation of an agreement or in breach of one's duty to the owner of the protected information, then the act of posting would be wrongful, and the perpetrator would likely be liable for the improper activity.

IN PLAIN ENGLISH

Cyberspace is the newest communication vehicle, but it is considered to be one of the most dynamic and effective.

PROTECTING CONSUMER INFORMATION

Legislation has been passed in an attempt to control the dissemination of personal information by nonprofit organizations. It is now required that all organizations provide customers with an opportunity to elect whether their personal information may be disclosed to others through opting out. In addition, California adopted legislation requiring any company doing business in California or affecting California commerce to disclose any breach in security that has potentially compromised personal information. This legislation applies to nonprofit organizations who gather personal information while subscribing members, accepting donations, etc. It is expected that this type of legislation will become far more widespread.

DOMAIN NAMES

Characterization of website names has also presented some vexing problems. It is unclear whether a domain name is merely an address (uniform resource locator [URL]) used for the purpose of locating the site or whether that name may be characterized as a trademark. In addition, the problem is compounded by the fact that, while there is only one Internet, each trademark is distinguished by the classification of goods or services it covers. There are thirty-four international classes of goods and twelve international classes of services.

Example: The American Bar Association, commonly referred to as the ABA, wished to register its acronym as its domain name. It was not able to do so, because the American Booksellers Association—also commonly known as the ABA—had already registered www.aba.org.

Domain names were originally registered with Network Solutions. Today, there are a number of different registrars. Competition for domain name registration is fierce. Prices for securing a domain name have become far more competitive. Generally, domain names are registered on a first-come, first-served basis. Many Internet host service providers can assist you in obtaining a domain name.

Initially, there were five top-level domain name categories for US-based registrants: .com for commerce; .org for organizations; .gov for government; .mil for military; and .edu for educational institutions. These suffixes were supposed to be made available only to those who qualified for their use. As the availability of popular domain names shrank, it became necessary to create additional opportunities by creating new suffixes, such as .pro for professionals, .biz for nonprofit organizations, .fm for radio, and the process continues. In fact, the number of suffixes is becoming rather large, though the initial five are still the most popular. In addition to all of the US designators, many other countries have distinctive suffixes as well, such as .uk for the United Kingdom, .ru for Russia, etc.

Disputes

There are several methods for resolving domain name disputes. These include litigation in federal district court, reliance on the anti-cybersquatting legislation, and the online arbitration process using the procedure established by ICANN (the Internet Corporation for Assigned Names and Numbers, which offers numerous resources at its website, www.icann.org). The anti-cybersquatting legislation is intended to prevent so-called cybersquatters from obtaining an inventory of domain name registrations for the purpose of reselling them to those who are likely to have a better right to that name as a URL. A lawyer specializing in online intellectual property issues should be consulted when these issues arise.

Trademarked Names

Generally speaking, obtaining a trademark registration for your organization's name will also provide you with leverage in both obtaining and keeping the organization's name as a domain name. Thus, for example, the National Audubon Society would likely have success in either obtaining the URL audubon.org or in defending that URL against another potential registrant of that domain name because Audubon is a registered trademark. As noted in chapter 7, on trademarks, it is possible today to register trademarks in seventy-eight countries throughout the world pursuant to the Madrid System through the US Patent and Trademark Office. One of the principal reasons for this expanded opportunity to obtain international trademark protection was the expanded use of trademarks in commerce on the Internet.

Under some circumstances, using your organization name as a domain name may be considered adequate for purposes of trademark registration. A number of cases have dealt with trademark issues online. In those cases, the applicability of federal trademark law and the question as to which jurisdiction was proper for purposes of litigating the wrongdoing were considered. While the issues have not been definitively resolved, the trend appears to be in favor of extending trademark laws to the Internet and holding infringers liable wherever their infringing activity can be accessed.

In a landmark case, an enterprising individual residing in Illinois decided to register a number of popular organization names as website domain names. When the organization owners who had previously registered those names as trademarks attempted to register their company names as domain names, they were told that they were too late. The entrepreneuring registrant then offered to sell these companies the domain names for their own registered trademarks. The companies filed suit in federal court in California, alleging that the appropriation of the protected trademarks as domain names by one who lacks authority from the trademark owner is an infringement. The court agreed and stated that this outrageous conduct would result in liability.

The defendant in this case objected to being sued in California, stating that he was located in another state and that all his activity actually occurred within his home state. The court made it clear that since the infringing site could be accessed in California and since the infringer was trying to extort money for sale of the marks from California, the case could properly be brought there.

At least one case appears to have taken a different stance regarding jurisdiction. In that situation, a European restaurant bearing the same name as a restaurant in the United States established a website. The American company sued, alleging trademark infringement, and the court held that it was unlikely the European restaurant would cause the kind of market confusion necessary to establish trademark infringement by advertising on the Web and having those advertisements viewed in the United States. This is consistent with intellectual property law in general since it would appear that, even online, it will be necessary to establish a likelihood of confusion and that the infringer somehow appropriates business from the owner of the protected trademark before liability will be imposed.

FRAMING

A number of other issues have generated web-based litigation. Framing is the mechanism whereby the contents of a website can be displayed on another's website. The content is not hosted on the framing website but rather, merely retrieved from the original owner's server. When Total News, Inc., decided to provide users with the ability to compare data from several news sources, such as the *Washington Post* and CNN, problems arose. The other services filed suit, complaining that while the material had not been copied onto Total News's server, the visual presentation of their material was framed within the host's site and that their protected material was, thereby, being retransmitted without their permission. The case was settled, with Total News agreeing to refrain from framing the protected material and the plaintiffs agreed to grant Total News licenses to link directly to their sites. Later cases have judicially established that framing is unlawful and can be legally redressed. The popularity of framing has declined since Internet speeds have increased and there is no legal theory left to justify framing as a non-infringing activity.

LINKING

In the Total News case, the question of linking, where one may jump from one site to another by simply clicking on an identifying icon or phrase, was raised but not resolved. The question has since been reconsidered. Early court decisions held that linking is unlawful when the link is established without the consent of the proprietor of the linked site. Later cases, however, have held that such linking is permissible.

ONLINE ADVERTISING

One of the most important distinctions of advertising on the Internet is the way digital advertising reaches consumers. Ads in other advertising forums, such as magazines, newspapers, radio, and television, are intended to affect conduct in the future. It is hoped that the consumer will purchase the product next time he or she goes shopping. Internet shoppers, on the other hand, can instantaneously make a purchase.

KEYWORDS

One of the more controversial practices that has occurred online is the use of trademarks as keywords in the metadata of competitors. For example, web developers for Pepsi may include the words Coke and Coca-Cola in the code of the website to increase search engine results and deflect Coca-Cola traffic to Pepsi's website. Some courts have held that this practice is unlawful passing off, whereas others have condoned it. The practice remains legally ambiguous, although search engines such as Google have placed restrictions on some services (such as Google AdWords) as to how a competitor's trademark can be used in advertising.

DISCLOSURES

The Internet has become a significant marketplace, and laws adopted for purposes of preventing deceptive advertising do apply online. The Federal Trade Commission (FTC) periodically surveys websites in conjunction with state attorneys general. The FTC requires certain disclosures in connection with traditional forms of advertising. These disclosures are easily lost online. A disclosure can be bypassed when linking from one site to another and required legends can be buried in text that users may just scroll through. In contrast, when a disclosure appears in a more traditional advertisement, the viewer sees the entire composite—and required disclosures are unlikely to be bypassed.

IN PLAIN ENGLISH

According to the FTC, it is a good idea to require website visitors to click through required disclosures whenever an advertising site is visited.

The FTC has announced that it will sue a website designer if that designer knows or should have known that the site he or she created violates the law. However, thus far users have not uniformly been pressed into having to read disclosures if they do not want to.

AUDITS

Some intellectual property practitioners suggest that an attorney who has expertise in working with websites be requested to conduct a so-called Internet traffic and web-content audit. This would include evaluating whether the appropriate permissions to display material have been obtained. For example, if copyrighted material is to be used, has the copyright owner granted permission for the work to be displayed online? If testimonials are to be displayed, then it is important to get written permission from the individual providing the testimonial.

LIABILITY INSURANCE

Organizations need to determine whether their existing liability insurance covers their online activity. Losses resulting from a crashed website are probably not covered in a traditional policy. Similarly, Errors and Omissions insurance should be considered for situations where an organization's website contains infringing work or defames someone.

INTERNATIONAL CONCERNS

Since websites are, by definition, worldwide, it is important to determine whether your site, the content of which is legal in the United States, may subject you to liability elsewhere. For example, comparative advertising is generally permissible and fairly common in the United States. Other countries, such as South Africa, are far more restrictive in what they permit in a comparative advertising spread.

In addition, activities that are legal in the United States can nonetheless subject a website owner to liability abroad.

Example: When eBay permitted auction sales of Nazi memorabilia, it was sued in France by Holocaust survivors for violating French law that prohibits such activities. The court was not sympathetic to eBay's position that it could not technologically isolate France from the rest of the world with respect to its online auctions. In fact, the judge believed the plaintiffs' expert, who said that technology was available to create such a block. The online auction house was found guilty and fined for its activities in France. eBay then filed suit in the United States for the purpose of preventing enforcement of the judgment.

The problem is clear—one who engages in Internet activity has, by definition, established a worldwide presence and must, therefore, comply with worldwide laws—a difficult process even for multimillion-dollar companies like eBay.

COPYRIGHT CONCERNS

The extent of litigation that has resulted from online activity suggests that care must be taken when establishing your presence online. This new dimension gives rise to increased and often desired exposure, but the ramifications of problems can be devastating for a small organization.

PERMISSIONS

Even the simple act of advertising a product for sale could have serious consequences if you are not careful. For instance, if you market or sell a copyrighted item—even if your organization has obtained permission to advertise this item for sale—the organization may still not have the right to post an image of that item on your website. It may be necessary for you to obtain specific permission to replicate the work in two dimensions before engaging online promotional activities.

Downloading and reusing material from other websites may also expose an organization to liability. Some organizations use electronic watermarks to place on the images they post on their websites in order to discourage anyone from attempting to capture and reuse those images without permission.

International Copyright Concerns

Similarly, you have to recognize the fact your organization's material may find its way into jurisdictions and geographical regions that do not have copyright treaty relations with the United States. In this event, you may find that your organization has lost control of protected work.

While the *World Intellectual Property Organization (WIPO)* has expanded the extent of protection available for intellectual property with the WIPO Treaty of 1996, not all countries have adopted or implemented it. As of the date of this writing, 191 countries belong to WIPO, yet few have ratified the treaty to expand protection for sound recordings, motion pictures, computer software, and other digitally transmitted literary works. Even where the treaty is in force, there is still some risk, since it is limited in scope. Additionally, not all countries can be expected to participate and enact this treaty without reservation. Some countries will certainly remain on the US watch list since they continue to disregard their current treaty obligations and there is no reason to believe these countries will adopt or respect the WIPO treaty.

PEER-TO-PEER PROBLEMS

Online music and video streaming have presented a host of problems. Many individuals have been involved in peer-to-peer activities whereby copyrighted music, videos, and films are made available to anyone who wishes to download them without the copyright owner's permission. The situation has been so ubiquitous that drastic steps have been taken. For example, the music industry began filing suit against individuals who were felt to be involved in the practice of music and video swapping. If the peer-to-peer network has a website that acts as a hub that hosts a directory of content, it may be possible to identify and remove infringing content. Often, however, peer-to-peer networks are distributed such that enforcing copyright becomes difficult. If your organization's intellectual property is being disseminated through peer-to-peer networks, it would be wise to contact an experienced intellectual property attorney to discuss your organization's options.

SERVER PROTECTION

One significant risk in maintaining a website is that it may serve as a window to your company's computer system. There are some safeguards that should be taken in order to prevent improper access and protect your organization's internal files.

IN PLAIN ENGLISH

If your organization hosts its site on its own server that is networked with your other organization computers, hackers could gain access to your entire system and all of your data.

Information you deem to be confidential and sensitive should be encrypted. Similarly, your system should always be protected by a password. Robust firewalls, which are electronic blocks preventing access to all but those who have the proper key, should be used and timely updated. Your organization should consult with an expert when designing its website and update themes, plug-ins, and code as soon as it becomes available in order to take advantage of the latest technology.

EMAIL

Email communications within an organization are commonplace and efficient. Internal, paperless transmissions of important messages throughout an office or plant help facilitate the day-to-day operations in many nonprofit organizations. In addition, some nonprofit organizations use intranets. These are websites available only to a defined network.

Because of the ubiquitous use of internal email, a nonprofit organization's handbooks and policy statements should deal with the proper use of email, as well as other related computer issues, especially when dealing with employees. For instance, it has been held that repeated transmission of sexually or racially explicit email messages by one employee to another may be deemed harassment and, if not controlled by the employer, may render the employer liable as well.

SPAM

Email is often abused. The persistent transmission of undesired electronic junk mail, commonly called spam, continued after a request to stop is an actionable wrong. In response to this problem, most of the major ISPs have developed spam filters and pop-up blockers. Similarly, software can be purchased to serve the same function.

Interestingly enough, the very word *spam*, which has been used to describe bulk email, usually advertising, itself became the subject of litigation. Hormel, the meat company that first developed the name Spam for its canned meat, filed suit for trademark infringement against a software manufacturer for using the word as part of the name of its spam-filtering product.

VIRUSES, WORMS, AND RANSOMWARE

One of the most serious problems to arise online is the prevalence of computer viruses, worms, and traps. These parasites are intended to interfere with computer use and, in some cases, to damage software and/or hardware. Briefly, viruses and worms are computer programs, usually transmitted via email and Internet downloads, often designed to damage a computer or computer system or hijack some or all of its capabilities. Again, Internet-use policies can help avoid some of the problems, while installing and updating firewall and antivirus software can avoid still more. In the case that a virus gets past your organization's defenses, there is insurance available that can protect against loss, help pay for any recovery or data breach requirements, and even help your organization if it becomes the victim of ransomware.

CYBERTERRORISM

The Department of Homeland Security has identified computer hacking and the infiltration of worms and viruses as one of the more significant problems to be faced by the free world today. Sadly, no computer system is immune from these unwanted intrusions and the havoc they wreak. Even software giants such as Microsoft have been forced to announce the discovery of vulnerabilities in their systems that have been exploited by hackers and those who produce worms and viruses. While hackers typically invade government sites and those computers belonging to large organization operations, worms, viruses, and ransomware can interfere with and cause significant damage to even a small organization's computer system or an individual's home computer. As quickly as they are identified and software developed or modified to block them, new ones appear.

SECURITY FOR ONLINE COMMERCE

Another reason for ensuring cybersecurity is the expanded use of online commerce. In the early days of cybercommerce, there was a great deal of fear among consumers with respect to the security of their credit card information being compromised on the Internet. Today, secure sites are the norm and companies such as PayPal and Visa have established certification programs for ensuring customers of a website's security.

By proceeding with good judgment and consulting with experienced intellectual property lawyers who have been involved with new technology and computer system specialists, your organization can remain on the cutting edge of cyberspace. For more information, you may wish to visit the authors' firm's website at www.dubofflaw.com.

CHAPTER 12

Insurance

Recent crime statistics show that even in rural areas, individuals and organizations may become the victims of burglary. The forces of nature—such as fires, floods, earthquakes—are undiscriminating in their targets. If a nonprofit organization sells products or provides services, the organization may be subjected to virtually unlimited liability to anyone who may be injured by the products or services, no matter how careful the organization may have been. Loss of revenue due to sickness or accident is a risk common to all organizations. These risks and others are far too often overlooked, but the potential cost makes even the slightest chance of these occurrences disastrous to a nonprofit organization. Fortunately, many of these risks can be insured against.

History contains too many gruesome stories of desperate or disturbed people obtaining insurance with an eye toward collecting the proceeds. Because of such insurance frauds, most kinds of insurance, particularly liability insurance, do not cover injuries that are intentionally caused by the policyholder.

BASICS OF INSURANCE LAW

Before analyzing the mechanics of choosing whether or not to insure a particular risk, a brief outline on the law of insurance is in order.

Insurable Interest

Public policy will not permit you to insure something unless you have what is called an insurable interest. To have an insurable interest, you must have a property right, a contract right, or a potential liability that would result in a real loss to you if a given event occurs. This is simply to minimize the temptation to cause the calamity against which you are insured.

The Contract

All insurance is based on a contract between the insurer and the insured whereby the insurer assumes a specified risk for a fee called a premium. The insurance contract must contain at least all of the following:

- a definition of whatever is being insured (the subject matter);
- the nature of the risks insured against;
- the maximum possible recovery;
- the duration of the insurance; and
- the due date and amount of the premiums.

When the amount of recovery has been predetermined in the insurance contract, it is called a valued policy. An unvalued or open insurance policy covers the full value of property up to a specified policy limit.

The very documents that a company uses to make insurance contracts are regulated from state to state. Sometimes the state requires a standard form from which the company may not deviate, especially for fire insurance. A growing number of states require that plain English be used in all forms. Plain English is measured in reference to the average number of syllables per word and the average number of words per sentence. Because of a federal ruling that all insurance contracts are, per se, fraudulent if they exceed certain maximum averages, the insurance companies are forced to write contracts that an average person can understand.

After Hurricane Katrina and several other catastrophic natural events, many individuals and organizations learned, to their horror, that the insurance coverage they thought they had was being denied. The litigation that resulted from the insurance companies' refusals to pay claims was even more traumatic than the disasters that gave rise to the claims. The moral is clear: Read your policy—and be sure that you understand it. If you have any doubt, review it with your broker, agent, or lawyer.

IN PLAIN ENGLISH

A *broker* is a person or entity who represents a number of insurance companies and is authorized by those companies to sell their policies. An *agent* is a person who is employed by a single insurance company for the purpose of selling its insurance. Brokers customarily shop the risk to a number of companies in order to obtain the best price for the policy.

After the insurance contract has been signed, its terms can be reformed (revised) only to comply with the original agreement from which the written contract may somehow have deviated.

ASCERTAINING RISK

The insurance contract does more than merely shift the risk from the insured to the insurance company. The insurance industry is regulated by state law so as to spread the risk among those subject to that same risk. The risk-spreading is accomplished by defining the method used for determining the amount of the premium to be paid by the insured. First, the insurance company obtains data on the actual loss sustained by a defined class within a given period of time. State law regulates just how the company may define the class. An insurance company may not, for example, separate white homeowners and nonwhite homeowners into different classes, but it may separate drivers with many accidents from drivers with few.

Next, the company divides the risk equally among the members of the class. Then the company adds a fee for administrative costs and profits. This amount is regulated from state to state. Finally, the premium is set for each policyholder in proportion to the likelihood that a loss will occur.

ADDITIONAL STATE REGULATIONS

Besides the method of determining premiums, state insurance laws usually specify the training necessary for agents and brokers, the amount of commission payable to them, and the kind of investments the insurance company may make with the premiums.

EXPECTATIONS VS. REALITY

One frequent result of the difficult language used in most insurance contracts is that the signed contract may differ in some respect from what the agent may have led the insured organization to expect. If you can prove that an agent actually lied, then the agent will be personally liable to your organization for the amount of promised coverage. In addition, the insurance company itself may be liable for the wrongful acts of its agents.

Most often, the agent will not lie, but will accidentally neglect to inform the insured of some detail. For instance, if your organization wants insurance for a weekend event in a park, the agent may sell you a policy that covers activities that occur only in the organization's facility—when you intended to hold activities in a park. In most states, the courts hold that it is the duty of the insured (your organization) to read the policy before signing. (In the example, if you neglect to read the clause that limits coverage to your organization's facility, you would be out of luck.)

In other states, this doctrine has been considered too harsh. These states will allow an insured to challenge specific provisions in the signed contract to the extent they do not conform to reasonable expectations resulting from promises that the agent made. In the example, it might be considered reasonable to expect that you would be insured for activities held in the park. If the agent did not specifically call your attention to this limitation in the contract, odds are that you would have a good case for getting rid of it. In addition, it is common for the insured to receive the policy only after the premium is paid or only after a specific request is made.

Other states follow a different approach for contract interpretation and attempt to ascertain the intention of the parties. The first step in interpreting an insurance policy is to examine the text and context of the policy as a whole. If, after that examination, two or more conflicting interpretations remain reasonable, the ambiguity is resolved against the insurer. A court in these states will assume that parties to an insurance contract do not create meaningless provisions and will favor the interpretation that lets all provisions have meaning.

IN PLAIN ENGLISH

Read the contract with the agent. If it is unintelligible, ask the agent to list on a separate sheet of paper all of the important aspects before you sign it. Keep that sheet with the policy.

OVERINSURING AND UNDERINSURING

If an insured accidentally overvalues its property, the insurance coverage will still apply. However, the recovery will only be for the actual value of the property. Overinsurance does not entitle your organization to a recovery beyond the actual value of the property insured. This is because one does not have an insurable interest beyond the actual value of an item.

Since your organization can, at best, break even with insurance, you might think it would be profitable to underinsure its property. The organization could gain by paying lower premiums and lose only in the event that the damage exceeds the policy maximum. This has been tried and failed.

Example: An insured organization stated the value of its unscheduled property as $9,950 and obtained insurance on that amount. (Unscheduled property means an undetermined collection of goods—for example, all of an organization's furniture—that may change from time to time.) A fire occurred causing at least $9,950 damage.

The insurance company investigated the claim and determined that the insured owned at least $36,500 in unscheduled property. The company refused to pay on the grounds that the insured obtained the insurance fraudulently. The court agreed with the insurance company, stating that the intentional failure to communicate the full value of the unscheduled property rendered the entire contract void. Therefore, the insured could not even collect the policy maximum.

Although at first glance this may seem harsh, its ultimate fairness becomes apparent with a little analysis. The chance of losing $9,950 out of $36,500 is greater than the chance of losing $9,950 out of $9,950 simply because most accidents or thefts do not result in total losses.

Various tests are used by the courts to determine whether an omission or misstatement renders such a policy void. In almost all cases, the omission or misstatement must be intentional or obviously reckless and it must be material to the contract. Materiality is typically measured with reference to the degree of importance that the insurance company ascribes to the omitted or misstated fact. If stating the fact correctly would have significantly affected the conditions or premiums that the company would demand, then the fact is likely material. In the above example, had the full value of the unscheduled property been stated, the insurer would either have demanded that the full value be insured or that a higher premium be paid for the limited coverage. Thus, the misstatement was clearly material.

UNINTENTIONAL UNDERVALUING

Not all undervaluations will be material. Many insurance contracts do allow some undervaluation where it is unintentional. This provision is designed to protect the insured from inflation, which causes property to increase in replacement value before the policy's renewal date.

A so-called coinsurance clause generally provides that the insured may recover 100 percent of any loss up to the face value of the policy provided the property is insured for at least 80 percent of its full value. For example, if a nonprofit's office building worth $100,000 was insured for $80,000 and suffered a $79,000 loss from a covered casualty, the insured would recover the full amount of the loss, or $79,000. If the property was only insured for $50,000, then a formula would be used to determine the amount of recovery. This formula requires you to establish a ratio between the amount of insurance coverage and the total value of the property and then multiply the resulting fraction by the loss to get the recovery.

IN PLAIN ENGLISH

It is important to carry insurance on at least 80 percent of the value of your organization's property. Considering inflation, it is wise to reexamine the coverage each year. Some policies automatically increase the coverage annually, based on some fixed percentage.

PROPERTY COVERED

All insurance policies are limited to certain defined subject matter and to losses caused to that subject matter by certain defined risks. Once the risks are recognized, it is a simple matter to decide whether or not to insure against them. However, correctly defining the subject matter of insurance is tricky business. Mistakes here are not uncommon and can result in anyone finding themselves uninsured.

SCHEDULING PROPERTY

The typical insurance policy will include various exclusions and exemptions. For example, most homeowner and auto insurance policies cover personal property but exclude business property. Business property in this context will include a nonprofit organization's property that is used for the nonprofit organization's stated purpose. This brings up the question for nonprofits when the organization's members or principals keep certain items at home for personal enjoyment—are they personal or business property? The answer depends on whether the person may sell or display any of these items. If any are sold or displayed, this may convert them all to business property.

In order to avoid the potentially uninsured loss of such property, the individual who actually owns the item may schedule the pieces that are held for personal enjoyment. Scheduling is a form of inventorying where the insured submits a list and description of all pieces to be insured with an appraisal of their value. The insurer assumes the risk of loss of all scheduled works without concern as to whether or not they pertain to the organization. Insurance on scheduled property is slightly more expensive than that on unscheduled property.

VALUING SCHEDULED PROPERTY

Many battles occur over the value of objects stolen, destroyed, or lost. In anticipation of such battles, you should maintain records of sales to establish the market price of goods and an inventory of all items on hand. In the case of certain kinds of property (artwork, rare books, or artifacts, for example), the value must be determined by an expert in the field. However, this will not avoid all problems, because the insurance company can always contest the scheduled value.

WHEN AND HOW TO INSURE

Three factors should be weighed to determine whether or not to obtain insurance. First, your organization must set a value on that which is to be insured. Health is of the utmost value and should always be insured. Material goods are valued according to the cost of replacement. If your organization keeps a large inventory of items or if it owns expensive equipment, it probably should be insured. Your organization may also want to consider obtaining business interruption insurance. The most elementary way to determine if the value is sufficiently high to necessitate insurance is to rely on the pain factor—if it would hurt to lose it, insure it.

Second, you must estimate the chances (risk) that a given calamity will occur. An insurance broker can tell you what risks are prevalent in your organization's area of performance or in your organization's neighborhood. You should supplement this information with your personal knowledge. For example, you may know that your organization's workshop is virtually fire-proof or that only a massive flood would cause any real damage. Although these facts should be weighed in your decision, you should not be guilty of audaciously tempting fate. If the odds are truly slim, but some risk is still present, the premium will be correspondingly smaller in most cases.

The third factor is the cost of the insurance.

KEEPING THE COST DOWN

As already explained, the premiums charged by an insurance company are regulated by the government. Nonetheless, it still pays to shop around. Insurance companies can compete by offering different packages of insurance and by hiring competent agents to assist you in your choice.

If there are enough nonprofit organizations in your area engaged in similar activity and of similar size, it may be possible for you to form a co-op insurance fund. To do this, you must estimate the total losses your co-op would sustain in the course of a year. Each member then contributes a pro rata share. The money is put into a bank to collect interest. If a disaster occurs and the losses are greater than the fund, each member must contribute to make up the difference. If there is money left over, it can be used to lessen the following year's premiums. This method is cheaper than conventional insurance because it eliminates insurance agents' commissions and the profit earned by the insurance company. Before you form your co-op, contact an attorney to determine what regulations exist in your state and be sure that the arrangement is memorialized by an understandable written agreement.

There are a number of different kinds of insurance that organizations should consider and there are some that are required by law. Workers compensation insurance is customarily required for every organization that employs individuals, including nonprofit organizations, though some states allow exceptions for the members of its board of directors. You should consult with your organization's lawyer or insurance professional regarding the law in your state.

If your organization owns its building, then it should certainly obtain insurance for that building. Even if it does not own its building, the contents of the building should be insured. As noted above, you should also consider obtaining *product liability* insurance as well if your organization distributes a product. In fact, most organizations purchase what is known as a general liability policy for the purpose of covering a host of risks. It is essential for you to work with an experienced lawyer in order to determine the kind of insurance that would best serve your organization's needs.

CHAPTER 13

Employees, Contractors, and Members

There comes a time in the life of almost every nonprofit when it is necessary to get help, be it brain or brawn. The help most commonly needed first is the bookkeeper or accountant who can handle taxes, billing, and the like. When things get a little hectic around the office, you might then hire someone to help with running errands and dealing with members. If fund-raising is not your greatest talent, you may engage the services of a professional. If this professional is really good, you will soon have to hire more employees to keep up with the expanding operation of your organization.

In this chapter, we will discuss the legal issues that arise when an organization hires employees, deals with contractors, and has the assistance of volunteers as well. The roles of these individuals are very important, and the organization should establish guidelines and prepare appropriate agreements for each of them when the relationship begins.

EMPLOYEES

An individual who works exclusively for your organization is likely an employee. An employee is anyone over whose work your organization exercises direct control—helpers, apprentices, fund-raisers who represent your organization alone, a bookkeeper who is a full-time member of your organization's staff, and so forth. The formation of this relationship entails nothing more than an agreement on your organization's side to hire someone and an agreement by that person to work. Although a written contract is generally not necessary, it is suggested that employment terms be put down in writing so that there are no misunderstandings later.

Liability

Unlike the situation where your organization has hired an independent contractor, your organization is vicariously liable for the negligence and, sometimes, even the intentional wrongdoing of your organization's employee when the employee is acting on your organization's behalf. This means that if your organization's employee is on the job and is involved in an automobile accident that is his or her fault, your organization, as well as your organization's employee, are legally liable. It would be wise to be extremely careful when hiring and to contact your organization's insurance agent to obtain sufficient insurance coverage for your organization's additional exposure. As discussed more fully in chapter 5, the wrongful conduct of volunteers, religious leaders, and the like have resulted in significant liability for a number of prominent nonprofits.

Employment Contracts

While there is no prescribed form that an employment contract must take, there are, nevertheless, certain items that should be considered.

Term

The first item of an employment contract is the term of employment. An employment contract may be either terminable at will or for a fixed duration, though if the employment is to be for more than one year, there *must* be a written contract specifying the period of employment; otherwise, either party may terminate the relationship at any time.

Making the contract for a fixed period gives the employee some job security and creates a moral and contractual obligation for the employee to remain for the term. Of course, if the employee chooses to quit or the employer chooses to fire the employee, the law will not compel fulfillment of the contract. Improper premature termination of a contract for a fixed period, however, will subject the party who is responsible for the wrongful act to liability for damages.

Wage

The second item is the wage. Unless you have financial activity of $500,000 or more or are engaged in interstate commerce (which is very broadly defined), your organization will not have to comply with federal minimum-wage laws. Most states, however, have their own minimum-wage laws with which your organization will still have to comply. Above the requirement imposed by this law, the amount of remuneration is open to bargaining.

In the event no salary is specified, the law will presume a reasonable wage for the work performed. Thus, your organization cannot escape paying its employees fairly by not discussing the amount they will earn. If your organization hires a security guard and the accepted salary in the region for a security guard is $20 per hour, then it will be presumed that the guard was hired for this amount unless your organization and that person have agreed to a different salary.

In addition to an hourly wage or monthly salary, other benefits can be given, such as health and life insurance or retirement pensions. Some legal advice in this area may be necessary in order to take advantage of tax laws.

Duties

Third, it is often wise to spell out the employee's duties in the employment contract. This serves as a form of orientation for the employee and also may limit future conflicts over what is and what is not involved in the job.

Noncompetition

Fourth, you may want the employee to agree not to work for someone else while working for your organization or, more importantly, not to compete against your organization at the end of the employment period. The latter agreement must be carefully drawn to be enforceable. Such an agreement must:

- not be overly broad in the kind of work the employee may not do;
- cover a geographic area no broader than that in which you actually operate; and
- be for a reasonable duration.

Some states have enacted special laws with respect to noncompetition restrictions during employment and after termination. You should, therefore, consult with an experienced lawyer when preparing an employment contract. Some states refuse to uphold noncompetition agreements. For example, California law states that a noncompetition agreement is void as against public policy unless it is coupled with a business sale of the purchase or sale of *stock*.

Employers may achieve some form of protection by restricting the use of the organization's intellectual property. This should include a prohibition on the use of any trade secrets, both during the term of employment and thereafter. These restrictions should be in writing. It has been held that trade secrets may include, among other things, memberships lists, donors lists, supplier lists, secret formulas, and know-how.

Termination

Finally, grounds for termination of the employment contract should be listed, even if the contract is terminable at will. You should clearly specify that the contract may be terminated either for the specified causes or at the will of the employer.

Employers should take some precautions to avoid being placed in the untenable position of having bound themselves to individuals in their employment when the relationship has soured. This can result from language in employee handbooks that might be construed as giving rise to a contractual right. It is also possible that oral statements made by recruiters or interviewers could give rise to contractual rights. To avoid this problem, an employer should have a legend placed in any employee handbook making it clear that the material is not an employment contract. It has also become common for employers to require prospective employees to sign a statement making it clear that the employment is at will and does not give rise to any contractual right.

If there is a probationary period, the employer should be careful to state that the probationary employee will become a *regular* or *full-time* employee rather than a *permanent* employee. In addition, if there is any evaluation of the employee after the probationary period has ended, it should be conducted fairly. When evaluations become merely pro forma, problems can and do arise. Employees may argue that they have received sparkling evaluations and are being fired for some invalid reason.

Other Considerations in Hiring

There are other issues you should consider when hiring an employee, most of which fall into the realm of accounting or bookkeeping responsibilities. You should, therefore, consult with your organization's accountant or bookkeeper regarding such items as the following:

- A Worker's Compensation policy for employees in the event of on-the-job injury or occupational illness. State laws vary on the minimum number of employees that trigger this very important requirement. The Worker's Compensation laws of many states provide that an employer who has failed to obtain or keep in force required Worker's Compensation insurance will be strictly liable even in the absence of negligence for on-the-job injury or illness. This includes not only medical expenses, but also damages for pain and suffering, lost earning potential, and other damages that are a consequence of on-the-job injuries or illnesses.

- Withholding taxes (federal, state, and local). Here too, the laws vary, and your organization must find out what is required in its locale. Employers are required to withhold employees' federal taxes, and failure to do so will expose the employer to liability for that amount plus interest and penalties. This is true even for nonprofit organizations that are otherwise tax-exempt.

- Social Security (FICA). There are some exemptions from this body of social legislation. Contact your nearby Social Security office to determine how these exemptions may affect your organization.

- Unemployment insurance (both federal and state). These also include certain technical requirements for subcontractors and the like.

- Health and safety regulations (both federal and state).

- Municipal taxes for specific programs such as schools or public transportation.

- Employee benefits such as insurance coverage (medical, dental, prepaid legal), retirement benefits, memberships, and parking.

- Union requirements, if your organization or its employees are subject to union contracts.

- Wage and hour laws (both federal and state). These include minimum wage and overtime requirements. In some states, the law also regulates holidays and vacations, as well as the method of paying employees during employment and upon termination.

As already noted, the requirements of these laws may vary dramatically from state to state. You are well advised to discuss them with your nonprofit's lawyer, accountant, and bookkeeper. In addition, your organization should find out if any other forms of employment legislation, such as licensing requirements, apply to it or its employees.

Hazards in the Workplace

While few organizations would intentionally injure a fellow human being, your organization may nevertheless find itself in an industry or using a process that involves hazardous activities. It is not uncommon to use toxic materials. Employees are often not aware of the potential hazard that may result from toxic materials. It is essential to research the potentially toxic effects of all substances your organization may encounter. Occupational Safety and Health Administration (OSHA) regulations require that all employers with hazardous chemicals in their workplaces provide labels and Safety Data Sheets (SDS) for their exposed workers and train them to handle the chemicals appropriately. (More information on this can be found at the OSHA website at www.osha.gov.) In other words, there is a regulatory duty to advise and train employees with respect to hazardous substances in the workplace. Further, many older buildings have lead paint and asbestos insulation. These items, if not properly dealt with, are extremely dangerous. OSHA regulations govern how an organization must deal with this as well.

Congress and federal administrative agencies are active in the field of regulation of hazardous substances. You should also be aware that the state Worker's Compensation agency and OSHA may have specific rules regarding your specific type of organization. It is critical to obtain a lawyer's assistance in determining whether any of these regulations apply to your particular organization. Your state's labor department may also be able to give you information regarding applicable workplace regulations.

If an employment contract is used, a paragraph containing the required disclosure regarding hazardous substances and the employee's acknowledgment of the known risks should be incorporated in the contract. A similar statement should also be included in any employee handbook.

While these documents would not provide a defense to a Worker's Compensation claim, they would sensitize employees to the need for caution in working with the toxic materials. Needless to say, your organization should take all precautions possible to protect the health and safety of its employees.

INDEPENDENT CONTRACTORS

Someone hired on a one-time or job-by-job basis is called an independent contractor. Although paid for their services by the hiring entity or individual, contractors remain their own bosses and may even employ others to actually do the work.

If you occasionally give donated items to an individual to sell on consignment, that individual is probably an independent contractor. If you hire a bookkeeper or accountant once or twice a year to go over your organization's records, that person, too, is an independent contractor. The fact that the person is independent and not your organization's employee means that your organization does not have to pay Social Security taxes, withhold income taxes, obtain a Worker's Compensation policy, or comply with the myriad rules imposed on employers.

More importantly, your organization is generally not liable for injuries to a third party resulting from the independent contractor's negligence or wrongful acts even while working for your organization. However, there are situations where, despite your organization's innocence, an independent contractor can render your organization legally responsible for his or her wrongful acts. Such situations fall into the following three basic categories:

1. If an employer is careless in hiring an independent contractor and a careful investigation would have disclosed facts to indicate that the contractor was not qualified, the employer may be liable when the independent contractor fails to perform the job properly and a third person is injured.
2. If a job is so dangerous as to be characterized as *ultrahazardous* or *inherently dangerous* (both legal terms) and is to be performed for the employer's benefit, then regardless of who performs the work, the employer will remain legally responsible for any injuries that occur during the performance of the work. A fireworks displayer, for example, cannot escape liability by having fuses lit or rockets aimed by independent contractors.
3. An employer may be required by law to perform certain tasks for the health and safety of the community.

These responsibilities are said to be *nondelegable*—that is, an employer cannot delegate them and, thus, escape liability for their improper performance.

If, therefore, a nondelegable duty is performed by an independent contractor, the employer will remain responsible for any injury that results.

A good example of a nondelegable duty is the law (common in many states) that homeowners and storekeepers are responsible for keeping their sidewalks free of dangerous obstacles. If a nonprofit church hires an independent contractor to fulfill this obligation by removing ice during the winter, the church is still legally liable if someone is injured on the slippery sidewalk even if the accident resulted from the contractor's carelessness.

VOLUNTEERS

Volunteers who participate in the activities of nonprofit organizations may also expose those organizations to liability for the volunteer's wrongful acts. As the material presented in chapter 5 makes clear, nonprofit organizations must be diligent in establishing safeguards to prevent any volunteers from using the individual's position in the organization for improper purposes. Thus, when Boy Scout leaders were permitted to use their leadership role for the purpose of taking advantage of the youngsters in their Scout troops and when religious leaders were able to use their position in the religious organizations for improper purposes, the organizations were held liable. Today, the Boy Scouts of America and all of its local councils have some of the best programs possible to prevent the past problems from reoccurring, and the vast majority of religious organizations have adopted safeguards for the same purpose. Your organization should be sensitive to the problems discussed in chapter 5, and it should take steps to address them as well.

Nonprofit organizations may be responsible for protecting volunteers who are exposed to harm because of their activities with the organization. Many nonprofits have insurance to deal with this type of situation, and your organization should determine whether it has adequate protection for its volunteers.

Whether a volunteer would be considered an employee or an independent contractor is not always clear. The distinction between these characterizations is important for numerous purposes including, for example, copyright ownership of works the volunteer creates, the volunteer's ability to bind the organization, and the like. Since the role of a volunteer is ambiguous, it is important for your organization to establish guidelines, specify the volunteer's position in the organization clearly, and have the description of the volunteer's task, role, and authority spelled out for the organization. That job description can be placed in the organization's bylaws, volunteer handbook, or other organizational documents. The role of a volunteer, as well as the volunteer's authority and the like, should also be spelled out in a written agreement between the organization and the volunteer. It is often said that good fences make good neighbors—and good contracts make for good relationships.

DISCRIMINATION

Nonprofit organizations that employ others must comply with numerous antidiscrimination laws, including the Civil Rights Act, the Equal Pay Act, the Age Discrimination in Employment Act (amended by the Older Workers Benefit Protection Act) and the Americans with Disabilities Act. The Equal Employment Opportunity Commission (EEOC) is responsible for enforcement of these laws. Antidiscrimination laws apply not only during the hiring processes but also during the employment itself, including considerations for transfer, promotion, layoff, and termination, as well as job advertisements, recruitment, testing, use of company facilities, training, benefits, and leave. These laws generally prohibit not only intentional discrimination but practices that have the effect of discrimination. Note that many antidiscrimination laws apply to independent contractors as well as to employees.

These laws make it clear that management may not legally retaliate against employees or job applicants who file discrimination charges against them. If an organization is found to have unlawfully discriminated, then that organization will likely be liable for lost wages, punitive and other damages, including attorney fees.

Many states, as well as some cities and counties, have also passed laws that reiterate and expand the federal government's protection against discrimination. These laws are often more protective of employees than federal laws. In addition, some categories not covered by federal law, including those with respect to sexual orientation, may be covered by state or local law.

Civil Rights Act

The Civil Rights Act prohibits discrimination based on race, color, religion, sex, or national origin.

With regard to religious discrimination, employers generally may not treat employees or applicants less or more favorably because of their religious beliefs or practices. Employees cannot be forced to participate or not participate in a religious activity as a condition of employment. Employers must reasonably accommodate employees' sincerely held religious beliefs and permit employees to engage in religious expression if employees are permitted to engage in other personal expressions at work. This law also requires the employer to take steps to prevent religious harassment of their employees, not only by other employees and management but also by vendors, volunteers, and patrons.

National-origin discrimination includes discrimination based on foreign accents and English fluency, as well as English-only rules, though there are exceptions if they are necessary for the safe or efficient operation of the organization.

Race-based discrimination includes discrimination based on skin color, hair texture, and facial features, as well as harassment and segregation. It also includes discrimination based on a person's marriage to or association with those of a different race.

The prohibitions against sex-based discrimination encompass pregnancy, birth, and related medical conditions, as well as sexual harassment.

The Equal Pay Act (part of the Fair Labor Standards Act of 1938, as amended) also prohibits sex-based discrimination; it prohibits sex-based wage discrimination among persons in the same establishment who are performing under similar working conditions. Virtually all employers are subject to this act.

More information about the Civil Rights Act and the Equal Pay Act can be obtained at the EEOC's website, www.eeoc.gov.

Membership Rules

Despite all of these laws, nonprofit organizations may establish rules that appear to discriminate, such as the requirement that clergy belong to a certain religion, or that members of a fraternity all be male or members of a sorority all be female. While these rules appear discriminatory, they are nevertheless enforceable. If your nonprofit desires to establish a rule restricting participation, it should consult with an experienced attorney in order to determine whether the rule is legal and enforceable.

HARASSMENT

One of the legal obligations of all nonprofit organizations is to create a nondiscriminatory work environment for employees, members, and participants. A policy should be established prohibiting any discriminatory language (i.e., ethnic jokes or racial slurs) or other offensive language or activities such as bullying.

Sexual harassment is one form of illegal discrimination, though harassment based on race and certain other characteristics also violates the Civil Rights Act. There are two basic types of sexual harassment: *quid pro quo* and that of a *hostile environment*. Quid pro quo refers to either a harasser asking for sexual favors in exchange for some advantage in the workplace, or a harasser penalizing another person for rejecting his or her sexual advances. A hostile environment, on the other hand, is more generalized in that the harasser creates or permits a hostile work environment through language, activities, and/or conduct.

An employer is subject to vicarious liability for a hostile work environment; for example, a thrift shop manager will be responsible for the actions and language of a supervisor that results in an employee's injury, harm, or damage. If a supervisor has harassed or permitted harassment of an employee and this situation has led to that employee's termination, relocation, or the like, the employer will be held liable for the discriminatory sexual actions of its supervisor. To avoid this form of liability, the employer must exercise reasonable care to prevent and promptly correct any harassment behaviors that are reported or otherwise become known to it, and the employee who was harassed must have taken advantage of all preventive programs or policies provided by the employer. There is a host of training and other resources available to nonprofit organizations. Check with your organization's attorney or state employment division. This not only applies to employees and independent contractors, but to volunteers and all other individuals who are involved with nonprofits.

Many states have anti-harassment policies as well. For example, California requires employers with fifty or more employees to provide certain sexual harassment training and education to supervisory employees. Details of the California sexual harassment laws can be obtained at www.dfeh.ca.gov.

More information on sexual harassment is available at the EEOC website (www.eeoc.gov).

AGE DISCRIMINATION

Federal age antidiscrimination laws apply to employers of twenty or more employees, as well as to government and union offices. These laws provide that persons forty years old or older may not be discriminated against due to their age in connection with any term, condition, or privilege of employment, including hiring, firing, layoffs, job compensation, benefits, job training, assignments and tasks, and promotions.

More information on age discrimination is available at www.eeoc.gov.

DISABILITIES DISCRIMINATION

The Americans with Disabilities Act (ADA) prohibits discrimination against disabled persons in public accommodations, transportation, telecommunications, and employment. This act applies to those who employ fifteen or more individuals. "An individual with a disability" means a person who has a physical or mental impairment that substantially limits one or more major life activity, has a record of such an impairment, or who is regarded as having such an impairment. A qualified individual with a disability is someone who, with or without reasonable accommodation, can perform the essential functions of the job.

Reasonable accommodation must be made so that a disabled job applicant or employee can perform the necessary and essential work of the job position. Reasonable accommodations include making existing employee facilities readily accessible to and usable by disabled employees, including the acquisition or modification of equipment or devices, job restructuring, and modifying work schedules.

A nonprofit organization is not required to provide reasonable accommodations if it results in an undue hardship. "Undue hardship" under the Americans with Disabilities Act refers to an action requiring significant difficulty or expense when considered in light of factors such as the employer's size and financial resources.

Under the ADA, complex rules apply to medical examinations and inquiries, so you should contact an attorney for more information if you plan to make such inquiries or require any physical examinations.

For more information concerning the Americans with Disabilities Act, see www.ada.gov. Many states have laws that are comparable to or more restrictive than the ADA. You should check with your organization's attorney or state employment division to determine whether your state has such legislation.

EMPLOYEE HANDBOOKS

As discussed elsewhere in this chapter, your organization should have an employee handbook. It should set forth, among other things, your policies on sexual harassment and nondiscrimination, hours of work, as well as security, overtime, and the like. The handbook should make it clear that it is not an employment contract and, in fact, that employment is "at will." It should also cover trade secret protection discussed earlier in this chapter. This document should be drafted or reviewed by an attorney since there are numerous requirements for legal notices and other areas that a layperson or even a handbook software program may fail to address properly.

If your organization plans to monitor its employees' Internet usage, emails, computer files, phone calls, voice mails, and the like, use video surveillance or conduct searches of employees' personal belongings (such as lockers), your organization should include a specific written employee privacy policy identifying the types of situations where employees should not have an expectation of privacy. Note that your organization's employees do have certain privacy rights, such as privacy in the restroom. Any monitoring must be done in a nondiscriminatory manner to ensure quality and equitably enforce policies and standards.

ZERO TOLERANCE POLICIES

A zero tolerance standard will best protect an employer from discrimination claims. An employee handbook containing policies against sexual harassment, offensive behaviors, and the like is a good starting point. A well-drafted discrimination policy will apply to behavior and oral and written (including electronic) communications. It will include procedures that provide employees with a way to confidentially report problems regarding offensive or harassing behavior and will direct management on how to investigate and resolve the issues. The process should include an employee appeals process for any adverse findings. The *complaint* and appeals procedures should direct an employee to contact someone other than the employee's immediate supervisor, since that supervisor may be the one responsible for such conduct.

Employees should be advised that both the complaints and appeals need to be put in writing so that there can be no misunderstandings, though the first step is often verbal. A well-drafted policy will state that the employer will, whenever possible, provide complaining employees and witnesses reasonable confidentiality, but it should be made clear that there can be no assurance of confidentiality, since it may become necessary for management to disclose the identity and testimony of relevant parties in any legal proceeding.

It is also essential for employers to provide employees with ongoing education with respect to employment relations, including harassment and discrimination issues.

THE FAMILY MEDICAL LEAVE ACT

The Family and Medical Leave Act of 1993 (FMLA) allows employees to take up to twelve weeks of unpaid leave each year for certain family or medical reasons if they have worked for the employer for a year and meet certain other eligibility requirements. FMLA must be followed by private sector employers who employ fifty or more employees during the current or preceding calendar year and who are engaged in interstate commerce or any activity affecting commerce.

An eligible employee may take his or her twelve-week leave due to the birth and care of his or her newborn, a foster child being placed with the employee, to care for a spouse, child, or parent with a serious health condition, or to take care of the employee's own serious health condition. FMLA defines "serious health condition" as an illness, injury, impairment, or physical or mental condition that brings about a period of incapacity and/or requires intensive and continual medical treatment, and specifically includes prenatal care.

When the worker returns to the job, the job may be the exact job that the employee left, or it may be an equivalent job—with equivalent duties, pay, benefits, and the like. The only employees to which this would not apply are "key" employees whose absence from their positions will cause "substantial and grievous economic injury" to the employer.

There are certain notice requirements, as well as rules for requiring medical certification of the need for leave. Further information can be found at www.dol.gov.

Many states have supplemental leave acts. Check with your organization's attorney or state employment division.

TERMINATION OF EMPLOYMENT AND MEMBERSHIP

Determining whether someone is an employee or an independent contractor is not always easy. One reason that the characterization is important is that employers are responsible for income-tax withholding, Social Security, Worker's Compensation, and the like, whereas one who hires an independent contractor is not.

Another reason that the characterization may be important regards how the employment relationship may end. If the individual working for your organization is merely an independent contractor, the contract between your organization and that person will govern the respective rights of termination. On the other hand, if the individual is an employee, care must be taken not to become responsible for a wrongful termination when dismissing the individual.

Wrongful Termination

Historically, an employee who was not under contract could be terminated for any reason whatsoever. Now an employee's job can be terminated for the right reason or for no reason at all, but cannot be terminated for the wrong reason. For example, an employee whose job was terminated for refusing to commit perjury before a legislative committee was entitled to recover against the employer for wrongful termination. The public policy of having individuals testify honestly was considered more important than the employer's right to control the employment relationship.

Courts have become even more protective of the rights of employees. In a 1983 case, *Novosel v. Nationwide Insurance Company*, the US Circuit Court of Appeals held that the power to hire and fire could not be used to dictate an employee's political activity and that even a nongovernmental entity is limited by the Constitution in its power to discharge an employee. The court, in essence, held that one's right to exercise constitutionally protected free speech was more important than the employer's right to control an employee's conduct.

Wrongful termination cases generally fall into certain categories. Employers may not legally terminate an employee's job for:

- refusing to commit an unlawful act, such as committing perjury or refusing to participate in illegal price-fixing schemes;
- performing a public obligation, such as serving on a jury or serving in a military reserve unit;
- exercising a statutory right, such as filing a claim for Worker's Compensation; or
- discrimination.

Some courts appear to go quite far in holding that an employer cannot discharge an employee unless there is just cause for termination. A number of states have considered the adoption of legislation that would restrict the employer's right to terminate an employee's job to cases in which there was just cause. Most states have laws that contain specific prohibitions on the termination of employment for whistle-blowing (e.g., cases in which employees notify government authorities of wrongful acts by the employer, such as tax evasion).

Progressive Discipline

Perhaps an employer who uses evaluations should employ what has been characterized as progressive discipline. In this procedure, the employer starts by orally warning a problem employee of his or her concern and progressively imposing disciplinary practices until termination becomes the only form of recourse left. Care should be taken not to violate the employee's rights since the liability for wrongful termination can be catastrophic to a nonprofit. When in doubt, an employer should contact an attorney with some experience in the field of employment relations. In this area, as with many others, pre-problem counseling can prevent a good deal of time-consuming and costly litigation.

The relationship between a nonprofit and its members should also be spelled out in a contract. In this way, the organization can establish appropriate rules and guidelines in order to avoid problems in the future. Here too, the assistance of an experienced attorney in preparing appropriate documentation is essential. The organization can avoid liability if it should become necessary to terminate the relationship between the organization and an individual member. The documentation should make it clear that participation in the organization's activity is a privilege that may be terminated by the organization or the individual without liability.

CHAPTER 14

Taxes

While chapter 3 explains how to establish tax-exempt status, this chapter will dive further into taxes for unrelated business income, appraisals, *joint ventures*, partnering and umbrella organizations, and tax shelters. The subjects discussed in this chapter are very complex, and each of them could easily fill an entire book on its own. By necessity, this discussion will merely assist you in identifying the issues to consider and attempt to point out the key factors involved so that you and your nonprofit team will be able to effectively work with an experienced tax attorney, accountant, or both.

UNRELATED BUSINESS INCOME

Not all activities of a nonprofit organization are necessarily exempt from tax once it obtains tax-exempt status. Whereas income derived from donations, admission fees, and membership dues are rarely questioned, income from certain commercial activities may be taxed as unrelated trade or business income. Nonprofit organizations commonly derive additional revenues from selling items in a gift shop, for example, logos on T-shirts, caps, and backpacks for a school's athletic team, pictures of birds or animals from a zoo's menagerie, and the like; licensing the copying and sale of items in their collection; operating dining facilities; and engaging in other dealings for profit. Revenues from these activities may become subject to scrutiny by the IRS.

The tax law makes all the *unrelated business income* of otherwise tax-exempt organizations subject to ordinary income tax. An *unrelated trade or business* is technically defined in the law but essentially means any trade or business not *substantially related* to the organization's charitable, educational, or other tax-exempt purpose.

In order to determine whether an organization's activities are *substantially related* to the exempt purpose, the tax law states that the test is whether the production or distribution of the goods from which the gross income is derived *contributes importantly* to the accomplishment of the exempt purposes of the organization. This test has been applied in several Internal Revenue Service rulings. In a key ruling issued in 1973, the sale of greeting cards bearing reproductions of artworks from the museum was not *unrelated business income*. The IRS found that although the activity was unquestionably commercial, it *contributed importantly* to the museum's educational purpose by stimulating and enhancing public awareness, interest, and the *appreciation* of art. The IRS also noted that a broader segment of the public may be encouraged to visit the museum itself to share in its educational functions and programs as a result of seeing the cards.

Present law enables many nonprofits to cover their operating costs by engaging in some profit-making activities, although the nonprofit still must be able to show that such activities *contribute substantially* to its exempt purpose that ultimately benefits the community. In a later revenue ruling, the IRS held that the profitable operation of a cafeteria or dining room, operated for a nonprofit's staff and the public visiting the nonprofit, was not an unrelated business activity.

However, while the sale of reproductions has been held to further a museum's exempt purpose, the IRS has distinguished the situation of a folk-art museum that sold scientific books and city souvenirs along with reproductions of pieces from its collection. According to the IRS, such sales were an unrelated business activity, even though other items sold in the shop were related to the museum's exempt function. Because the scientific books and souvenirs did not bear a relationship to the museum's artistic endeavor, their sale did not *contribute importantly* to the organization's exempt purpose. The rule was thus established that sales of a particular line of merchandise could be considered individually to determine their relatedness to the institution's exempt purpose.

IN PLAIN ENGLISH

If your organization has a gift shop, each item sold in that gift shop must be individually evaluated to determine whether its sale is or is not related to the organization's exempt activity in order to determine whether the income earned by its sale will be taxed.

In 1997, the tax court ruled that affinity credit card payments by a bank to a charity are royalties and not subject to unrelated business income tax. Similarly, the IRS issued a private letter ruling that held that links from an exempt organization's website to the websites of businesses that provide services to its members do not create unrelated business income and that such links do not affect the exempt status of royalties or qualified sponsorship payments.

As these rulings make clear, the sales activities, licensing, and promotional activities that generate income for the nonprofit must be carefully evaluated in order to determine whether income derived from them is exempt from taxation or taxable as unrelated business income. Your organization should work with experienced tax advisors in order to establish a plan that best fulfills the organization's mission, needs, and objectives.

DONATIONS

The vast majority of nonprofit, tax-exempt organizations obtain donations from individuals and organizations. The donations can be in the form of cash, securities, or property. Donors may take a tax deduction for donations to certain qualified charitable organizations. In fact, as the value of art collections, precious metals, and other properties have gone up, owners reluctant to take a huge hit in capital gains taxes are choosing to donate the items instead of selling them.

The aggregate amount of such deductions is governed by certain percentage limitations. Corporations may deduct a maximum of 10 percent of their taxable income. Individuals may deduct up to 50 percent of their adjusted gross income for contributions to churches, educational organizations, governmental units, and other defined organizations but may deduct only 30 percent for contributions to other charities. Furthermore, contributors of capital gain property, such as artwork, crafts, precious metals, antiquities, and the like, are limited to a 30 percent deduction for contributions to churches, schools, and so forth (or alternatively, 50 percent, if deducting the tax basis of the property rather than the fair market value), but contributors may deduct only 20 percent of contributions made to other charities.

Some types of contributions are not deductible. Individuals asked to donate their time should know that no charitable deduction is allowed for the value of services, although out-of-pocket expenses incurred in performing the services can be deducted. The IRS requires a written statement from a charity acknowledging the taxpayer's out-of-pocket expenses if the taxpayer's expenses on behalf of that charity total more than $250 in a year.

A gift of a future interest in tangible personal property, for example, stating that the charity will only be entitled to receive that property after the donor dies, is deductible only after all intervening interests in the use, possession, or enjoyment of the property either have expired or are held by someone other than the donor or his or her family. That is, the event that must occur in order for the charity to receive the property must actually occur before the deduction can be taken. In the above example, the donor must die and the property must transfer to the charity before the deduction can be taken by the decedent's estate.

It is possible to transfer an undivided present interest in property and still be eligible for a charitable deduction. A treasury regulation provides a useful example of a contribution of a painting to a museum for three months out of each year. The contribution was considered made when the contract was signed by all parties; however, for this arrangement to work, the first period of possession by the museum cannot be deferred by more than one year.

If the donation is cash, then issues rarely arise if the donation is properly documented and used by the organization to fulfill its charitable mission. If securities are donated, and the organization properly documents the donation, it will be able to hold those securities and dispose of them when it determines that the proceeds of their sale should be realized. The person or entity donating the securities may enjoy enhanced benefits in situations where the securities have appreciated since they were initially acquired.

The organization should not provide tax advice to donors. Instead, it should counsel them to obtain their own independent information regarding the donation they intend to make. Issues to be considered when securities are involved include whether the securities are publicly traded, traded over the counter, or are privately held. Your organization's attorney and tax advisor should be consulted in order to establish appropriate guidelines for dealing with securities.

When tangible property is to be donated, the amount of a particular charitable deduction is generally considered to be its fair market value but may have to be reduced depending on the character of the contributed property in the hands of the donor and its use by the nonprofit organization. If the donated property would have produced short-term capital gains or ordinary income if sold, the deduction for its donation is limited to the property's *adjusted basis*—that is, the item's original cost reduced by any *depreciation* taken for that item over time and increased by any improvement to the item over time as well. If the property is given to a private foundation or if it is tangible personal property and its use is unrelated to the purpose or function of the nonprofit organization (such as a gift of livestock to a church or a gift of an antique chair to Heifer International), then the amount of the deduction is reduced by the amount of any gain that would have been realized had the property been sold. It is essential for individuals who donate tangible property that exceeds $5,000 in value to obtain appropriate appraisals. This will be discussed more fully later in this chapter.

As the above discussion points out, this is a very technical area of the law, and nonprofit organizations are well-advised to work with experienced tax and legal advisors in order to establish appropriate guidelines for the nonprofit organization. In addition, many nonprofit organizations provide members and others who are interested in the organization's well-being with presentations laying out the benefits, obligations, and recommendations that would be helpful for prospective donors to know in order to encourage them to support the nonprofit organization. Here too, it would be appropriate for your organization to enlist the aid of an experienced attorney, accountant, or investment advisor to assist in presenting this type of program.

APPRAISALS

Donations valued in excess of $5,000 must be substantiated by a qualified appraisal document made within sixty days of the donation, which includes a description of the item, its physical condition, a statement that it was made for tax purposes, the date of contribution, the terms of any agreement concerning the item made by the parties, the appraiser's name, address, and qualifications, the date of appraisal, the appraised value, the method of appraisal, and the basis used in determining value. It is often the case with donations of tangible property that experts disagree as to the fair market value of a particular item. Fortunately, the taxpayer may deduct the cost of appraisal fees for a charitable contribution. As with any tax dispute, the taxpayer has the burden of proving that the amount claimed as a deduction is appropriate.

Moreover, if an item is substantially overvalued, the taxpayer may be assessed a penalty. The tax law provides a penalty in the form of an addition to the tax assessed against an individual, a closely held corporation, or a personal service corporation for underpayments of income taxes that are attributable to valuation overstatements. The penalty applies if the value of the property as claimed on the taxpayer's return is 200 percent or more of its correctly determined value and the underpayment of tax attributable to the total of all overvaluations made by the taxpayer for the taxable year amounts to $5,000 or more. The amount of the penalty is 20 percent of the underpayment if the claimed property value is 150 percent or more of its true value. A 40 percent penalty applies if the claimed property value is 200 percent or more of its true value. Thus, there are strong incentives for taxpayers to value items donated to charities as accurately as possible.

Valuation problems customarily fall into two general categories: Either the experts disagree with each other and the IRS on the value of the donated item, or the authenticity of the donated item is questioned. In order to resolve such problems with respect to art, the IRS has established valuation guidelines, as well as special panels to review the deductions taken by the donor. These art advisory panels are often inconsistent, typically recommend lowering the value for works claimed by taxpayers as charitable donations and increasing the values for works contained within decedents' estates. When Alexander Calder died in 1976, the art advisory panel valued 1,292 gouache paintings in his estate at $897,230. Six weeks after Calder's death, his widow received 1,226 of the paintings and made gifts in trust of them for the couple's children and grandchildren. For gift tax, she valued them, as did the estate, at $897,230, but the IRS insisted that the art's value was $2.3 million and assessed Mrs. Calder for $459,419 more in gift tax.

After the death of art dealer Ileana Sonnabend, the IRS appraised *Canyon*, by Robert Rauschenberg, at $65 million, although the artwork cannot legally be sold because it includes a taxidermied bald eagle. Sonnabend's heirs were able to work out an arrangement with the IRS whereby they avoided the $29.2 million tax bill (plus penalties) by donating the work to the Museum of Modern Art in New York and forgoing the tax deduction.

When the IRS art advisory panel determines that an overvaluation has resulted in an underpayment of tax, not only is the taxpayer liable for penalties, but the appraiser can, under certain circumstances, be liable for civil and criminal penalties. For these reasons, donors of tangible property should be cautious about the valuation attributed to the donated work, and they should always enlist the services of a qualified, experienced, and conservative appraiser.

JOINT VENTURES, PARTNERING, AND UMBRELLA ORGANIZATIONS

Some nonprofit organizations find it beneficial to work with business organizations in order to achieve a designated objective. For example, a local nonprofit theater company may work with a local for-profit restaurant in order to provide patrons with the opportunity to attend the theater and have dinner either before or after the presentation. In situations such as this, it is important for the nonprofit organization to work out an acceptable arrangement with the restaurant so that both organizations benefit from the program. If the restaurant pays the nonprofit for the referrals, then the issues to be considered are the method for determining which restaurant patrons went to the restaurant because of the theater and how much should be paid for the referral. This should be negotiated before the arrangement is implemented and the parties should consider the extent of advertising, promotion, and the like, in order to determine a fair arrangement. In addition, the payment by the restaurant to the nonprofit is likely to be considered a royalty or referral fee; the tax consideration of this type of payment was discussed above in the section on unrelated business income.

Some nonprofit organizations operate under an umbrella organization, which is an association of institutions who work together formally to coordinate activities or pool resources. Sometimes, the umbrella organization is responsible for the groups under its care. Generally, the umbrella organization is a nonprofit, tax-exempt entity and the organizations it works with may either be other nonprofit organizations or business entities. An example of this type of arrangement is when a nonprofit hospital works with a group of medical professionals who are structured as a for-profit professional corporation. The arrangement between these organizations requires a great deal of thought, and that arrangement should be formalized in an appropriate document that addresses the business, legal, and ethical rules that apply to all of the organizations involved. It is essential for the nonprofit organization to work with a team of professionals including lawyers, accountants, and business advisors. These professionals should prepare appropriate documentation to be sure that the entire arrangement complies with all relevant laws.

TAX SHELTERS

Periodically, entrepreneurial individuals determine that they have come up with a plan to reduce taxable income by creating programs that take advantage of provisions in the tax law. These programs are designed to exploit ambiguities in the law rather than to take legitimate deductions. Tax shelters do not ordinarily relieve a taxpayer of the obligation of paying tax; rather, they are designed to postpone or defer tax liability. They generally accomplish this in two ways: (1) postponing current tax liability by accelerating deductions in the early years of the investment, rather than matching deductions with the income as it is generated, and (2) using leverage to increase the basis upon which the tax benefits are calculated without increasing the cash cost of the investment. These devices utilize loopholes in the tax law. Although shelters involving charitable donations can be very advantageous to the taxpayer, Congress and the IRS are extremely diligent in closing such loopholes as they are exploited. You should, therefore, be aware that this area is very dynamic, and should keep in regular contact with your tax attorney or accountant if believe you or your organizations is involved with a tax shelter.

One of the major limitations of tax shelters is the at-risk provision of the law. Without detailing the law, it may be said that it covers most taxpayers (including individuals, *partners*, *S-corporations*, and *limited liability companies [LLCs]* electing taxation as partnerships, but excluding regular corporations) and a wide variety of activities (including activities that are part of a trade or business or activities that are engaged in for the production of income). The law limits a taxpayer's deduction of losses to the amount the taxpayer has at risk and could actually lose from the activity. The IRS applies different rules to different types of taxpayers, but, generally speaking, the amount considered to be *at risk* is the amount of cash the taxpayer contributes to the activity, the adjusted basis of property contributed to the activity, and the amount borrowed by the taxpayer for the activity on which he or she is personally liable.

The at-risk provision affects tax shelters in the following manner: In a typical example, for a stated purchase price the investor in art reproductions would receive the right to (1) an entire limited edition of prints or sculptures, (2) the original master lithographic plate or mold (although the artist may insist on the right to deface or "strike" the plate or destroy the mold in order to make certain that the number of copies will be limited), and (3) the copyright in the master, including the exclusive right to use, manufacture, sell, distribute, promote, advertise, and license the master, mold, prints, or sculptures. If the purchase price were $100,000, it would normally be payable with a 10 percent cash investment, and the balance of $90,000 would be payable in the form of a note payable out of the profits derived from the sale of the works and the ancillary rights to market the work. The note used may be either a recourse note, which is one bearing the personal liability of the drawer, or a nonrecourse note, which is one not bearing the personal liability of the drawer but providing the holder security against the works themselves.

If the note is a recourse note, the depreciation tax benefits would be calculated on the basis of the total $100,000 purchase price. If, on the other hand, the $90,000 note is nonrecourse, only $10,000 would be at risk. Under the at-risk law, the losses stemming from the depreciation deduction (assuming the shelter produced no income) would be limited to the $10,000 at-risk amount. Those planning to be involved in these types of activities should consult with a tax advisor since there are additional limitations under in the tax law that relate to this type of arrangement.

In addition to the at-risk limitation, there are several other potential pitfalls to this type of tax shelter. For example, the law specifies different depreciation rates for property in different useful life classes. The investor must be careful that the IRS does not conclude, as it did in a 1979 ruling, that the property, there a lithographic plate master, is not eligible. Similarly, the law accords less attractive treatment to income produced from passive activity.

Certain property can also be subject to depreciation recapture. If depreciated tangible personal property is resold and the value of the property exceeds its adjusted basis, the depreciation is recaptured, which requires that the amount of gain attributable to the depreciation be characterized as ordinary income rather than as capital gain.

Another means by which a taxpayer can shelter income is to donate appreciated property. If, for example, an individual is lucky enough to purchase a valuable piece of jewelry for an amount less than its fair market value, he or she may hold the piece for one year and then donate it to a qualified charity. The tax deduction that may be taken for this donation is based on the fair market value of the work on the date of the donation. As discussed in the appraisals section above, valuation is an important consideration, and a substantial penalty can be imposed if an underpayment of tax occurs as a result of overvaluation.

A taxpayer may take this donation concept one step further and set up a systematic plan of donations involving limited edition prints, books, or sculptures. In this situation, the investor purchases the prints or sculptures, probably at a discount, or the books at cost, holds them for twelve months plus one day, and then donates them to museums or charities. He or she then may expect to take a charitable deduction in the amount of fair market value of the items on the date of contribution and in the amount of retail list price of the books. However, two revenue rulings make it clear that the investor's activity with respect to these types of art shelters makes him or her substantially equivalent to a dealer who sells the objects in the ordinary course of a trade or business. Therefore, the items contributed would be treated as ordinary income property held by the donor for sale to customers in the ordinary course of the donor's trade or business, regardless of whether the donor is actually engaged in such a trade or business.

Under the tax law, the taxpayer's charitable deduction would be reduced by the amount of gain that would not have been long-term capital gain had the objects been sold by the investor at their fair market value. Instead of taking a deduction in the amount of the fair market value on the date of contribution, the taxpayer may take only a deduction in the amount of his or her cost. The IRS evidently will look at bulk acquisitions and subsequent disposal of substantial parts of, for instance, a limited edition of prints, and probably will find that the activities are equivalent to those engaged in by an art dealer.

Another type of tax shelter involves an investment tax credit for qualified rehabilitation expenditures. This is one of the few shelters that Congress appears to favor. It is a means by which the legislature can encourage rehabilitation activities that it deems beneficial. In these situations, the taxpayer deducts the tax credit directly from taxes owed. The amount of investment tax credit is 20 percent for certified historic structures and 10 percent for other qualifying structures. To qualify, most buildings must be nonresidential at the time rehabilitation begins; however, certified historic buildings can be either residential or nonresidential. The building also must have been placed in service before the beginning of the rehabilitation, and it must have been substantially rehabilitated, with 50 percent or more of the existing external walls retained as external walls. Also, the taxpayer must elect to use a straight-line method of depreciation rather than accelerated methods. For certified historic structures, approval of the rehabilitation must be obtained from the Secretary of the Interior.

Other tax shelters include free ports and temporary loans. Taxpayers can avoid paying taxes and duties on items during the time it is stored in a *free port*, which is a secure warehouse located in one of the free trade zones offered by many countries. In addition, in some cases, a taxpayer can take advantage of a use-tax exemption in his or her home state simply by loaning newly purchased items to a nonprofit in a state without a use tax (Alaska, Delaware, Montana, New Hampshire, Oregon) for a set period, usually three months. Unfortunately for taxpayers, not all states have a *first use* exemption.

Of course, taxpayers need to be sure that their plans to avoid or reduce taxes are legal. After Tyco International's former chief executive L. Dennis Kozlowski was accused of failing to pay more than $1 million in state and city sales taxes on art purchases, the Manhattan District Attorney conducted a sales tax investigation beginning in 2002, resulting in numerous art dealers being charged with tax fraud and the collection of millions of dollars in unpaid sales taxes. The dealers were falsely stating that the purchases had been shipped out of state in order to avoid the payment of state sales tax.

There are many other ways to structure tax shelters and to reduce one's tax liability. New schemes are constantly being devised by creative lawyers and accountants. As indicated above, not all of these schemes produce the effects intended; when they do, the tax laws frequently are changed. Nonprofit taxpayers, therefore, should plan their transactions carefully. With proper awareness of the tax laws, significant amounts of money can be saved—though the risks of having an improper tax shelter disqualified are also very significant. You should, therefore, be sure that your nonprofit organization does not become involved in questionable tax shelter activities since the consequences for an organization can be significant and they could even jeopardize its tax-exempt status.

CHAPTER 15

Zoning

It is not uncommon for nonprofit organizations to have an office or storage facility in a home or garage, especially with the increased sophistication of computer systems. Telecommuting has become a viable option for many organizations. Online activities can also be conducted through home computers.

Problems raised by the multiple uses of a dwelling can be divided into two basic areas: local *zoning* regulations legally allow working and living in the same place, and whether the income tax laws recognize the realities of home-based businesses. This latter situation would apply to business organizations but not to nonprofits. This chapter covers the problem of zoning and similar laws.

LOCAL ZONING RESTRICTIONS

For the person who wants to live and work in the same space, local zoning ordinances can be a significant issue. Some city ordinances flatly prohibit using the same space as a business and as a dwelling. In this context, *business* is defined as including the activities of nonprofit organizations. In some commercially zoned areas where low-cost spaces are available, it is illegal to maintain a residence in the same space. In residential areas, regulations may require permits and restrict the size and use of the workspace. Since municipal and county ordinances vary, the nonprofit organization should check with the appropriate local government agency to determine specific requirements. The fire department, for example, would likely have to approve the use of a kiln.

For the person who wants to maintain an office or storage facility in the garage or basement of a residence, several types of restrictions may apply. The space devoted to the work activity may be limited to a certain number of square feet. Outbuildings may or may not be allowed. The type of equipment used may also be restricted. Noise, smoke, and odor restrictions may apply. Approval may be required from all or some of the neighbors. If remodeling is contemplated, building codes must, of course, also be considered.

Your organization may also have to obtain a home occupation permit or, in many areas, a license. The application fee for either of these will normally be a flat fee or a percentage of annual receipts from the activity. Depending upon the success of the activity, this could become a substantial expense. In addition, your homeowner's or renter's insurance policy will typically contain some restrictions relating to commercial activity that may very well incorporate your nonprofit organization's activity. You should contact your insurance broker to find out whether or not your policy contains such limitations and what can be done to deal with them.

In commercially zoned areas, nonprofit organizations may have more flexibility in the types of activities they conduct, particularly if they produce noise or odors that would be offensive to others in a residentially zoned location. But if your organization also wishes to use the workspace for eating and sleeping, as would be the case for homeless shelters, for example, zoning ordinances may prohibit such use.

FEDERAL REGULATIONS

Additional regulations that can adversely affect those who want to work at home are federal laws that inhibit so-called *cottage industries*. The US Department of Labor actively enforces a 1943 regulation that forbids individuals from producing in their homes for profit the following six categories of goods: embroidery, women's apparel, gloves and mittens, buttons and buckles, jewelry, and handkerchiefs. While this situation appears to apply to commercial activity, it may affect nonprofits that employ individuals to produce these goods. For example, there are a number of nonprofit workshops that employ disabled individuals to create products for sale. The proceeds of those sales are entitled to special tax treatment, as more fully discussed in chapter 14. These so-called sheltered workshops are currently being phased out in many communities and must comply with minimum-wage laws.

The regulation was originally enacted many years ago when the Department of Labor found that minimum-wage violations were widespread in industries in which working at home predominated. The minimum wage is mandated by the federal Fair Labor Standards Act and requires employers to pay their employees no less than a set hourly rate. Overtime, which is usually at one-and-one-half times the employee's hourly rate, is also mandated for hours worked over forty hours per week.

In 1981, the Department of Labor proposed repealing all regulations that prohibited cottage industries, but bitter labor union opposition resulted in the continuation of the regulation for all the targeted crafts except knitted outerwear.

The remaining regulations may create serious difficulties for people who want to work at home. In recent years, the disputes between labor unions, principally the International Ladies Garment Workers Union, and women who make their livings from cottage industries have become quite heated. The unions argue that they merely want to prevent sweatshop conditions, but many people believe that the real issue is nonunionized home labor competing with union members who work in unionized factories.

In order to fall within the scope of the regulation, the worker must be an employee. This does not mean, however, that a person can avoid the effect of the regulation simply by labeling him or herself an independent contractor. Under the Fair Labor Standards Act, the test of employment is the economic reality of the relationship. Volunteers are not employees and are thus not covered by the law.

IN PLAIN ENGLISH

For a website that makes handmade items available for sale, see Etsy.com.

TELECOMMUTING AND WEB-BASED ORGANIZATIONS

As noted above, telecommuting has become popular for many organizations. It makes it possible for individuals to maintain a traditional employment relationship while working at home and enabling individuals to reside anywhere they wish. Thus, for example, many nonprofit organizations that solicit donations from individuals and organizations in high-rent areas are themselves based in less expensive rural communities. The cost savings to the organization in rent is obvious; the lifestyle benefits to the employee are also clear.

There is at least one tax issue that has arisen for telecommuting employees in particular. When a telecommuter is located in Nashville, for example, working for a New York organization, which jurisdiction's income tax will apply to the salary earned? The highest court in the State of New York held that since the salary was derived from New York sources and the telecommuter chose to live in Nashville, New York income tax was due on 100 percent of the income earned by the out-of-state employee. The result might have been different if the employee had been transferred to Nashville rather than voluntarily choosing to live in that state for the employee's own convenience. This issue is important for the nonprofit when determining employee withholding tax.

Web-based organizations can be run from anywhere. It is quite common for individuals to conduct those activities from home. All that is needed is a telephone, computer, and Internet connection.

Various forms of independent contractors establish their base at home. Since the zoning laws that prohibit the operation of home-based activities were generally enacted for the purpose of preserving a residential quality in residential neighborhoods, including air quality, traffic flow, and noise, it is not clear whether these laws would be violated by the types of home-based activities described above. Technically, the laws state that any business activity would be a violation, yet the purpose of the law is not affected by organizations that do not result in increased air pollution, traffic, or noise. Thus, it would seem that a modernization of the legislation would be appropriate or, at the very least, a clear legislative exemption for these types of organizations should be enacted.

Notwithstanding the logic of this position, there is a risk in establishing any home-based operation without complying with the laws as they are written or obtaining a proper exemption from them.

Your organization should consult with an experienced lawyer if it desires to operate out of a home or if you wish to live in your place of business.

CHAPTER 16

Renting Space

At some point in the life of your organization, it will probably be necessary to evaluate the terms and conditions of a commercial lease. Commercial leases are much more subject to negotiation and pitfalls than residential leases, which are more tightly regulated in most states. You should consult an attorney with experience in negotiating commercial leases before signing one.

Landlords typically employ the services of a broker when attempting to rent commercial space. In addition, many nonprofits hire brokers to assist them with lease negotiations. This discussion is intended to alert you to some of the topics that should arise in your discussion with your nonprofit's lawyer or real estate broker.

PREMISES

To begin with, the exact space to be rented should be spelled out in detail in the lease. Determine whether there is a distinction between the space leased and the actual space that is usable. Often, tenants are required to pay rent on commercial space measured from wall to wall (commonly referred to as a vanilla shell) even though, after the area is built out, the resulting usable space may be significantly smaller.

If your space is in a shopping center or office building and you share responsibility for common areas with other tenants, your responsibilities for the common areas should be explained. Such matters as who will be responsible for cleaning and maintaining them, when will the common areas be open or closed, and when other facilities, such as restrooms and storage, are available must be spelled out.

COST

Another important item is the cost of the space. A flat monthly rental or one that will change based on your earnings at the location, as is often the case in shopping centers and office buildings, must be determined. In the case of nonprofit organizations, *earnings* are likely not to be an issue, but care should be taken to be sure that donations are not deemed *earnings* within the lease's definitions. In order to evaluate the cost of the space, you should compare it with other similar spaces in the same locale. Do not be afraid to negotiate for more favorable terms. Care should be taken not to sign a lease that will restrict your organization from opening another facility close to the one being rented.

Nonprofit organizations enjoy tax benefits in many jurisdictions. That is, they are provided with the privilege of having the real estate tax reduced when they lease space. This benefit can and should be used by your organization to obtain more favorable terms from the landlord when negotiating a lease.

TERM

It is also important for your organization to consider the period of the lease. If, for example, your organization is merely renting a booth at a convention, then you are only concerned with the short term. On the other hand, if your organization intends to rent for a year or two, it is a good idea to get an option to extend the lease because, when you advertise and promote your organization, your location is one of the things about which you will be telling people. Moving can cause a lot of problems with mail and telephone numbers. Besides, if your organization moves every year or two, some patrons or supporters may feel that your organization is unstable, and individuals who visit on an irregular basis may not know where to find your organization after the lease period ends. Worse still, they may find a competitor in your old space. In fact, goodwill is often defined as including a stable location.

Long-term leases are recordable in some states. Recording, where permitted, is generally accomplished by having the lease filed in the same office where a deed to the property would be filed. Check with a local real estate title company or real estate attorney for the particulars in your locale.

RESTRICTIONS

It is essential for you to determine whether there are any restrictions on the particular activity your organization wishes to perform on the leased premises. For example, the area may be zoned so as to prohibit you from selling donated merchandise. It is a good idea to insist on a provision that puts the burden of obtaining any permit or variances on the landlord or, if your organization is responsible for them, the inability to obtain them should be grounds for terminating the lease without penalty.

Be sure the lease provides that your organization is permitted to use any sign or advertising on the premises or spells out any restrictions. It is not uncommon, for example, for historic-landmark laws to regulate signs on old buildings. Some zoning laws also prohibit signs.

REMODELING

You should also be aware that extensive remodeling may be necessary for certain spaces to become suitable for your organization's use. If this is the case, then it is important for your organization to determine who will be responsible for the costs of remodeling, who will determine the contractors to be used, and who owns the tenant improvements. In addition, it is essential to find out whether it will be necessary for your organization to restore the premises to its original, pre-remodeled condition when the lease ends. This can be expensive and, in some instances, impossible.

AMERICANS WITH DISABILITIES ACT

The Americans with Disabilities Act of 1990 (ADA), which was discussed in the context of employment in chapter 13, also covers real estate. The ADA requires places of public accommodation to be reasonably accessible. The law is broadly interpreted and includes virtually every type of organization, including nonprofit organizations. The term *reasonable accommodation* is not precise and, thus, it is important to determine what must be done in order to fulfill the requirements of this federal statute. Typically, approximately 25 percent of the cost of any covered remodel must be allocated to items that aid accessibility. These would include, among other things, levered door openers, Braille signs, larger bathroom stalls, wheelchair ramps, approved disability-accessible doors, and elevators. You should determine whether the cost of complying with the ADA will be imposed on the landlord, the tenant, or shared.

ENVIRONMENTAL LAWS

Environmental laws will inhibit the use of your space for certain organizations. It is essential for you to determine whether any of the materials used in your organization will violate federal, state, or local rules with respect to hazardous materials. In addition, there can be hazardous materials cleanup problems resulting from prior uses of the space to be occupied by your organization. For example, space previously used by a dry cleaner, chemical company, automotive repair organization, or the like may require an expensive cleanup operation prior to any occupation. Other issues, such as whether the building contains any asbestos, lead-based paint, or the like may exist. These present specialized problems in the costs of remodeling. It is essential for the lease to spell out who will bear the costs of any environmental compliance.

UTILITIES

If your organization needs special hookups, such as water or electrical lines, you should determine whether the landlord will provide them or whether your organization will have to bear the cost. Of course, even if the leased premises already has the necessary facilities, you should question the landlord regarding the cost of these utilities and whether they are included in the rent or are they to be paid separately.

In some locations, garbage pickup is not a problem, since it is one of the services provided by the municipality. On the other hand, it is common for renters to be responsible for their own trash disposal. In commercial spaces, this can be quite expensive and should be addressed in the lease.

Customarily, the landlord will be responsible for the exterior of the building. It will be the landlord's obligation to make sure that it does not leak during rainstorms and that it is properly ventilated. Notwithstanding this fact, it is important for your organization to make sure the lease deals with the question of responsibility if, for example, the building is damaged and some of your property is damaged or destroyed.

IN PLAIN ENGLISH

If your organization has to take out insurance for the building, as well as its contents, the cost will greatly increase. Determine who will be responsible for insuring the building.

Similarly, you should find out whether or not it will be your organization's obligation to obtain liability insurance for injuries that are caused in portions of the building that are not under your control, such as common hallways and stairwells. Your organization should, of course, have its own liability policy for accidental injuries or accidents that occur on its leased premises. See chapter 12 for a discussion of organization insurance.

SECURITY AND ZONING

A good lease will also contain a provision dealing with security. If your organization is renting indoor space in a shopping center or office building, it is likely that the landlord will be responsible for external security, although this is not universally the case. If your organization is renting an entire building, it is customarily its responsibility to provide whatever security it deems important. You should address the question or whether the lease permits your organization to install locks or alarm systems.

If your organization is dealing with large, bulky items and it is accepting deliveries or making them, the lease should contain a provision that will give it the flexibility it desires.

If the place your organization wishes to rent will be used as both a personal dwelling and an organizational office, such as a homeless shelter, other problems may arise. It is quite common for zoning laws to prohibit certain forms of commercial activities when the area is zoned residential (see chapter

15). You should consult with your organization's attorney before attempting to operate out of a residential home or allowing residential occupation in a building zoned for commercial use.

WRITTEN DOCUMENT

Finally, it is essential for your organization to be sure that every item agreed upon between your organization and the landlord is stated in writing. This is particularly important when dealing with leases since many state laws provide that a long-term lease is an interest in land and can be enforced only if in writing. Further, as mentioned above, many jurisdictions permit leases to be recorded. You should determine whether your organization wants its entire lease to be a matter of public record or whether your organization would prefer only to have a summary of it available for others to see.

The relationship between landlord and tenant is an ancient one that is undergoing a good deal of change. Care should be taken when examining a potential location to determine exactly what your organization can do on the premises and whether the landlord or municipal rules will allow your organization to use the location for its intended purpose.

DONATED FACILITIES

Some nonprofit organizations are fortunate enough to have a benefactor that will provide the organization with a building to be used for its charitable purposes. If your organization is fortunate enough to have such a benefactor, then it is important to determine whether that building is adequate for its purposes, the zoning laws permit the activity your organization intends to engage in, and whether the location is right for your organization. After evaluating these and other factors that may be unique to your organization's activity, you can determine whether that building will fit your organization's needs and use it, or whether another facility should be obtained. In the latter case, it is important for your organization to determine whether it can dispose of the donated property, exchange it for a more suitable location, or whether your organization may not dispose of that property, in which event, it may need to lease that property to another user and find a property which is suitable for it.

Your organization should spend as much time as necessary determining its facility needs and whether the donated real estate will fit those needs. If your organization is not fortunate enough to be provided with a real estate donation and it requires a facility to conduct its charitable mission, then it must still evaluate its needs, determine the best location, and research the availability of acceptable space in that location and negotiate an appropriate lease as discussed in this chapter.

CHAPTER 17

Estate Planning

No matter what activity you are involved with and no matter how successful you are, the time that you will work with your organization is limited by either retirement or death. Prudent individuals will make appropriate plans for both. Nonprofit organizations should also encourage the individuals involved with the organization to establish estate plans that consider donations to the organization when the individuals pass on.

Many organizations provide this type of incentive by having free seminars for members and supporters. Others offer present rewards or recognition to an individual who promises to include a significant bequest in the individual's will or after-life trust. A number of organizations actually have standard provisions for identifying the organization as a beneficiary that a donor can easily add to his or her will. Others will arrange for the assistance of a volunteer attorney to draft appropriate language to accomplish the gift or donation. Nonprofit organizations are continuously developing incentives and looking for ways to make it easier for individuals to provide for the organization with after-life donations.

All individuals should give some thought to estate planning and take the time to execute a proper will. Without a will, there is simply no way to control the disposition of one's property. Sound estate planning may include transfers outside of the will since these types of arrangements typically escape the delays and expenses of probate. Certain types of trusts can be valuable will substitutes, but they may be subject to challenge by a surviving spouse.

Proper estate planning will require the assistance of a knowledgeable lawyer and, perhaps, also a life insurance agent, an accountant, a real estate agent, and a bank trust officer. What help will be needed and from whom will depend on the nature and size of the estate. This chapter considers the basic principles of estate planning. This discussion is not a substitute for the aid of a lawyer experienced in estate planning; rather, it is intended to introduce you to the basic principles, alert you to potential problems, and aid in preparing you to work with your estate planner(s).

While every other chapter in this text is directed at the nonprofit organization itself, this chapter is intended to educate the individuals who work with and are involved with the nonprofit so that they can be aware of the laws of succession while considering their ability to provide for the nonprofit organization after they pass away.

THE WILL

A will is a legal instrument by which a person directs the distribution of property in his or her estate upon death. The maker of the will is called the *testator*. Recipients of gifts are known as *beneficiaries* or *legatees*. Gifts given by a will are referred to as *bequests* (personal property) or *devises* (real estate).

Certain formalities are required by state law to create a valid will. About half the states require formally witnessed wills, that is, that the instrument be in writing and signed by the testator in the presence of two or more witnesses. The other states allow either witnessed or *holographic* wills. A will that is entirely handwritten and signed by the testator is known as a holographic will.

A will is a unique document in two respects. First, if properly drafted, it is ambulatory, meaning it can accommodate change, such as applying to property acquired after the will is made. Second, a will is revocable, meaning that the testator has the power to change or cancel it at any time. Even if a testator makes a valid agreement not to revoke the will, the power to revoke it remains. If the testator uses that power, he or she may be liable for breach of contract.

Generally, courts do not consider a will to have been revoked unless it can be established that the testator either (1) performed a physical act of revocation, such as burning or tearing up a will with the intent to revoke it or (2) later executed a valid will that revoked the previous will. Most state statutes also provide for automatic revocation of a will, in whole or in part, if the testator is subsequently divorced or married.

To change a will, the testator must execute a supplement, known as a *codicil*. It has the same formal requirements as those for creating a will. To the extent that the codicil contradicts the will, the contradicted parts of the will are revoked.

PAYMENT OF TESTATOR'S DEBTS

When the testator's estate is insufficient to satisfy all the bequests in the will after debts and taxes have been paid, some or all of the bequests in the will must be reduced or even eliminated entirely. The process of reducing or eliminating bequests is known as *abatement*. The priorities for reduction are set by state law according to the category of each bequest. The legally significant categories of gifts are generally as follows:

- specific bequests or devises, meaning gifts of identifiable items (*I give to X all the furniture in my home*);
- demonstrative bequests or devises, meaning gifts that are to be paid out of a specified source unless that source contains insufficient funds, in which case the gifts will be paid out of the general assets (*I give to Y $1,000 to be paid from my shares of stock in ABC Corporation*);
- general bequests, meaning gifts to be paid out of the general assets of an estate (*I give Z $1,000*); and
- residuary bequests or devises, meaning gifts of whatever is left in the estate after all other gifts and expenses are satisfied (*I give the rest, residue, and remainder of my estate to Z*).

Intestate property (property not governed by a will but part of the testator's estate) is usually the first to be taken to satisfy claims against the estate. (If the will contains a valid residuary clause, there will be no such property.) Next, residuary bequests will be taken. If more money is needed, general bequests will be taken, and, lastly, specific and demonstrative bequests will be taken together in proportion to their value. Some states, however, provide that all gifts, regardless of type, abate proportionally.

DISPOSITION OF PROPERTY NOT WILLED

If the testator acquires more property during the time between signing the will and death, the disposition of such property will also be governed by the will. If such property falls within the description of an existing category in the will (i.e., *I give all my stock to X; I give all my real estate to Y*), it will pass along with all similar property. If it does not and the will contains a valid residuary clause, such after-acquired property will go to the residuary legatees. If there is no residuary clause, such property will pass outside the will to the persons specified in the state's law of intestate succession.

INTESTATE SUCCESSION

When a person dies without leaving a valid will, this is known as dying *intestate*. The estate of a person who dies intestate is distributed according to the state law of intestate succession. These laws specify who is entitled to what parts of the estate. In general, intestate property passes to those persons having the nearest degree of kinship to the decedent. An intestate's surviving spouse will always receive a share, generally at least one-third of the estate. An intestate's surviving children generally get a share. If some of the children do not survive the intestate, the grandchildren of the intestate may be entitled to a share by *representation*.

Representation is a legal principle meaning that if an heir does not survive the intestate but has a child who does survive, that child will represent the non-surviving heir and receive that parent's share in the estate. In other words, the surviving child stands in the shoes of a dead parent in order to inherit from a grandparent who dies intestate.

If there are no direct descendants surviving, the intestate's surviving spouse will take the entire estate or share it with the intestate's parents. If there is neither a surviving spouse nor any surviving direct descendant of the intestate, the estate will be distributed to the intestate's parents or, if the parents are not surviving, to the intestate's siblings by representation. If there are no surviving persons in any of these categories, the estate will go to surviving grandparents and their direct descendants. In this way, the family tree is constantly expanded in search of surviving relatives.

If none of the persons specified in the law of intestate succession survive the testator, the intestate's property ultimately goes to the state. This is known as *escheat*.

The laws of intestate succession make no provision for friends, in-laws, or stepchildren. Children adopted by the testator are treated the same as natural children for all purposes.

SPOUSE'S ELECTIVE SHARE

State law will often provide a testator's surviving spouse with certain benefits from the estate even if the spouse is left out of the testator's will. Historically, these benefits were known as *dower*, in the case of a surviving wife, or *curtesy*, in the case of a surviving husband. In place of the old dower and curtesy, modern statutes give the surviving spouse the right to elect against the will and, thereby, receive a share equal to at least one-fourth of the estate. Here again, state laws vary. In some states, the surviving spouse's elective share is one third. The historical concepts of dower and courtesy are in large part a result of the law's traditional recognition of an absolute duty on the part of the husband to provide for the wife. Modern laws are perhaps better justified by the notion that most property in a marriage should be shared because the financial success of either partner is due to the efforts of both.

ADVANTAGES TO HAVING A WILL

A will affords the opportunity to direct distribution of one's property and to set out limitations by making gifts conditional. For example, if an individual wishes to donate certain property to a specific charity but only if certain conditions are adhered to, a will can make such conditions a prerequisite to the donation. Nonprofit organizations may wish to educate the individuals who are involved with it to provide for the organization in their will. Many organizations have programs specifically for this type of arrangement. For example, many Boy Scout Councils provide immediate recognition for those adult leaders who agree to donate a specified amount of money to the organization when they pass. Church groups frequently arrange for lectures so that members will be educated on how to make bequests to the church when they pass. It is not uncommon for nonprofit organizations to provide as much help as possible for supporters, members, and others interested in helping the nonprofit organization with estate planning guidance. In this way, nonprofit organizations are able to benefit the individuals who are interested in helping the organization while benefiting the organization as well.

A will permits the testator to nominate an *executor*, called a *personal representative* in some states, to watch over and administer the estate in accordance with the testator's wishes and the law of the state where the will is being handled. If no executor is named in the will, the court will appoint one. A will permits the testator to give property to minors and to regulate the timing and uses of the property given (i.e., funds to be used exclusively for education).

If the testator has unusual types of property, such as antiques, artwork, publishable manuscripts, or intangibles, such as copyrights, trademarks, patents, and the like, it is a good idea to appoint joint executors, one with financial expertise and the other with expertise in valuation in the genre in question. If joint executors are used, some provision should be made in the will for resolving any deadlock between the two. For example, a neutral third party might be appointed as an arbitrator who is directed to resolve any impasses after hearing both sides.

It is also advisable to define the scope of the executor's power by detailed instructions. A lawyer's help will be necessary to set forth all of these important considerations in legally enforceable, unambiguous terms. It is essential in a will to avoid careless language that might be subject to attack by survivors unhappy with the will's provisions. A lawyer's assistance is also crucial to avoid making bequests that are not legally enforceable because they are contrary to public policy (i.e., if an individual gets married, the bequest will fail).

ESTATE TAXES

In addition to giving the testator significant posthumous control over the division of property, a carefully drafted will can greatly reduce the overall amount of estate tax paid at death. The following information on taxing structures relates to federal estate taxation. State estate taxes often contain similar provisions, but state law must always be consulted for specifics. The tax law is continuously changing and must be consulted when preparing an estate plan. The plan should also be monitored and revised as the tax laws change. It is important for you to work with experienced estate planning lawyers and accountants.

GROSS ESTATE

The first step in evaluating an estate for tax purposes is to determine the so-called *gross estate*. The gross estate will include all property over which the deceased had significant control at the time of death. In addition to certain bank accounts, examples would include properly held residences, investments that have been structured to avoid probate, certain life insurance proceeds and annuities, jointly held interests, and revocable transfers.

Under current tax laws, the executor of an estate may elect to value the property in the estate either as of the date of death or as of a date six months after death. The estate property must be valued in its entirety at the time chosen. However, if the executor elects to value the estate six months after death and certain pieces of property are distributed or sold before then, that property will be valued as of the date of distribution or sale.

VALUATION

Fair market value is defined as the price at which property would change hands between a willing buyer and a willing seller when both buyer and seller have reasonable knowledge of all relevant facts. Such a determination is often very difficult to make, especially when items such as a non-publicly traded organization, artwork, antiques, other collectibles, and intangibles such as intellectual property are involved. Although the initial determination of fair market value is generally made by the executor when the estate tax return is filed, the Internal Revenue Service may disagree with the executor's valuation and assign assets a much higher fair market value.

When an executor and the Internal Revenue Service disagree with regard to valuation, the court will decide the matter. In most cases, the burden will be on the taxpayer to prove the value of the asset. Thus, expert testimony and evidence of the sale of the same or similar properties will be helpful. In general, courts are reluctant to determine valuation by formula.

THE TAXABLE ESTATE

Figuring the *taxable estate* is the second major step in evaluating an estate for tax purposes, after determining the gross estate. The law allows a number of deductions from the gross estate in determining the amount of the taxable estate. The taxable estate is the basis upon which the tax owing is computed. Some of the key deductions used to arrive at the amount of the taxable estate are discussed below.

Typical deductions from the gross estate include funeral expenses, certain estate administration expenses, debts and enforceable claims against the estate, mortgages and liens, and, perhaps most significant, the marital deduction and the charitable deduction.

Marital Deduction

The marital deduction allows the total value of any interest in property that passes from the decedent to the surviving spouse to be subtracted from the value of the gross estate. The government will eventually get its tax on this property when the spouse dies but only to the extent such interest is included in the spouse's gross estate. The spouse, of course, may limit or eliminate the estate tax on his or her estate by implementing certain estate-planning procedures. This deduction may occur even in the absence of a will making a gift to the surviving spouse since state law generally provides that the spouse is entitled to at least one-fourth of the overall estate regardless of the provisions of the will.

Charitable Deduction

The charitable deduction refers to the tax deduction allowed upon the transfer of property from an estate to a recognized charity. Since the definition of a charity for tax purposes is quite technical, it is advisable to insert a clause in the will providing that, if the institution specified to receive the donation does not qualify for the charitable deduction, the bequest shall go to a substitute qualified institution at the choice of the executor.

Calculating the Tax

Once deductions are figured, the taxable estate is taxed at the rate specified by the Unified Estate and Gift Tax Schedule. The unified tax imposes the same rate of tax on gifts made by will as on gifts made during life. It is a progressive tax, meaning the percent paid in taxes increases with the amount of property involved. Whether the estate tax will eventually be repealed altogether, be fixed at an intermediate amount, or revert to a former form will depend on future congressional action.

Paying the Tax

There is also an additional exemption for families with qualifying nonprofit organizations or farms. These exemptions, combined with the unlimited marital deduction, allow most estates to escape estate taxes altogether. For those estates with estate taxes due, generally, estate taxes must be paid when the estate tax return is filed (within nine months of the date of death). Arrangements may be made to spread payments out over a number of years, if necessary.

IN PLAIN ENGLISH

It is not uncommon for executors to be forced to sell properties for less than full value in order to pay taxes. This can be avoided by obtaining insurance policies, the proceeds of which can be set up in a trust.

DISTRIBUTING PROPERTY OUTSIDE THE WILL

Property can be distributed outside the will by making *inter vivos gifts* (given during the giver's lifetime), either outright or by placing the property in an irrevocable trust prior to death.

Advantages

A potential advantage of distributing property outside of the will is that the property escapes the delays and expense of probate, the court procedure by which a will is validated and administered. It used to be that there were also significant tax advantages to making inter vivos gifts rather than making gifts by will, but, since the estate and gift tax rates are now unified, there are few remaining tax advantages. One remaining advantage to making an inter vivos gift is that if the gift appreciates in value between the time the gift is made and death, the appreciated value will not be subject to estate tax. If the gift were made by will, the added value would be taxable since the gift would be valued on the estate tax return as of the date of death (or six months after).

IN PLAIN ENGLISH

This difference in value can represent significant tax savings for the heirs of someone whose assets suddenly increase in value.

Annual Exclusion

The other advantage of making an inter vivos gift involves the *yearly exclusion*. A yearly exclusion per recipient is available on inter vivos gifts. A married couple can combine their gifts and claim a yearly exclusion of twice the individual exclusion. You should check with your accountant to determine what the actual amount of the exemption is on the date the gift is made.

Three-Year Rule

Gifts made within three years of death used to be included in the gross estate on the theory that they were made in contemplation of death. Amendments to the tax laws, however, have done away with the three-year rule for most purposes. The three-year rule is still applicable to gifts of life insurance and to certain transfers involving stock redemption or tax liens. The rule also applies to certain valuation schemes, the details of which are too complex to discuss here.

Gift Tax Returns

The donor must file gift tax returns for any year in which gifts made exceeded a certain amount to any one donee. It is not necessary to file returns when a gift to any one donee amounts to less than that amount. However, where it is possible that the valuation of the gift will become an issue with the IRS, it may be a good idea to file a return anyway.

Filing the return starts the three-year statute of limitations running. Once the statute of limitations period has expired, the IRS will be barred from filing suit for unpaid taxes or for tax deficiencies due to higher government valuations of the gifts. If a taxpayer omits includable gifts amounting to more than 25 percent of the total amount of gifts stated in the return, the statute of limitations is extended to six years. There is no statute of limitations for fraudulent returns filed with the intent to evade tax.

In order to qualify as an inter vivos gift for tax purposes, a gift must be complete and final. Control is an important issue. If a giver retains the right to revoke a gift, the gift may be found to be testamentary in nature, even if the right to revoke was never exercised (unless the gift was made in trust). The gift must also be delivered. Actual, physical delivery is best, but a symbolic delivery may suffice if there is strong evidence of intent to make an irrevocable gift. An example of symbolic delivery is when the donor puts something in a safe and gives the intended recipient the only key.

TRUSTS

Another common way to transfer property outside the will is to place the property in a trust that is created prior to death. A trust is simply a legal arrangement by which one person holds certain property for the benefit of another. The person holding the property is the *trustee*. The trustee can be an individual or an institution, and in some situations, it may be beneficial to have more than one trustee. Those for whose benefit the trust is held are the *beneficiaries*. To create a valid trust, the giver must identify the trust property, make a declaration of intent to create the trust, transfer property to the trust, and name identifiable beneficiaries. If no trustee is named, a court will appoint one. The *settlor* (creator of the trust) may also be designated as trustee, in which case segregation of the trust property satisfies the delivery requirement. Trusts can be created by a will, in which case they are termed *testamentary trusts*, but these trust properties will be probated along with the rest of the will. To avoid probate, the settlor must create a valid *inter vivos trust*.

Inter Vivos Trusts

Generally, in order to qualify as an inter vivos trust, a valid interest in property must be transferred before the death of the creator of the trust. If the settlor fails to name a beneficiary for the trust or to make delivery of the property to the trustee before death, the trust will likely be termed testamentary. Such a trust will be deemed invalid unless the formalities required for creating a will were complied with.

A trust will not be termed testamentary simply because the settlor retained significant control over the trust, such as the power to revoke or modify the trust. For example, when a person makes a deposit in a savings account in his or her own name as trustee for another and reserves the power to withdraw the money or to revoke the trust, the trust will be enforceable by the beneficiary upon the death of the depositor, providing the depositor has not, in fact, revoked the trust.

IN PLAIN ENGLISH

Many states allow joint bank accounts with rights of survivorship to serve as valid will substitutes.

As Part of the Gross Estate

Property transferred and passed outside the will need not go through probate. However, even though such an arrangement escapes probate, the trust property will probably be counted as part of the gross estate for tax purposes because the settlor retained significant control. In addition, if the deceased settlor created a revocable trust for the purpose of decreasing the share of a surviving spouse, in some states, the trust will be declared *illusory*—in effect, invalid. The surviving spouse is then granted the legal share from the probated estate and from the revocable trust.

Life Insurance Trusts

Life insurance trusts can be used for paying estate taxes. The proceeds will not be taxed if the life insurance trust is irrevocable and the beneficiary is someone other than the estate, such as a friend or relative in an individual capacity or an organization. This is especially important, since, without a life insurance trust, their survivors might be forced to sell estate assets for less than their real value in order to pay estate taxes.

PROBATE

Briefly described, probate is the legal process by which a decedent's estate is administered in a systematic and orderly manner and with finality. The laws that govern the probate process vary among the states. One of the principal functions of probate administration is to provide a means to transfer ownership of a decedent's probate property. Accordingly, probate administration occurs without regard to whether the decedent died testate or intestate.

In the course of probate administration, the following occurs:

- a decedent's will is admitted to probate as the decedent's last will;
- someone (referred to as the personal representative, executor, or administrator) is appointed by the court to take charge of the decedent's property and financial affairs;
- interested persons are notified of the commencement of probate administration;
- information concerning the decedent's estate is gathered;
- probate property is assembled and preserved;
- debts and taxes are determined, paid, and/or challenged;
- claims against the decedent's estate are paid and/or challenged;
- conflicting claims of entitlement to the decedent's property are disposed of; and

- at the conclusion of the process, remaining estate property is distributed to the appropriate persons or entities.

While probate administration is pending, distributions of the decedent's property are suspended to allow *creditors*, claimants, devisees, and heirs the opportunity to protect their respective rights.

Probate property consists of the decedent's solely owned property as of the date of death. Property jointly held by the decedent and another person with the right of survivorship (i.e., a residence or *stock certificates* owned jointly with right of survivorship) passes to the survivor and is not a part of the decedent's probate estate. Likewise, the proceeds of life insurance on the decedent's life are not part of the probate estate (unless the estate is the designated beneficiary). It is, therefore, possible for a wealthy individual to die leaving little or no probate property.

As noted throughout, this chapter is intended to benefit you, the reader, so that you can make appropriate disposition of your assets when you pass on. It is also intended to provide you with information about charitable donations so that you can determine whether to provide for the nonprofit organization you are involved with and, if so, the extent of that disposition.

CHAPTER 18

Finding a Lawyer and an Accountant

Most nonprofit organizations expect to seek the advice of a lawyer only occasionally, for counseling on important matters such as employment contracts or real estate considerations. If this is your concept of the attorney's role in your nonprofit organization, you need to reevaluate it. Most organizations would operate more efficiently and effectively in the long run if they had a relationship with an attorney more like that between a family doctor and patient. An ongoing relationship that allows the attorney to get to know the nonprofit well enough to engage in preventive legal counseling and to assist in planning makes it possible to solve many problems before they occur.

If your organization is small or financially challenged, it is doubtless anxious to keep operating costs down. Your organization probably does not relish the idea of paying an attorney to get to know the nonprofit if it is not involved in an immediate crisis. However, it is a good bet that a visit with a competent lawyer right now will result in the raising of issues vital to the future of your organization. There is a good reason why larger, successful organizations employ one or more attorneys full-time as in-house counsel. Ready access to legal advice is something you should not deny to your nonprofit organization at any time, for any reason.

An attorney experienced in nonprofit law can give you important information regarding the risks unique to your nonprofit. Furthermore, a lawyer can advise you regarding your organization's rights and obligations in its relationship with present and future employees, the rules that apply in your state regarding the hiring and firing of employees, rules regarding donations, and so forth. Ignorance of these issues and violation of the rules can result in financially devastating lawsuits and even criminal penalties. Since each state has its own laws covering certain nonprofit practices, state laws must be consulted on many areas covered in this book. A competent local nonprofit attorney is, therefore, your best source of information on many issues that will arise in the running of your organization. Many law firms have attorneys who are licensed in several jurisdictions, and others have relationships with attorneys in other locales.

IN PLAIN ENGLISH

Most legal problems cost more to solve or defend after they arise than it would have cost to prevent their occurrence in the first place. Litigation is notoriously inefficient and expensive. Your organization does not want to sue or to be sued if it can help it.

FINDING A LAWYER

If you do not know any attorneys, ask other people if they know any good ones. Your organization wants either a lawyer who specializes in nonprofit law or a general practitioner who has many satisfied nonprofit clients. Finding the lawyer who is right for your organization may require that you shop around a bit. Most local and state bar associations have referral services. A good tip is to find out who is in the nonprofit law section of the state or local bar association or who has served on special bar committees dealing with law reform. It may also be useful to find out if any articles covering the area of law with which you are concerned have been published in either scholarly journals or continuing-legal-education publications and if the author is available to assist your organization.

It is a good idea to hire a specialist or law firm with a number of specialists rather than a general practitioner. While it is true that you may pay more per hour for the expert, you will not have to pay for the attorney's learning time. Experience is valuable. In this regard, you may wish to keep in mind that it is uncommon for a lawyer to specialize in nonprofit practice and also handle criminal matters. Thus, if someone within your organization is faced with criminal prosecution for the death of an employee, you should be searching for an experienced criminal defense lawyer.

EVALUATING A LAWYER

One method by which your organization can attempt to evaluate an attorney in regard to representing nonprofit clients is by consulting the *Martindale-Hubbell Law Directory* in your local county law library or online at www.martindale.com. While this may be useful, the mere fact that an attorney's name does not appear in the directory should not be given too much weight, since there is a significant charge for being included and some lawyers may have chosen not to pay for the listing. You can also consult Avvo (www.avvo.com), Google (www.google.com), and Yelp (www.yelp.com). Many law firms have established websites. The larger firms usually include extensive information about the firm, its practice areas, and its attorneys.

After you have obtained several recommendations for attorneys, it is appropriate for you to talk with them for a short period of time to determine whether your organization would be comfortable working with them. Do not be afraid to ask about their background, experience, and whether they feel they can help your organization.

USING A LAWYER

Once you have completed the interview process, select the person who appears to best satisfy your organization's needs. One of the first items you should discuss with your organization's lawyer is the fee structure. You are entitled to an estimate. However, unless your organization enters into an agreement to the contrary with the attorney, the estimate is just that. Nonprofit lawyers generally charge by the hour, though you may be quoted a flat rate for a specific service, such as creating the organization or assisting with a lease.

Many state bar associations require or strongly recommend that attorneys in that jurisdiction provide some free or pro bono service to qualified organizations or individuals. You may wish to check with the local bar association whether it has such a requirement and, if so, how you or your organization might be able to take advantage of that program. In this way, you and your nonprofit organization might be able to obtain the services of an experienced and skilled attorney without incurring significant costs or even for free. In fact, some states have volunteer lawyer's organizations in specific areas of law. You should also determine whether your jurisdiction has organizations such as this and, if it does, contact that organization for assistance as well.

Contact your organization's lawyer whenever you believe a legal question has arisen. The attorney should aid your organization in identifying which questions require legal action or advice and which require organizational decisions. Generally, lawyers will deal only with legal issues, though they may help you to evaluate other related issues.

Some attorneys encourage clients to feel comfortable calling at the office during the day or at home in the evening. Other lawyers, however, may resent having their personal time invaded. Some, in fact, do not list their home telephone numbers. You should learn the attorney's preference early on.

The *attorney-client* relationship is such that your organization should feel comfortable when confiding in its attorney. This person will not disclose any confidential communications; in fact, a violation of this rule, depending on the circumstances, can be considered an ethical breach that could subject the attorney to professional sanctions.

If your organization takes the time to develop a good working relationship with its attorney, it may well prove to be one of its more valuable assets.

FINDING AN ACCOUNTANT

In addition to an attorney, most organizations will need the services of a competent accountant to aid with tax planning, the filing of periodic reports, and annual tax returns. Finding an accountant with whom your nonprofit is compatible is similar to finding an attorney. You should ask around and learn which accountants are servicing organizations similar to yours. State professional accounting associations may also provide a referral service or point you to a directory of accountants in your area. You should interview prospective accountants to determine whether your organization feels that it can work with them and whether your organization feels their skills will be compatible with the nonprofit's needs. Like attorneys, many accountants contribute their time to qualified nonprofit organizations. You should check with the local accounting board to determine whether your area has volunteer accountants who may be able to assist your organization without charge or for a reduced rate.

Like your attorney, your accountant can provide valuable assistance in planning for the future of your nonprofit organization. It is important to work with professionals you trust and with whom you are able to relate on a professional level.

For an online newsletter that covers many of the issues discussed in this book and updates that information on a regular basis, go to www.dubofflaw .com/subscribe.

Glossary

123

401(k) is a type of plan provided by an employer for its employees that requires periodic payments during employment so that the employee can obtain post-retirement income benefits. Its name is derived from the initial section of the Internal Revenue Code, which created it.

A

Acceptance is a term used in contract law to describe an element of a contract, which occurs after an offer has been made. See *contract, offer.*

Accountant is a trained professional who provides accounting services such as setting up and maintaining a company's books and tax preparation. See *certified public accountant.*

Accounts Payable is an accounting term used to define monetary obligations owed by one to another. See also *accounts receivable.*

Accounts Receivable is an accounting term used to define monetary obligations that one is entitled to from another. See also *accounts payable.*

Action, sometimes referred to as "cause of action," is the legal claim or right that one has against another. It is frequently written in the form of a legal document known as a complaint, which is filed in court and is used to begin a lawsuit.

Addendum is a document attached at the end of another document and is customarily intended to supplement the terms of the document to which it is attached. See *contract.*

Adjusted basis is a term used to describe a tax concept. The "basis" of an item is its cost or fair market value that is "adjusted" for tax purposes by deducting depreciation and other offsets allowable under the Internal Revenue Code. This concept is frequently used when valuing property for tax or related purposes. See also *tax.*

Affidavit is a statement sworn to or affirmed by the party making the statement, who is known as an "affiant." Affidavits are written, and the signature is notarized. Because of this, affidavits carry a great deal of weight and may be used in legal proceedings or other official purposes, such as in real estate transactions or in legal proceedings when a sworn oath is required. See also *declaration, notary.*

Agency is the relationship between one person, known as the *principal*, and another, known as the *agent*. Customarily, the agent works for or on behalf of the principal and is subject to the principal's control or right of control. Typically, the agent owes a duty to the principal. See also *principal.*

Agent. See *agency, principal.*

Agreement is an arrangement, written or oral, whereby two or more parties reach an understanding. When conforming to the requirements of contract law, it is known as a *contract*. If one or more of the requirements for a legal contract are missing, the agreement may be subject to certain legal defenses and, thus, not enforceable. See also *contract.*

Amendment is the term used to when an agreement is modified, as when a contract is changed. See also *contract.*

Americans with Disabilities Act of 1990 (ADA) is a federal statute enacted by Congress for the purpose of providing individuals with defined disabilities the opportunity to obtain fair treatment in employment, housing, transportation, and the like. The courts have been wrestling with the definition of "disability" for purposes of interpreting the statute and with the amount of "reasonable accommodation" required to be provided under the act.

Antidilution is a term used in trademark law to describe one of the forms of protection available to trademark owners under the law. It prohibits another from weakening, tarnishing, disparaging, or otherwise undermining the strength and credibility of the protected trademark. See also *trademark.*

Antitrust laws are the laws used to prevent monopolies and unlawful arrangements that are intended to manipulate or control a particular market and unlawfully affect pricing, as well as other key market factors. The antitrust laws are enforced by both government regulation (federal and state) and by through litigation.

Apparent authority is a legal term used to define the authority an agent appears to have when dealing with third persons. This is intended to protect the third person's reasonable expectations when dealing with the agent and is available for third-person protection even when contrary to the express instructions of the principal. See also *agency, principal.*

Appreciate and **appreciation** are financial and accounting terms used to define the increase in value of property, whether tangible or intangible, that occurs over time. Thus, a house frequently appreciates in value as real estate prices increase. Similarly, a copyright, which is intangible, may increase in value when the protected work has received positive critical acclaim or popularity. See also *depreciate, depreciation.*

Articles of incorporation are created in a legal document filed with the state in which a company desires to do business as a corporation and is the "charter" or creating instrument for the corporation. It defines the authority granted by the state for the company to be conducted in the corporate form and is analogous to a constitution. All business corporations are created under the law of the state in which they are incorporated and may do business in other states by filing the appropriate document(s) in those states as a "foreign" (corporation chartered in another state) corporation doing business in that state. The only entities incorporated under federal law are federally charted banks and certain federally mandated organizations, such as the Smithsonian Institution and the Postal Service. See also *articles of organization, bylaws, corporation, partnership.*

Articles of organization are created in a legal document filed with the state in which a business desires to do business as a limited liability company (LLC) and is the "charter" or creating instrument for the LLC. It defines the authority granted by the state for the company to be conducted as an LLC and is analogous to a constitution. All LLCs are created under the law of the state in which they are created and may do business in other states by filing the appropriate document(s) in those states as a "foreign" (LLC chartered in another state) LLC doing business in that state. See also *articles of incorporation, bylaws, limited liability company, partnership.*

Asset is a financial or accounting term used to describe cash or property. The property can be tangible, such as real estate and office equipment, or intangible, such as intellectual property and goodwill. See also *intellectual property, goodwill.*

Assignment for the benefit of creditors is a legal term used in bankruptcy and collections law to define an arrangement whereby assets of a debtor are assigned to another, either the creditor, trustee, or receiver, for the benefit of one or more creditors. This can take the form of a formal court-administered plan or an informal arrangement worked out between the parties. See also *bankruptcy, debt, receiver, trustee.*

Attorney, also known as "lawyer," is a professional who has been licensed to practice law in the state or other jurisdiction by which the license has been issued and whose conduct is regulated by state bar associations and the highest court of the state or jurisdiction. Attorneys must be licensed to practice in every court in which they appear. Customarily, attorneys are graduates of post-graduate law schools and have passed one or more bar examinations.

Attorney-client privilege is a legal doctrine established for the purpose of enabling a client to communicate freely with his or her attorney. All communications between the client and attorney (or attorney's staff) that are not in the presence of any other person are privileged and may not be disclosed by the attorney without the client's permission.

Attorney-in-fact is a person who is not actually a lawyer but, rather, is a person authorized to perform a specific act or combination of acts described in a document known as a "power of attorney" on behalf of the person granting the power. The person granting the power must sign this document, and that person's signature must be notarized. The power may be general or specific, as defined in the document. In some jurisdictions and for some purposes, a power of attorney may be "recorded"; that is, filed with the appropriate governmental agency.

Audit is an accounting term used to describe a review, typically of financial statements or tax returns. The audit is intended to verify the accuracy of the document and is conducted by an auditor, who is typically a skilled professional.

Authority is the power granted by law or by a principal to a person to perform a prescribed act or combination of acts. The act or combination of acts, when performed, will be legally binding. See also *agency, attorney-in-fact, principal.*

B

Bankruptcy is the legal term defining the consequences of insolvency. In other words, when liabilities are greater than assets or when bills cannot be paid in the ordinary course of one's business, one is technically insolvent or bankrupt. Laws have been enacted that provide relief for those who are insolvent, as well as for their creditors. See also *Chapter 7, Chapter 11, Chapter 13, receiver, trustee.*

"Blue sky" law is a common term used to define state securities laws enacted for the protection of those who invest in businesses. The term comes from a statement in Congress during the aftermath of the 1929 Depression that referred to the victims of the financial crash who bought securities whose values were artificially inflated as people who obtained nothing more than chunks of "blue sky."

Board of directors is the governing board of a business entity charged by statute with responsibility for administering the business and affairs of that entity. It is frequently used in the context of corporate boards of directors, though it can refer to the administrative board of other types of entities, such as nonprofit corporations, limited liability companies, or the like. See also *corporation, limited liability company, partnership.*

Branding is the term used to describe the identification and reputation of a product or service. This modern accordion concept has been used by businesses to describe the process of identifying the qualities, unique characteristics, reputation, market awareness and the like of specific products or services. One of the most famous "brands" in the world today is Coca-Cola.

Business plan is a document used to describe the process of developing a new or existing business. The plan typically includes the items set forth in chapter 3.

Buy-sell agreement is a document customarily used by business organizations for the purpose of establishing a formal arrangement whereby the ownership interest in the business may be sold or transferred only in accordance with the terms of the agreement. These agreements typically impose restrictions on the sale or transfer to "outsiders" and establish methods for valuing the interest when the owner desires to transfer the interest, dies, or becomes incapacitated. These agreements are frequently used in closely held businesses, as distinguished from those that are publicly traded.

Bylaws are formal documents adopted by corporations for administering the internal affairs of the company. They typically cover the rules and regulations for calling meetings, defining key positions, and the like. Bylaws may not be broader in scope than the company's articles of incorporation. Articles of incorporation are analogous to a constitution and define the boundaries of a company's power and authority. The bylaws are analogous to laws and statutes and are the rules and regulations for implementing the powers and authority. Bylaws are not filed with any governmental agency but are kept in the corporation's minute book. See *articles of incorporation, corporation.*

C

Cash discount is a reduction granted a customer for paying cash on delivery, rather than obtaining credit and delaying payment.

Cashier's check is purchased from a bank and is issued by the bank. See also *certified check, money order.*

Certificate of incorporation is the document issued by many states evidencing the formation of a corporation in that state. It is used to establish that a corporation is "in good standing" in that state. It may be required when a corporation desires to do business in another state.

Certified check is a check that has been "certified" by the issuing bank, which means that the bank segregates adequate funds from the depositor's account to pay the check, and the certification means that the bank is guaranteeing payment of the check. See also *cashier's check, money order.*

Certified public accountant (CPA) is a professional who has passed the examinations required by the appropriate state agency to provide kinds of accounting services. These services include, for example, setting up and maintaining a company's books and tax preparation. One of the services unique to CPAs is providing audited financial statements. See *accountant, audit.*

Chapter 7 is a type of federal bankruptcy for individuals and businesses whereby all "non-exempt" assets are made available to creditors, who are paid in a prescribed order according to an approved schedule, and the debtor is "discharged" from all further outstanding obligations to the listed creditors. See also *Chapter 11, Chapter 13.*

Chapter 11 is a type of federal bankruptcy for businesses, which permits the debtor to propose a plan to pay creditors according to a specific schedule and "discharge" all outstanding debts. See also *Chapter 7, Chapter 13.*

Chapter 13 is a type of federal bankruptcy for individuals, which permits the debtor to propose a plan to pay creditors according to a specific schedule and "discharge" all outstanding debts. See also *Chapter 7, Chapter 11.*

Check is a financial instrument whereby the payor (person writing the check) instructs the bank to pay the defined amount to the order of the designated payee (person or entity to whom the check is written).

Civil law is the body of law adopted in some jurisdictions, including Louisiana and California, based on the Napoleonic Code and following prescribed rules or statutes, rather than adhering to past practices or precedent, as in the "common law." See also *common law*.

Civil liability is the legal process for recovery of money or property or compelling the doing of things for the benefit of individuals and businesses, rather than imposing penalties or extracting obligations to the governmental jurisdiction. It is administered by private attorneys and individuals, rather than through a district or prosecuting attorney on behalf of the government.

Closely held business is a business owned by a small number of people or other business, rather than one that is publicly held or traded on the stock markets. It is frequently a business arrangement between one or more family groups or groups of friends, though the term could describe a larger group of owners, so long as the group is small enough to avoid the necessity of complying with the technical requirements set forth in the state and federal securities laws for publicly held businesses. See also *corporation, limited liability company, partnership*.

Collateral is the term used to define assets of a borrower which may be available to a lender as a means of repaying a loan. For example, when a bank is asked to lend money, it will usually require the prospective borrower to provide a list of the borrower's available assets in order to determine whether the borrower has sufficient assets, if liquidated, to repay the loan. The bank may or may not require the assets to be "secured" or "encumbered" for the purpose of guaranteeing repayment. See also chapter 4.

Collective works are works defined by the federal copyright statute as including periodicals, anthologies, or encyclopedia in which contributions consisting of separate and independent works themselves are assembled into a collective whole. See chapter 8; see also Section 101 of the Copyright Revision Act of 1976, as amended.

Collusion is a legal term defining an unsavory arrangement between two or more entities for an improper purpose.

Commingling means combining assets from two or more sources. The commingling could be legitimate where, for example, a husband and wife have a joint checking. It could also be improper, as in situations where a "mom and pop" corporation pays the personal obligations of the owners from corporate funds and/or corporate obligations from the owners' individual funds.

Common law is the legal system based on "English Common Law" and follows past practice or legal precedent, known as *stare decisis*. In this process, rules established in court cases become binding and are followed until modified, extended, or reversed. This should be distinguished from "civil law," which is based upon the Napoleonic Code and is limited to statutory pronouncements. See *civil law*.

Common stock is the form of stock issued by a corporation that has unrestricted voting rights, dividend rights and ownership in the corporation. It is the kind of stock every corporation must have, and is distinguished from "preferred stock," which must, by definition, must have some form of "preference" in either dividends or distribution on dissolution, or both. See also *preferred stock*.

Complaint is the legal document filed in a court that begins a lawsuit. This document, along with the summons, must be properly served on behalf of the complainant (plaintiff) on the other party (defendant) in order to continue the lawsuit.

Confirming memorandum is a written document sent by one party to another for the purpose of confirming the terms of an oral arrangement.

Conflict of interest is an ethical concept whereby a party has divided loyalties. For example, when a partner in a partnership is given a cash payment of $10 for a service rendered and belatedly realizes that, instead of one crisp $10 bill, there were two stuck together, the partner is forced to decide whether he should disclose to his partner the fact that the client overpaid. A lawyer who represents two parties who have opposing interests is in a conflict of interest and may, under the rules of many bar associations, be required to suspend representation of both parties. Alternatively, if the conflict is merely theoretical, then most bar associations permit the lawyer to continue representing both parties, provided the facts are disclosed to both parties in writing and there is an appropriately written waiver of the theoretical conflict by all.

Consideration is a contract element, which requires the giving or receiving of something of value by one party in exchange for something of comparable value from the other party. Consideration can be in the form of money, property, services, or an agreement to refrain some action. Historically, consideration did not have to be comparable, as when "token" consideration was used for transactions, such as the classic use of "a single peppercorn." Today, the law tends to require the parties to give or receive things of comparable potential value in order for the "consideration" to be deemed valid.

Consignment is a legal arrangement whereby the property of one party is entrusted to another for purposes of sale. The person who entrusts the property, who must be the owner or lawful possessor, is known as the consignor, and the person receiving the property is known as the consignee. The consignment agreement may be oral or written and, if in writing, it may be recorded with the appropriate government office. Many states have enacted special legislation dealing with unique forms of consignment, such as fine art, crafts, and collectibles. See also chapter 3.

Consumer Price Index (CPI) is a financial tool used to define the increase or decrease in a defined list of consumer products and services in a particular geographic area during a specified period of time.

Contract is a legal concept whereby one offers consideration to another in exchange for the other providing comparable consideration. To be legally valid, all contracts require an offer, acceptance, and consideration. They may be oral or written. The are other legal requirements for certain types of contract; for example, contracts for the sale of real property (land) and contracts for personal property worth $500 or more must be in writing. See *acceptance, consideration, offer*; see also chapter 6.

Cooling-off period is a concept whereby a consumer is given a specified period of time to reflect on an otherwise valid contract and, if desired, rescind it before it is performed by either party. For example, many states permit a three-day period within which a consumer may cancel contracts obtained by door-to-door salespeople.

Copyright is the right whereby any original work of "authorship" that is put in a tangible form is protected by law. In the United States, the copyright laws have been enacted pursuant to the enabling provision set forth in Article I of the United States Constitution. The most recent copyright statute was enacted in 1976 and became effective on January 1, 1978. This law continues to evolve and has been amended a number of times. It is known as "the Copyright Revision Act of 1976, as amended." There are numerous treaties throughout the world dealing with copyright on a multinational level. See also chapter 8.

Corporate shield and **corporate veil** are the terms used to define the limited liability available for those who conduct business through corporate or other business entities. It is said that shareholders in corporations and owners of limited liability companies are "shielded" by the limitation of liability available to them when they properly conduct business through these entitles.

Creditors cannot "pierce the corporate veil" or "penetrate the corporate shield" without establishing a valid legal reason to do so, and the reasons available are very limited.

Corporation is a business entity created by one or more persons pursuant to the corporate code of the state in which the business is to be formed. See *common stock, preferred stock, articles of incorporation, certificate of incorporation*; see also chapter 1.

Counteroffer is an offer presented by an "offeree," or recipient of an offer, from another, which rejects the original offer and provides a new offer. It converts the original "offeror" into an "offeree." Once the "give and take" is completed and an agreement is reached, there is a contract. See *contract, offer*; see also chapter 6.

Creditor is one who is owed an obligation by another, known as a "debtor." In business, the term is more commonly used to define one who is owed money.

D

Damages is the compensation sought or awarded for legal injury sustained.

Debentures and **bonds** are legal debt instruments frequently used by corporations to evidence debt. When the debt is secured by one or more identified assets, such as a mile of railroad track, the instruments are "bonds." When the debt is secured by all of the debtor's assets, the instruments are known as "debentures." Bonds are also issued by governmental entities for specific designated purposes, such as building libraries, schools, and the like, or funding a particular project. See also *debt*.

Debt is an obligation owed by one ("debtor") to another ("creditor"). See also *creditor, debtor*.

Debtor is one who owes an obligation to another, known as a "creditor." In business, the term is more commonly used to define one who owes money.

Defined benefit plan is a retirement plan that pays a specific amount after the employee retires. This payment stream is used to determine the method and amount necessary to fund the plan. See also *defined contribution plan*.

Defined contribution plan is a retirement plan that establishes the amount to be paid into the plan, and the benefits then flow from the pre-retirement contribution. See also *defined benefit plan*.

Depreciate and **depreciation** are financial and accounting terms whereby the useful life of an item is "guesstimated" and the value of the item is reduced on a yearly basis according to a prescribed schedule. For tax purposes, the Internal Revenue Service has established prescribed periods of depreciation for various items. See chapter 14; see also *appreciate, appreciation.*

Derivative work is a copyright concept whereby a work is taken from, or based on, a prior work. See chapter 8; see also Section 101 of the Copyright Revision Act of 1976, as amended.

Design defect is a defect in the design of a product that results in the product being defective and may result in liability for the designer of the product. This should be distinguished from a manufacturing defect, where liability would fall to the manufacturer of the product.

Discharge is the legal concept whereby a debtor in bankruptcy is permitted to extinguish all pre-bankruptcy debts when the legal requirements of the bankruptcy law are followed. See *bankruptcy, creditor, debtor.*

Disclaimer is a legal device whereby a party may avoid responsibility for warranties that have either been expressly given or are implied by law. In order for a disclaimer to be valid, it must comply with the legal requirements set forth in the statute governing warranties and disclaimers. See also Article 2 of the Uniform Commercial Code.

Dissolution. An entity, such as a corporation, limited liability company, limited partnership, or the like, may end its existence by a formal process known as "dissolution." This can either be mandatory, by court order, or voluntary. It can also be involuntary, as when the annual report required by state law and the accompanying annual fees are not tendered.

Dividend preference is a payment defined by a preferred stock instrument setting forth the amount (in either dollars or percentage) which must be paid to the holders of the preferred stock before any dividends are paid to the holders of common stock. See *common stock, preferred stock.*

E

e-commerce is shorthand for "electronic commerce," which is the practice of engaging in commercial activities using the computer network known as the Internet and/or World Wide Web.

Electronic signature is the electronic communication adopted by a party for purposes of taking advantage of the E-Sign statute and consummating contracts through "e-commerce." See *e-commerce, Electronic Signatures in Global and National Commerce Act (E-Sign Act)*.

Electronic Signatures in Global and National Commerce Act (E-Sign Act) is a federal statute that prescribes a method whereby an "electronic signature" may be used for purposes of validating contracts in cyberspace, which contracts are binding in the same manner as they would be if entered into through traditional means.

Employee stock option plan (ESOP) is a plan established by a business entity using the company's stock for purposes of funding an employee retirement plan.

Express warranty is a statement of fact or representation by a seller with the respect to quality or other attributes of particular goods to be sold. See also *implied warranty*.

F

Fair use is a copyright concept developed by case law and codified in the Copyright Revision Act of 1976, as amended, to provide a defense for one who copies the protected work of another when the copying satisfies the guidelines set forth in the statute. See chapter 8; see also the Copyright Revision Act of 1976, as amended.

Federal Trade Commission (FTC) is the federal agency charged by Congress with responsibility for policing interstate commerce and trade within the United States and at its borders. It has also assumed responsibility for policing activities on the World Wide Web when those activities affect commerce in the United States.

Fiduciary is the term used to define one who owes a duty to another. The scope of that duty varies from relationship to relationship and has been more carefully defined in the myriad of cases dealing with individuals who owe or are owed the duty. Classic examples of fiduciary relationships are the agency relationship (where both parties owe a fiduciary duty to each other) and the trust relationship (where the trustee is held to owe a fiduciary duty to beneficiaries).

First sale doctrine is a copyright concept whereby the copyright owner may control the first sale of a copyrighted work. Resales of that work, absent an agreement to the contrary, may be made without involving the copyright owner. For example, a book publisher may, by virtue of the copyright in the book, control the first sale of that book but, absent some agreement to the contrary, a purchaser may resell the book without involving the publisher in the resale. See chapter 8.

Foreign corporation. See *corporation.*

Franchising is a process whereby a successful business pattern is licensed by the originator (franchisor) so that a licensee (franchisee) can create comparable businesses. In order for a franchising arrangement to be legal, the franchisor must comply with federal and state requirements and provide potential franchisees with the disclosures, known as a franchising disclosure document, required by those laws. Classic examples of successful franchises include McDonald's, Burger King, KFC, and other purveyors of fine foods.

Full disclosure is the concept of providing all relevant and pertinent information when securities are offered for sale or sold. It was first discussed by the US Congress, later by state legislatures, and the securities laws require "full and fair disclosure of all material facts" relevant to the transactions involved.

G

General partner is the person or entity who has full personal liability in a partnership. A general partner can be one of the parties involved in a general partnership, which is defined as two or more persons who are co-owners engaged in a business for profit, or the person or entity who runs a limited partnership and has full personal liability for the acts, contracts, or omissions of that business entity. See also *limited partner.*

Goodwill is an intangible, which has been defined in cases as the propensity of customers to return to a business. It has also been defined as including the business's reputation, marketability, and success.

Gray market is the market that develops when a legally licensed product is introduced into a market other than the one in which it is licensed. For example, a trademark owner in the United States may license the use of its mark in Canada, since the owner has captured the US market. If the Canadian licensee begins selling the Canadian-licensed products in the United States, those sales of otherwise legally licensed merchandise in the restricted market of the United States would be gray market sales.

H

Holographic will is defined as a will that does not comply with the laws for a classic will. Typically, it is handwritten, signed by the person writing it, and not properly witnessed.

I

Implied contract is a contract created by the law for the purpose of preventing injustice. It is a contract that the parties may or may not have expressly agreed to. For example, when a merchant sells a product without an appropriate disclaimer, the law implies a contract whereby the purchaser may expect the product to be "merchantable," even though merchantability was never specifically bargained for. See also *contract*.

Implied warranty is a warranty implied by law and exists whether or not the parties have negotiated for it. Classic implied warranties are the implied warranty of merchantability, the implied warranty of fitness for a particular purpose, the implied warranty of title, and the implied warranty that the item is not infringing the intellectual property rights of another. Implied warranties may, if the party against whom it is enforceable complies with the statute, be disclaimed. See also *express warranty*.

Independent contractor is a person who engages in his or her own independent business and provides goods or services to another. An independent contract must be distinguished from an employee, who is employed by another for the purpose of providing goods or services. The legal distinction between these two categories is that an employer has the right of control over the conduct of an employee's activities, whereas the employer does not have a right of control over the conduct of an independent contractor's activities; rather, the employer contracts for the results. For example, an in-house bookkeeper who provides bookkeeping services for only the employer and is subject to the employer's direction and control is an employee, whereas a bookkeeper who provides similar services for several businesses and is not subject to the employer's control is likely an independent contractor.

Inherently dangerous activities are ultrahazardous or perilous activities that are so dangerous that regardless of who performs the work, the employer will remain legally responsible for any injuries that occur during the performance of the work. A fireworks displayer, for example, cannot escape liability by having fuses lit or rockets aimed by independent contractors.

Intellectual property is the body of law that deals with "products of the mind." It includes patent law, copyright law, trademark law, trade secret law, and other forms of protection for creative works. See *copyright, patent, trade dress, trade secret, trademark*; see also chapters 7 and 8.

Internet Service Provider (ISP) is a business that provides access to the Internet/World Wide Web, usually for a fee. Examples of ISPs include AT&T, Comcast Xfinity, and Verizon.

Inter vivos trust is a trust created by one during his or her lifetime.

Intestate is the legal term defining a person who dies without a will.

Individual Retirement Account (IRA) is a form of pension account created by Congress by individuals.

J

Joint and several is the term used to define the liability of two or more individuals who are each liable for the entire amount of any damages awarded, or a pro rata share of those damages, depending on the wishes of the person in whose favor the damages are awarded.

Joint venture is an arrangement between two or more persons to accomplish a specific task. It is distinguishable from a partnership, in that a partnership is established for the purpose of conducting an ongoing business, whereas a joint venture is created for the purpose of achieving a specific goal. Thus, if two or more persons get together for the purpose of building an apartment complex, it would be a joint venture; if the agreement goes on to say that they will continue to manage it on an ongoing basis, it would be a partnership. A joint venture can be expressed, when the parties work out their terms, or implied, when the parties merely perform the identified task.

Joint work is the term defined by Section 101 of the Copyright Revision Act of 1976, as amended, as a work created by two or more persons contributing their creative elements and intending that those elements be combined into a unitary whole. Cases have established that the contributions of each must be independently copyrightable. A classic example of a joint work is an illustrated text, where one creates the illustrations and the other prepares the text.

Judgment creditor is a person or entity in whose favor a court has rendered a money judgment.

Judgment debtor is a person or entity against whom a court has awarded a money judgment.

Jurisdiction is the word used to define a place where a lawsuit may be properly filed, a corporation may be created, a building may be erected, or the like. It is a geographic area that has been defined by statute or case law for specific purposes. In the context of litigation, "jurisdiction" refers to court system within which a case may be filed; for example, the US District Court will accept jurisdiction of only those cases that deal with federal questions or involve citizens of different states or foreign countries, and amounts in excess of $75,000; state and local courts, on the other hand, have different jurisdictional requirements. See also *venue*.

K

Key-person insurance is a type of insurance procured on the life of a person key to a business. It is typically obtained by the business entity to compensate it for the loss it will sustain when the key person dies.

L

Lawyer. See *attorney, attorney-in-fact*.

License is a permitted use. In business, licensing is typically used to permit one to use the intellectual property of another. For example, a copyright owner may license the use of a copyrighted use. Licensing may also refer to other permitted uses—for example, states issue driver's licenses and municipalities issue business licenses.

Life insurance trust is a form of trust created for the purpose of owning a life insurance policy and distributing the proceeds of that policy when the insured party dies.

Limited liability company (LLC) is a business form that allows those who conduct business through it to enjoy the benefits of limited personal liability while electing the method by which the entity is to be treated for tax purposes. It was created to overcome the restrictions imposed on small business that could qualify for so-called "S-corporation" status.

Limited liability partnership (LLP) is similar to a limited liability company except that it was created for the purpose of allowing partners in partnerships to have a personal liability shield similar to those who conduct business through corporations.

Limited partner is a person or entity who owns an interest in a limited partnership but who is a passive investor and who enjoys limited liability.

Limited partnership is a partnership having one or more general partners with full personal liability and one or more limited partners who may enjoy limited liability but may not play an active role in conducting the business of the limited partnership. It is created by statute, and the partnership must comply with the limited partnership statute of the jurisdiction in which it is created.

Liquidation is the process of converting assets to cash and distributing the cash. It should be distinguished from "dissolution," which refers merely to the legal relationship between those who are conducting the business. For example, when a general partner in a general partnership dies, there is a dissolution by virtue of the death of a partner. The remaining partners may, if their agreement permits, continue the partnership or, if the agreement does not or they do not wish to, they may then liquidate the partnership by converting its assets to cash and properly distributing the cash.

Litigation is the term used to describe filing and prosecuting a lawsuit.

M

Magnuson-Moss Warranty Act is a federal statute that imposes requirements for warranties when products are sold in interstate commerce.

Merger and **Acquisition** are the terms used to define corporate and other business entity arrangements whereby two or more entities are formally combined, or one entity is acquired by another. A merger is a situation where two or more business entities are combined together and the combined entity emerges as a single entity. Acquisitions are when one business entity acquires another business entity or only the assets of another entity. Both mergers and acquisitions are regulated by statute. That is, the business organization statutes regulate the process and the federal, as well as state, securities laws also impose requirements on entities covered by them.

Minutes. State statutes governing corporations, LLCs, and other business entities typically require those entities to have annual meetings and permit those entities to have periodic meetings. Written records of these meetings are known as "minutes" and are customarily kept in the organization's "minute book."

Money order is a financial instrument purchased from an authorized seller, which includes banks, post offices, and many retailers. See also *cashier's check, certified check.*

Multilevel marketing (MLM) is a form of doing business whereby a product or service is distributed through a multitiered structure. The structure is referred to as a "down line" and, customarily, each person in the line receives some compensation for "down line" sales. It is referred to "multilevel marketing," since each person is able to both sell product or service and enlist "down line" distributors, who can establish their own sales and distribution networks as well. The consumer who pays for the product or service is actually providing a revenue stream that flows up through all distribution levels. Classic examples of successful multilevel marketing are Amway and Mary Kay Cosmetics.

O

Offer is an element of contract whereby one party, known as the "offeror," presents an opportunity, known as the "offer," to another party, known as the "offeree." If the offer is accepted, a contract is made. See *contract, counteroffer.*

Operating agreement is the document that defines the internal workings of a limited liability company. By statute, the agreement can be extremely flexible, and the law provides the parties creating the agreement the ability to determine whether the organization will be run by its owners, a panel of owners, or a single manager; whether the organization will be taxed as an "entity" or not. In fact, the law makes it clear that the drafters have extraordinary flexibility in creating the organizational arrangement they desire, so long as the limited legal requirements of the law are adhered to. This document is not filed with any governmental agency but is kept in the organization's minute book.

P

Partner. See *general partner, limited partnership, limited liability partnership.*

Partnership. See *general partner, limited partnership, limited liability partnership, partnership.*

Partnership agreement is the agreement between two or more persons who desire to conduct business in a partnership form. A partnership agreement can be expressed when the parties work out the arrangements between themselves; implied when they merely conduct their business as a partnership; and oral or written. When the parties do not work out the details of a formal partnership agreement, the law imposes certain terms on the relationship.

Patent or **letters patent** is a legal document issued by the government to those who comply with the strict and technical requirements of the patent law. It is a form of intellectual property.

Pension plan is a plan adopted for the purpose of providing a pension for individuals who retire so they can augment the Social Security payments obtained from the government.

Preferred stock is a form of stock that contains some form of preference. The preference can either be in the payment of a dividend; that is, the holders of this type of stock must receive a dividend payment before any dividends may be paid to holders of common stock. The preference may also be in the form of a liquidation payment; that is, when the entity is dissolved and liquidated, holders of preferred stock with liquidation preferences must be paid the preference before holders of common stock will receive any payment on account of their interest in the liquidated company. Preferred stock can have either or both of these forms of preference.

Principal is the term used to define the person on whose behalf an agent acts and who controls or has the right to control the conduct of the agent. This term also refers, in a financial context, to the amount upon which interest is calculated. It may also be used to describe the job held by a school administrator.

Product liability is the legal doctrine that applies to situations where a defective product results in injury to person or property. The defect can be a design defect or a manufacturing defect.

Profit-sharing plans are plans whereby business owners agree to share business profits with participants in the plan. These plans are very technical and require specialists to assist in their formation and administration.

Q

Qualified plan refers to a pension or other plan that qualifies for special tax treatment under the Internal Revenue Code and state taxing statutes.

R

Receiver is a person who is appointed on an interim basis to administer a business for the benefit of creditors or others. A receiver is typically appointed by court order and reports to the court.

Reorganization is the process whereby a business may be restructured for the purpose of satisfying its creditors when it is unable to pay them in the regular course of business. Reorganizations can involve use of the business entity's stock or ownership interest as vehicles for payment. Non-insolvency reorganizations can occur when businesses are restructured for the purpose of accomplishing other goals; for example, a business may reorganize in order to change its business form, add or delete new product lines, or the like.

Royalties are periodic distributions paid pursuant to a licensing agreement.

S

S-corporations are corporations that comply with the requirements set forth in the Internal Revenue Code and elect to be treated, for tax purposes, as if they were still run as sole proprietorships or partnerships.

Securities and Exchange Commission (SEC) is a federal agency, charged by Congress with responsibility for policing the securities market.

Securities exemption is the term used to define specific and technical requirements necessary to avoid having to register securities with either the federal Securities and Exchange Commission or the state securities agency (in every state in which the security is to be sold). The two most common federal exemptions are the so-called "intrastate offering exception," for securities that are offered for sale and sold only within the boundaries of one state, and the exemption available for those potential purchasers of the security who are deemed "sophisticated" or wealthy enough not to need the protection of the securities laws.

Security interest is the interest created by statute in favor of a party, known as the "secured party," in the assets of another for the purpose of protecting an obligation owed the secured party by the other party. A security interest may be "perfected" by having the proper document filed with the appropriate governmental agency.

Service mark is a trademark used to identify a particular service with its provider. Service marks may be registered with the federal Trademark Office and appropriate state offices. Classic examples of service marks for airlines providing travel services are Western Airlines' slogan "The only way to fly" and Braniff's "We move our tail for you."

Shareholder is the person or entity owning stock in a corporation.

Shareholders' agreement is the agreement between a corporation's shareholders and the corporation governing certain rights and restrictions of the owners with respect to their stock.

Shareholder's derivative action is a cause of action provided the owner of stock in a corporation to vindicate a right or redress a wrong to the corporation. A shareholder's derivative action may be brought by the holder of even one share of stock in a corporation, though certain procedural restrictions are imposed when the ownership interest is small.

Shareholder or **annual meeting** is the meeting required by the state corporation code for every corporation. It must be held at least once a year for the purpose, among other things, of electing the corporation's board of directors.

Simplified Employee Pension Plan (SEPP) is a type of pension plan permitted by statute for employees.

Sole proprietorship is the term used to define a business owned by a single individual.

Statute of Frauds is a law that was first enacted in England for the purpose of preventing fraud and perjury. It recognized the fact that certain transactions are so touched with the public interest that they should not be permitted enforcement over the objection of a party unless they were evidenced by a writing signed by that party, though parties could voluntarily perform the transactions if they wished. Since the English feudal system was a governmental process based on land ownership, one of the first transactions covered by the law was real estate transfers. The law was later extended to cover transactions in goods in excess of a certain value. The law also prohibited oral wills, since it would be too easy for unscrupulous individuals to misstate the wishes of a dead person. These laws have been refined and adopted in the United States.

Stock refers to the ownership interest in a corporation and, traditionally, was evidenced by a stock or share certificate. The stock can be common or preferred. In addition, both common and preferred stock may be issued in different "classes," typically identified by alphabetical designations.

Stock or **share certificate** is the document used to evidence stock ownership in a corporate. Historically, it was a steel-engraved form, though some companies created unique and distinctive versions of their certificates. For example, Playboy Enterprises uses stock certificates with "Playmates" depicted on them. Today, many stock transactions are electronic, and no physical certificates are issued.

Stock option is a method by which an individual or business may acquire the right to obtain corporate stock at a defined price for a limited period. Options themselves are tradable and, in fact, there is an option exchange. Those who deal in options are said to "trade on equity," since their exchanges are for the appreciation in the value of the underlying stock, rather than trading in the stock itself.

Stockholder. See *shareholder*.

T

Tax is the term used to define a government's right to extract payment from its citizens. In the United States, the federal income tax was initially declared unconstitutional, as "confiscatory," and voided. Unfortunately, for the taxpayer, the Constitution was amended to permit an income tax.

Trade dress is a form of intellectual property law that was initially developed through cases for the purpose of protecting the unique and nonfunctional characteristics of product packaging. It was later extended, by case law, to cover everything from product design to the "look and feel" of businesses. It has even been used to protect the distinctive characteristics or "look and feel" of an artist's distinctive style.

Trademark is any words, phrases, name, symbol, logo, or combination of them when used to identify a product or service. When used in connection with services, they are referred to as "service marks."

Trust is a legal arrangement whereby a person, referred to as the "settlor," "trustor," or "creator," conveys property to another, referred to as the "trustee," for the benefit of one or more persons or entities, known as "beneficiaries." The trustee is a fiduciary, owing a duty to the beneficiaries.

Trustee. See *trust*.

Truth-in-Lending Act is a federal statute requiring certain lenders (usually institutional lenders) to comply with its requirements when loans are made.

U

Uniform Commercial Code (UCC) is a body of commercial law, adopted in every state of the United States, though its periodic modifications may not have been universally accepted.

Uniform Offering Circular is the document required by statute to be used when franchises are offered for sale.

Unincorporated association is an association of two or more persons who have not adopted a legal business form. Since the individuals are conducting business without having the benefit of a liability shield, such as through corporations, LLCs, or the like, they are legally partners and, thus, have full personal liability for the debts and other obligations of the business.

V

Venture capital is funding obtained from business speculators who provide money in exchange for ownership interest, control, and other defined benefits of the business. Since venture capitalists frequently provide large sums of money in a single block, they are customarily in a position to extract more rewards than individuals or businesses that invest modest amounts. Many venture capitalists were "burned" by the so-called "technology meltdown" and, thus, the availability of venture capital today is limited.

Venue is the legal requirement imposed in litigation defining the specific court where a case must be filed and tried.

Vesting is the process whereby an individual's interest in a retirement or pension plan is secured. For example, many pension plans provide that plan participants are "vested" 20 percent per year for five years; thus, an employee who leaves the company after three years will be 60 percent vested and entitled to receive only 60 percent of the amount that would otherwise have been available to a fully vested participant.

Voting trust is an arrangement whereby shareholders or owners of interests in other business entities pool those interests and agree to have them voted in a particular way. These are typically formal arrangements embodied in technical documents that comply with the business code of the state in which the entity is created.

W

Warranty is a form of guarantee that is either expressed or implied by law and provides protection to the purchaser when the characteristics warranted are not present.

Winding up is the process whereby a business completes its activities and prepares to end its operations. This can be a technical dissolution and liquidation.

Works made for hire is the copyright term used to define works created by employees within the scope of their employment, or by independent contractors whose work is specially ordered or commissioned and the arrangement is embodied through a written contract, which arrangement falls into one or more of the categories enumerated in the statute.

World Intellectual Property Organization (WIPO) is a multinational organization created for the purpose of administering the interface of copyright laws between its member nations.

Z

Zoning is the government's designation of limitations on the use of land and structures. Classic examples of zoning laws are those that prohibit commercial activities in residential areas and those that prohibit individuals from living in commercial structures.

About the Authors

Leonard D. DuBoff, founder of the law firm The DuBoff Law Group, PC, graduated magna cum laude from Hofstra University with a degree in engineering and summa cum laude from Brooklyn Law School, where he was the research editor of the *Brooklyn Law Review*. He was a professor of law for almost a quarter of a century, first teaching at Stanford Law School, then at Lewis & Clark Law School in Portland, Oregon. He also taught at the Hastings College of Civil Advocacy and lectured for the AAA of the Hague Academy of International Law. He is the founder and past chairperson of the Art Law Section of the Association of American Law Schools; the founder and past president of the Oregon Volunteer Lawyers for the Arts; the former president of the Tigard, Tualatin, and Sherwood Arts Commission; past member of the board of the Oregon Committee for the Humanities; former Special Projects Coordinator for the National Endowment for the Arts; and a recipient of the governor of Oregon's prestigious Arts Award in 1990. DuBoff has testified in Congress in support of many laws, including the Visual Artist's Rights Act of 1990. In fact, he assisted in drafting that law as well. He is also responsible for drafting and testifying in support of numerous states' art laws and is a practicing attorney specializing in the field of art law, business law, and publishing law. DuBoff was on the task force that drafted the Oregon Corporation Code, Oregon Nonprofit Corporation Code, and began work on the Oregon LLC statute. He has represented numerous prominent businesses as well. His scholarly articles and books are frequently cited by courts and commentators. DuBoff is a pioneer of the field of art law and remains one of its most important and influential scholars in that field. He is a prolific author of law review articles and other publications as well and has written numerous books on art law, business law, and other related subjects. For more information about his writing, you can consult Amazon.

Amanda-Ann Bryan graduated from Brigham Young University with a degree in music and received her master's degree in writing with an emphasis in book publishing from Portland State University. She graduated magna cum laude from Lewis & Clark Law School with a certificate in intellectual property law. Amanda was the National Jurist Law Student of the Year for Oregon and was the recipient of numerous academic scholarships and awards. She was the ghostwriter for a book on entertainment law while in law school and edited a case book on copyright law. She is a practicing lawyer representing clients from all over the world specializing in intellectual property including copyright, trademark, and related subjects. Amanda ran a digital publishing services company for many years, has taught digital publishing, ebook production, and legal publishing at Portland State University, and has presented continuing legal education programs for attorneys.

Index

123

401(k), 197

A

accountant, 15, 19, 30–32, 34–35, 197
  certified public accountant
    (CPA), 202
  finding, 194–195
  volunteer, 194
accounts
  payable, 197
  receivable, 197
action, cause of, 197
addendum, 197
Adidas, 102
adjusted basis, 157, 160–161, 197
Adobe, 64
advertising, 97–103
  attorney, 97, 103
  celebrity endorsements, 99
  comparative, 98–99
  consumer protection laws, 97
  environmental, 99
  insurance, 102–103
  and Internet, 120
  locations, geographic, 100
  medicinal, 98
  photograph, permissions and
    releases, 99–100
  privacy, right to, 99–100
  publicity, right to, 99–100
  purpose, 97
  regulations, 97–98
  trade dress, 100–102
  trade dress, celebrity, 102
  trademark, licensing, 100
  trademark, unauthorized use
    of, 100
  truth in, 97
affidavit, 197–198
Age Discrimination in Employment
  Act, 145
agency, 47–53, 198
  actual authority, 48
  actual notice of termination, 52
  apparent authority, 48
  authority, 47–49
  contracts, 48
  disclosure, 50
  disclosure, partial, 50
  employees and volunteers, 50–51
  general agent, 48
  inherent authority, 48
  power coupled with an interest,
    and termination, 52
  power of attorney, 48
  ratification, 49
  reasonable notice of termination,
    52
  renunciation, 52
  revocation, 52
  servants, 50–51
  special agent, 48, 53
  termination, 51–53

agent, 198. *See also* Agency
agreement, 198
agricultural and horticultural
    organizations, 31
airports, local, 30
alcohol, 43
Allen, Woody, 99
amateur sports organization, 24
amendment, 198
American Bar Association (ABA), 117
American Booksellers Association
    (ABA), 117
American Geophysical Union v.
    Texaco, Inc., 93
Americans with Disabilities Act
    (ADA), 148, 171–172, 198
    reasonable accommodations, 172
annual meeting, 20, 213, 217
antidilution, 72, 78–79, 198
antitrust laws, 198
apparent authority, 198–199
appreciation, 154, 199, 207, 218
articles of
    incorporation, 5, 199, 201
    organization, 199
Art Law in a Nutshell, Vol. 6, 40
Ashton-Tate Corp. v. Ross, 85
Aspirin, 77
assets, 19, 199
assignment for the benefit of
    creditors, 199–200
attorney, 1, 9, 13, 15, 18, 21, 30–32,
    34–35, 37, 42–43, 53, 61, 68, 80,
    91, 97, 103, 106, 121, 139, 142,
    146–147, 156–157, 168, 177, 200
    attorney-client privilege, 200
    attorney-client relationship, 194

conflict of interest, 204
    evaluating, 193
    fees, 193
    fees, award of, 92
    finding, 191–192
    need for, 191–192
    pro bono, 193
    referral services, 192
    using, 193–194
attorney-in-fact, 200
auctions, 39–40
    bids, 40
    records, 40
    sale "as is," 40
audit, 110, 121, 200, 202
authority, 200
Avvo.com, 193

B
bank account, 6
    with right of survivorship, 187
bankruptcy, 46, 199, 200:
    Chapter 7, 202
    Chapter 11, 202
    Chapter 13, 202
    discharge, 202, 207
Bd of Trustees of Univ. of N.C. v.
    Heirs of Prince, 4
Berne Convention, 82, 94
Better Business Bureau, 9
    Wise Giving Alliance, 8
Blue Mountain Greeting Card
    Company, 101
"blue sky" law, 201
board of directors, 10, 20–21, 27,
    134, 201, 217
bonds, 206

Boy Scouts of America, 42, 45–47, 67, 100, 144, 181

Boys & Girls Club, 67

branding, 67, 201

Buchwald, Art, 109

Buchwald v. Paramount Studios, 109

Buenos Aires Convention, 94

business
    name, 15–16
    plan, 201

buy-sell agreement, 201

bylaws, 1, 6, 11–12, 19, 145, 201

C

Cadillac, 78

Calder, Alexander, 158

Canyon (Rauschenberg), 158

capitalization, 19

cars, 99

Cascade Pacific Council, 46

cash discount, 202

cashier's check, 202

Catholic Church, 46–47

celebrity, 99

certificate of incorporation, 202

certification marks, 67, 70

certified check, 202

chambers of commerce, 31

charity evaluation, 8–9

Charity Navigator, 8

CharityWatch, 8

check, 202

checklist, 15–21

Chicago Board of Trade, 31

Chipotle, 101

Church of Jesus Christ of Latter-Day Saints, 46–47

Church of Scientology, 115–116

City of the Dalles, 46

civil law, 202–203

civil liability, 203

Civil Rights Act, 145–147

Cleveland Creative Arts Guild v. Commissioner, 27–28

closely held business, 203

CNN, 119

Coca-Cola, 100, 102, 111, 120, 201

collateral, 203

college fraternities and sororities, 32

collusion, 203

Coming to America, 109

commerce, online, 126

commingling, 203

Commissioner of Trademarks, 75

Commission of Patents and Trademarks, 106

common law, 5, 71, 203–204

community associations, local, 30

Community for Creative Non-Violence v. Reid, 86

complaint, 204

conflict of interest, 204

consignment, 205

Constitution, 81, 205, 218

Consumer Price Index (CPI), 205

consumer protection laws, 64–65

contracts, 55–66, 205
    acceptance, 55, 57, 197, 204
    attorney, 61
    authority, 55
    breach, 55
    cancellation, 65
    confirming memorandum, 61–63, 204

consideration, 55, 57, 60, 204–205
consumer protection laws, 64–65
cooling-off period, 65, 205
counteroffer, 206
date of agreement, 60
defined, 55
employment, 138–140
express, 56
forms, 61
goods, defined, 60
goods or services, description, 60
goods valued at $500 or more, 60
implied, 56–57, 210
mail-order sales, 66
merchant, 62
no-cost written contract, 61
offer, 55, 57–58, 204, 206, 214
offeree, 206, 214
offeror, 206, 214
online, 64
oral, 56–59, 62–63
parties identification, 60
performance in one year, 59–60
proving agreement, 58–59
remedies, 55
signatures, 60
sweetheart, 8
terms spelled out, 63
written, 56, 58–59, 62–64
written, essentials, 60–61
written, required, 59–60
cooperative corporations (co-ops), 1,
  12–13, 15
  agreement, 16–18
  capital, 17
  check signing, 17
  description, 16
  dissolution, 18
  distribution of funds, 17
  duration, 17
  duties of participants, 18
  liquidation, 18
  management, 17–18
  meetings, 17
  name, 16
  as nonprofit corporation, 18
  as partnership, 18
  principal participants, 16
  prohibited acts, 15
  as public trust, 18
  reorganization, 18
  tax-exempt status, 25, 28–30
  voting power, 17
cooperative telephone companies, 35
co-ops. See Cooperative
  corporations (co-ops)
copyright, 81–95, 205
  application, 89–90
  attorney, 91
  attorney fees award, 92
  author, 82
  Berne Convention, 82
  collective work, 86–87, 203
  computer software, 82
  damages, 92
  deposit requirement, 89–90
  derivative work, 87, 207
  exemptions, 93–94
  fair use, 92–93, 208
  fair use and motion pictures, 93
  first sale doctrine, 83–84, 208–209
  history, 81–82
  impoundment, 92
  independent contractor, 86

infringement, 91–94
injunction, 92
international, 94
international and Internet, 123
and Internet, 115–116, 122
joint work, 84, 211
material, 82–83
notice requirement, 88–89, 94
originality, 83
ownership, 84–87
permissions, 109
photographs, 90
product packaging, 101
protection, period, 91
protection, scope, 83–84
publication, 82
registration, delaying, 90–91
registration, reasons for
    immediate, 90–91
right to display publicly, 84
right to distribute copies, 83
right to perform publicly, 84
right to prepare derivative works, 83
right to reproduce, 83
sale of copyright vs. sale of work,
    84
statute of limitations, 92
symbol, 88
three-dimensional designs, 87
utilitarian objects, protection,
    87–88
utility, items of, 100
and volunteers, 86, 144
work made for hire, 85–86
works made for hire, 220
Copyright Act of 1909, 88, 91–92
Copyright Office, 81, 89–90, 106

Copyright Register, 89
Copyright Revision Act of 1976,
    82–84, 88–89, 91–92, 203, 205,
    207–208, 211
corporation, charitable, 5, 15, 19–21,
    204, 206. See also Tax-exempt
    status
administrative officers, 19
annual meeting, 217
articles of incorporation, 5, 199
bank account, 6
board of directors, 5, 10, 20
bylaws, 1, 6, 11–12, 19, 145, 201
capitalization, 19
certificate of incorporation, 202
chief operating officer, 19
corporate seal, 6
corporate shield, 205–206
corporate veil, 205–206
creation, 5
creditors, 206
debts, 5
director, 10–11, 19
director, liability, 11–12
director, number of, 20
dissolution, 7, 207
and donors, 8–9
employee benefits, 20
executive director, 19
foreign corporation, 209
governing board, 20
housekeeping, 20
laws, 5
liability, 19, 24
liquidation, 5
membership, 9, 21
minutes, 214

officers, 6, 10, 19
organizational meeting, 5
purpose, 5
S-corporation, 216
structure, 9–10
structure, internal, 10
tax-exempt non-profit
    corporations, 6–9, 20–21
tax-exempt status, 6–9
tax-exempt status and politics
    and lobbying, 8
trustees, 10–11, 21
corporation, nonprofit. *See*
    Corporation, charitable
country clubs, 32
Crawford, Susan, 37
creditor, 206
    judgment creditor, 211
cyberspace. *See* Internet
cy pres doctrine, 42

D
damages, 46, 206
    copyright, 92
debentures, 206
debt, 206
    and estates, 179
debtor, 206
    judgment debtor, 212
depreciation, 207
disclaimer, 207
disclosure, full, 209
discrimination, 145–146, 149
    age discrimination, 147–148
    Age Discrimination in
        Employment Act, 145

Americans with Disabilities Act
    (ADA), 145, 148
appeals, 149
attorney, 146, 148
Civil Rights Act, 145–146
communication procedures, 149
complaint, 149
confidentiality, 150
disabilities discrimination, 148
education, 150
enforcement, 145
Equal Pay Act, 145–146
Fair Labor Standards Act, 146
membership rules, 146
national-origin, 146
Older Workers Benefit Protection
    Act, 145
race-based, 146
reasonable accommodations, 148
religious, 145–146
reporting, 149
sex-based, 146
undue hardship, 148
zero tolerance policy, 149–150
dissolution, 207, 213
Docusign, 64
domain names, 116–119
    disputes, 117–118
    and trademarked names,
        118–119
donations, 19, 38–39, 155–157. *See
    also* Estate planning
    adjusted basis, 157
    appraisals, 157–158
    appreciated property, 161–162
    attorney, 156–157
    auction, 40

cash, 156
charity evaluation, 8–9
coins, 41
copyrights, 39
cy pres doctrine, 42
estate plan, 42
facilities, 174–175
fair market value, 156
future interest in tangible
    personal property, 156
gifts in exchange, 41–43
intangibles, 39
intellectual property, 39
and lease earnings calculations, 170
marketable securities, 38
to other charities, 155
out-of-pocket expenses, 156
patents, 39
precious metals, 41–43
present interest in property, 156
securities, 156
services, 40
tangible property, 39
taxes, 38–40, 42–43
of time, 155
time frame, 42
trademarks, 39
duty of
    diligence, 18
    loyalty, 18
    obedience, 18

E
eBay, 122
e-commerce, 207
educational organizations, 24
electronic signature, 208

Electronic Signatures in Global and
    National Commerce Act (E-Sign
    Act), 64, 208
Elks Club, 33
email, 124
    spam, 125
Empire State Building, 100
employee, 137–142, 210
    age discrimination, 147–148
    attorney, 139, 142, 149
    benefits, 139, 141
    confidentiality, 150
    contract, 137–140
    contract term, 138
    defined, 137
    disabilities discrimination, 148
    discrimination, 145–146, 149
    duties, 139
    education, 150
    evaluation, 140, 152
    Family Medical Leave Act of 1993
        (FMLA), 150
    handbook, 140, 142, 149
    harassment, 146–147, 149
    hazards in workplace, 142
    insurance, 138
    labor department, 142
    liability, 138
    noncompetition, 139–140
    Occupational Safety and Health
        Administration (OSHA), 142
    overtime, 167
    parking, 141
    permanent, 140
    privacy policy, 149
    probationary period, 140
    progressive discipline, 152

regular or full-time, 140
regulations, health and safety, 141
retirement, 141
Safety Data Sheets (SDS), 142
Social Security (FICA), 141
and stock, 139
taxes, municipal, 141
taxes, withholding, 141
termination, 140, 151–152
termination, just cause, 152
termination, wrongful, 151
termination reasons, 151
unemployment insurance, 141
unions requirements, 141
wage, 138–139, 166–167
wage and hour laws, 141
whistle-blowing, 152
at will, 140, 149
worker's compensation, 134, 141
Worker's Compensation agency, 142
zero tolerance policy, 149–150
Employer Identification Number, 7
employment groups, 33
    local, 30
Energy Star, 67
environment, safe, 47
environmental laws, 172
Equal Employment Opportunity
    Commission (EEOC), 145, 147–148
Equal Pay Act, 145–146
Escalator, 77
estate planning, 42, 177–189
    abatement, 179
    attorney, 177
    awards, 177
    bank accounts with right of
        survivorship, 187

beneficiaries, 178, 187
bequests, 178–179
calculating tax, 184
charitable deduction, 184
codicil, 178
creditors, 189
curtesy, 181
debt payment, 179, 188
devises, 178
distributions outside the will,
    185–186
dower, 181
estate taxes, 182
executor, 181–182, 188
gifts, 185
gifts, annual exclusion, 185
gifts, three-year rule, 186
gift tax returns, 186
gross estate, 182–183
gross estate deductions, 183
holographic will, 210
intestacy, 179–180, 211
intestacy succession, 180
intestate succession,
    representation, 180
legatees, 178
marital deduction, 184–185
paying tax, 184–185
personal representative,
    181, 188
probate, 185, 188–189
property not willed, 179–180
seminars, 177, 181
settlor, 187
spouse's elective share, 180–181
taxable estate, 183–184
trustee, 186

trusts, 177, 186–188
Unified Estate and Gift Tax
    Schedule, 184
valuation, 183
will, 177–178, 181–182
Etsy.com, 167
European Union, 79

F
Fair Labor Standards Act, 167
Family Medical Leave Act of 1993
    (FMLA), 150
Fat Boys, 99, 102
Federal Trade Commission (FTC),
    97–98, 120–121, 208
fiduciary, 208
financial statement, 43
First Amendment, 70
Food and Drug Administration
    (FDA), 98
Ford Foundation, 38
FoundationCenter.org, 38
franchising, 106
fraternal beneficiary societies,
    orders, or associations, 33
fraternal-style organizations, 34
fraud and deceit, 51, 68
fund-raising expert, 37–38
    contract, 37
    government organizations, 38
fund-raising plan, 37–44
    alcoholic beverages, 43
    auction, 39–40
    borrowing money, 43
    brainstorming meeting, 38
    compliance with law, 43
    confidentiality, 38

donations, 38–39
minutes of meetings, 38
obtaining funds, 38
precious metals, 41–43
private organizations, 38
proposal, 38
source of funds, 38
tax shelters, 43

G
General Motors, 78
gift, 185
    annual exclusion, 185
    shop, 154
    tax returns, 186
    three-year rule, 186
Girl Scout Cookies, 71
*Goldsboro Art League, Inc v.
    Commissioner,* 26–28
Good Housekeeping Seal of
    Approval, 67, 70
goodwill, 209
Google AdWords, 120
Google.com, 193
grants, 19, 23
gray market, 209
greeting cards, 101
GuideStar, 8

H
Hallmark Greeting Card Company,
    101
handbook, 124, 140, 142, 145, 149
harassment, 146–147
    attorney, 147
    Civil Rights Act, 147
    education, 150

hostile environment sexual
   harassment, 147
liability, 147
policy, 147
quid pro quo sexual harassment,
   147
racial harassment, 147
reasonable care to prevent, 147
sexual harassment, 147, 149
state laws, 147
hazards in workplace, 142
hobby and dinner clubs, 32
holding companies, 24
homeowners associations, 32
hunting and fishing clubs, 32
Hurricane Katrina, 128

I
incorporating, 5
independent contractors, 47, 86,
   143–144, 210
bookkeeper, 143
consignment sales, 143
and cottage industries, 167
defined, 143
liability, 143
nondelegable responsibilities,
   143–144
qualifications, 143
Social Security, 143
and telecommuting, 168
termination, 151
ultrahazardous or inherently
   dangerous jobs, 143
inherently dangerous activities, 210
injunction, copyright, 92
insurance, 127–135

advertising, 102–103
agent, 128–129
broker, 128–129
building insurance, 134
business interruption insurance,
   133
co-insurance, 132
commissions, 129, 134
contract, 128–129
contract interpretation, 129
co-op insurance fund, 134
cost, 134–135
coverage, 132
dental insurance, 141
duration, 128
employee acts, 138
errors and omissions, 121
expectations and reality, 129–130
health insurance, 133
insurable interest, 127
investments, 129
key-person insurance, 212
liability, Internet, 121
liability insurance, 173
life insurance, 188, 212
medical insurance, 141
misstatement, 131
omission, 131
overinsuring, 130–131
plain English requirement, 128
premium, 128–129, 134–135
prepaid legal insurance, 141
product liability insurance,
   134–135
records, 133
recovery, 128
reevaluation yearly, 132

regulations, 128–129
rental insurance, 173
revision to policy, 129
risk, 128–129
risk assessment, 133–134
scheduled property, 132–133
underinsuring, 130–131
understanding your policy, 128
undervaluation, 131–132
unemployment insurance, 141
unvalued or open policy, 128
valuation, 133
valued policy, 128
value of property, 132
voiding a policy, 131
whether to obtain, 133
workers compensation insurance,
    134, 141, 143
intellectual property, 39, 211.
    See also Copyright; Patent;
    Trademark; Trade secrets
    and the Internet, 115–116
    restriction of by employer, 140
    treaty obligation watch list, 108
Internal Revenue Code, 6, 23
    501(c)(1), 23–24
    501(c)(2), 24
    501(c)(3), 24–30
    501(c)(4), 30–31
    501(c)(5), 31
    501(c)(6), 31
    501(c)(7), 32
    501(c)(8), 32–33
    501(c)(9), 33
    501(c)(10), 33–34
    501(c)(11), 34
    501(c)(12), 35

Internal Revenue Service (IRS), 21,
    154–155, 158, 160, 183, 215
    art advisory panel, 158
    Form 1023, Application for
        Recognition of Exemption
        Under Section 501(c)(3), 6, 29
    Form 1024-A Application for
        Recognition of Exemption
        Under Section 501(c)(4), 31
    Form 1024 Application for
        Recognition of Exemption
        Under Section 501(a), 31–35
    Form 8283 Noncash Charitable
        Contributions, 39
    Form SS-4, Application for
        Employer Identification
        Number, 6–7
    Priv. Ltr. Rul. 8634001, 28
    Priv. Ltr. Rul. 201516066, 28–29
    Rev. Rul. 71-395, 25–26
    Rev. Rul. 76-152, 25
    Rev. Rul. 80106, 28
International Ladies Garment
    Workers Union, 167
Internet, 115–126
    advertising, online, 120
    attorney, 121
    audits, 121
    consumer information,
        protecting, 116
    and copyright, 122
    cybercommerce, 126
    cybersquatting, 117–118
    cyberterrorism, 125–126
    disclosures, 120–121
    domain names, 116–119
    e-commerce, 208

electronic signature, 208
email, 124
encryption, 124
framing, 119
hacking, 124–125
insurance, 121
and intellectual property laws,
    115–116
international issues, 121–123
Internet Service Provider (ISP),
    116, 211
keywords, 120
linking, 119–120
online commerce security, 126
peer-to-peer, 123
permissions, 122–123
ransomware, 125
server protection, 124
spam, 125
viruses, 125
website, 115
worms, 125
Internet Corporation for Assigned
    Names and Numbers (ICANN),
    117–118
intestacy, 179–180, 211
    succession, 180

J
joint venture, 211
jurisdiction, 2, 212

K
*Kerry Lewis v. Boy Scouts of
    America,* 45
King Tut exhibit, 106–107
Knights of Columbus, 33

Knights of Pythias, 33
Kodak, 69
Kozlowski, I. Dennis, 163

L
labor unions, 31
Lanham Act of 1946, 72, 75, 78, 80, 102
lawyer. *See* Attorney
leases, 169–175
    cost, 170
    and disabilities, 171–172
    donated facilities, 174–175
    environmental laws, 172
    and insurance, 173
    and liability, 173
    premises, 169
    recording, 170–171
    remodeling, 171–172
    restrictions, 171
    security, 173
    tax reductions, 170
    terms, 170
    utilities, 172–173
    written, 174
    and zoning, 173–174
liability, 1, 24, 45–53
    agency, 47–53
    clergy malpractice, 47
    due care, 51
    employees and volunteers, 50–51
    fraud and deceit, 51
    hazardous activities, 51
    individual, 45
    issues, 47
    joint and several, 211
    law schools, 47
    leases, 173

organizational for wrongful acts
of individuals, 45–46
politicians, 47
product liability, 215
servant, 50–51
waiver, 53
Library of Congress, 89–90
licensing, 105–114, 212, 216
accounting report, 110
acknowledgment of ownership,
110
attorney, 106
basics, 106
currency, 110
design defects, 108
exculpatory clause, 108
franchising law, 106
gray market, 106, 209
international, 108–109
music, 108
naked license, 109
nature of the work, 107
opportunities, 106–107
patented technology, 108
payment, method of, 109
quality control, 110
recording, 106
royalty, 109
scope, 106
signature, 110–111
sublicensing, 107–108
trade secrets, 111–114
written, 106
Licensing Expo, 105
life insurance organizations, local, 35
limited liability company (LLC),
160, 212–213, 219

dissolution, 207
minutes, 213
operating agreement, 214
limited liability partnership (LLP),
212–213
liquidation, 213
litigation, 213
loans, 43
lobbying, and tax-exempt status, 8
logo, 67
Lourim v. Swenson, 45

M
Madrid System, 79, 118
Magnuson-Moss Warranty
Act, 213
*Managing the Future: A Leader's
Guide* (Crawford), 37
marks. *See* Trademarks
Martindale-Hubbell Law Directory,
193
Maxtone-Graham v. Burtchaell, 93
McDonald's, 102
members, 99, 111, 129, 132, 146, 177,
181
co-op, 12–13
liability, 45–53
personal information, 116
powers of, 9, 18–20
public trust, 21
relationship with, 153
termination, 152
membership, 9, 141
rules, 146, 152
termination, 151–152
merger and acquisition, 213
metals, precious, 41–43

Metropolitan Museum of Art, 24, 100, 105
Midler, Bette, 102
minutes, 201, 213–214
money order, 214
motion pictures and fair use, 93
multilevel marketing (MLM), 214
Murphy, Eddie, 109
Museum of Modern Art, 158
music
    industry, 123
    licensing, 108
mutual irrigation companies, 35

N
National Audubon Society, 118
National Endowment for the Arts and Humanities, 38
National Football League (NFL), 31
National Gallery of Art, 106–107
Nationwide Insurance Company, 151
Network Solutions, 117
nondelegable duty, 143–144
Novosel v. Nationwide Insurance Company, 151

O
Occupational Safety and Health Administration (OSHA), 142
Official Gazette of Trademarks, 73, 77
Older Workers Benefit Protection Act, 145
Onassis, Jackie, 99
operating agreement, 214
Order of the Eastern Star, 34

organization, 1–13
    documents, 1
    legal structure, 2–9
    structures, 1

P
Paramount Studios, 109
partner, 214
    general partner, 209
    limited partner, 213
partnership, 214. *See also* Limited liability partnership (LLP)
    agreement, 1, 214–215
    dissolution, 207
    limited partnership, 213
patent, 39, 106, 109–111, 182, 211, 215
    design defect, 207, 215
    letters patent, 215
    licensing patented technology, 108
    permissions, 109
PBS, 41–42
Pepsi, 120
perfumes, 98
photograph, 89–90, 112
    copyright, 90
    permissions, 99
    permissions and releases, 99–100
    release, 99–100
Playboy Enterprises, 218
politics, and tax-exempt status, 8
power of attorney, 7, 48, 200
Pregnant By Mistake (Maxtone-Graham), 93
prevention of cruelty to children or animals organization, 24
principal, 198–199, 215
privacy, right to, 99, 149

private operating foundation, 30
product design, 101–102
profit-sharing plan, 215
property, 24
   holding companies, 24
   leased and tax-exempt status, 7
   value of for insurance, 132
publicity, right of, 99, 102
public trust, 1–3. *See also* Charitable
   trust
   documents, 1

R
Rauschenberg, Robert, 158
receiver, 216
Red Cross, 67, 107
Register of Copyrights, 90
religion, 145–146
religious organizations, 24
reorganization, 216
Restatement (Third) of Trusts, 2
restaurant, 101
retirement plan
   defined benefit plan, 206
   defined contribution plan, 206
   Individual Retirement Account
     (IRA), 211
   pension plan, 215
   qualified plan, 215
   Simplified Employee Pension
     Plan (SEPP), 217
   teacher retirement funds, local, 34
   vesting, 219
Rock and Roll Hall of Fame, 102
Rockefeller Foundation, 38
Rotary Club, 31
royalties, 24, 39, 109–110, 159, 216

S
safeguards, 45–47, 53
salary. *See* Wages
Salvation Army, 107
scientific organizations, 24
S-corporation, 216
Securities and Exchange
   Commission (SEC), 216
securities exemption, 216
security interest, 216
servant, 50–51
service marks, 67, 76, 216–217
sexual abuse, 46–48
shareholders, 9, 205, 217, 219
   agreement, 217
   derivative action, 217
   meeting, 217
Shell, 69
Shriners, 34
The Slants, 70
Smithsonian Institution, 23
Social Security (FICA), 141, 143
sole proprietorship, 217
Sonnabend, Ileana, 158
Sony Corporation, 93
Space Needle, 100
Springmaid, 24, 105–106
Statute of Frauds, 59–60,
   62–63, 217
Stern v. Lucy Webb Hayes Nat'l
   Training School for Deaconesses
   and Missionaries, 12
stock, 139, 217–218
   certificate, 218
   classes, 217
   common stock, 204, 217
   dividend preference, 207

employee stock option plan
     (ESOP), 208
full disclosure, 209
option, 218
preferred stock, 204, 215, 217
reorganization, 216
shareholder, 217
stockholder, 218

T
T. R. v. BSA, 46
Tannehill, James Donald, 46
taxes, 1, 153–163, 218
     appraisals, 157–158
     at-risk provisions, 160–161
     attorney, 163
     basis, 160
     capital gain, 162
     deductions, 155, 159–163
     depreciation, 161
     donations, 38–40, 42, 155–157
     estate taxes, 182
     exemption, state, 7
     first use exemption, 163
     free ports, 162
     gift shop, 154
     gift tax, 185–186
     income contributes importantly
          test, 154
     income tax, 218
     income that is not tax-exempt, 153
     joint ventures, 158
     and leased property, 7
     loopholes, 160
     municipal, 141
     partnering with other
          organizations, 158

payroll taxes, 32–35
penalties for appraisal
     overvaluation, 157–158
qualified rehabilitation
     expenditures, 162
real estate tax on leases, 170
state, 21
substantially related activities,
     153–154
systematic plan for donations,
     161–162
tax-exempt non-profit
     corporations, 6–9, 21, 153
tax-exempt non-profit
     corporations, abusing status, 8
tax shelters, 43, 159–163
and telecommuting, 168
temporary loans, 162–163
umbrella organization, 158
unrelated business income, 153–155
unrelated trade or business, 153
valuation, 157–158
valuation guidelines, 158
withholding taxes, 25, 141, 143
tax-exempt non-profit corporations.
     See Tax-exempt status
tax-exempt status, 23–35
     accounting, 29–30
     by act of Congress, 23–24
     art galleries, 25–29
     benefits, 35
     benevolent life insurance
          companies, mutual ditch
          or irrigation companies,
          cooperative telephone
          companies, and cooperative
          electric companies, 35

business leagues, 31–32
charitable organizations, 24–30
consignment, 28
cooperative corporations (co-
    ops), 25, 28–30
domestic fraternal societies,
    33–34
federal, 23–36
fraternities, 32–33
fund-raising, 34
grants, 23
holding companies for other
    nonprofits, 24
insurance benefits, 33
labor, agricultural, and
    horticultural organizations, 31
liability, 24
payroll taxes, 32–35
political activity, 29
postage, 23
propaganda, 29
recordkeeping, 23
salaries and commissions, 25,
    31–35
social and recreational clubs, 32
social welfare organization,
    30–31
teachers' retirement fund
    associations, 34
voluntary employee's beneficiary
    associations, 33
teacher retirement funds, local, 34
telecommuting, 167–168
Thermos, 77
torts, 50–51
Total News, Inc., 119
toxic materials, 142

trade boards, 31
trade dress, 100–102, 218
    celebrity trade dress, 102
    registering, 102
trademark, 67–80, 218
    abandonment, 77–78
    actual use, 73–74
    advertising, 71
    affixing to product, 71
    antidilution, 72–73, 78–79
    applications, opposition to, 74
    assignments, 76
    attorney, 68, 80
    certification mark, 67, 70
    confusingly similar, 72
    constructive use, 75–77
    damages, 78
    deceptive and misleading, 70
    descriptive, 69–70
    distinguishable, 69
    and domain names, 118–119
    duration, 76–77
    extension of registration, 74–75
    famous mark, 78
    generic words, 69
    goodwill, 68
    history, legal, 67–68
    infringement, 78–79
    intent-to-use, 74–77
    international, 79, 118
    Lanham Act of 1946, 72, 75, 78, 80
    licensing, 100
    loss of, 77
    naked license, 100, 109
    obscene or scandalous, 70
    opposition, 77
    permissions, 109

Principal Register, 73–74, 76
priority, 75
priority right of use, exceptions to, 76
prohibited, 69–70
protecting, 71
registered trademark, 76
registers, 73
registration, federal, 72–73
registration, state, 80
registration benefits, 76
search, 68
secondary meaning, 70
statement of use, 75
Supplemental Register, 73, 77
symbol, 76
token use, 73
trade dress, 100–102
unauthorized use of, 100
use in commerce, 69, 71, 77
use of, 71
Trademark Law Revision Act of 1988 (TLRA), 72–74
trade secrets, 111–114, 140
confidentiality agreements, 113
confidential mark, 112
demonstrations, preventing, 112
elements of, 111
employee access, 112
fragmenting information, 113
and Internet, 115–116
law, 114
misappropriate of, 114
physical security, 112
protection, 111–113
vague labeling, 113
Trump, Donald, 29

trust, 42, 177, 186–188, 218
amendment, 4
beneficiaries, 218
creator, 218. See also Trustees
and gross estate, 186–187
illusory, 187
inter vivos, 187
inter vivos trust, 187, 211
life insurance, 188
life insurance trust, 212
settlor, 218
testamentary, 187
trustor, 218
voting trust, 219
trust, charitable, 2–12, 15, 21, 30
amendment, 4
assets, 3–4
board, 9
corporate form, 5–6
creation, 3
cy pres doctrine, 3–4
director, 10
equitable deviation doctrine, 5
laws, applicable, 5
membership, 9
name, 21
purpose, 2–5
structure, internal, 9–10
trustees, 3, 9–11
trustees, liability, 11–12
trustees, 3, 21, 218
liability, 11–12
Truth-in-Lending Act, 218
TV Guide, 70
Two Pesos v. Taco Cabana, 101
Tyco International, 163

U

UL mark, 67
ultrahazardous activities, 51, 143, 210
Uniform Commercial Code (UCC), 61, 219
Uniform Offering Circular, 219
Uniform Trust Code, 2
unincoporated association, 219
unions, 141
United States Code Title 18, Section 331, 41
Universal Copyright Convention, 94
Universal Studios, et al., v. Sony Corporation, et al., 93
US Congress, 114
US Department of Labor, 166–167
US Patent and Trademark Office (PTO), 68–69, 73–74, 77, 79, 118, 216–217
US State Department, 108
US Supreme Court, 93, 101

V

venture capital, 219
venue, 219
Veterans Administration, 23–24
volunteers, 50–51, 144–145

W

wages, 138–139
warranty, 220
  express warranty, 208
  implied warranty, 210
Washington Post, 119

Washington Redskins, 70
Western Airlines, 217
will, 42, 177–178
  advantages of, 181–182
  holographic, 178
  holographic will, 210
  revocation, 178
  and Statute of Frauds, 217
winding up, 220
WIPO Treaty of 1996, 123
works made for hire, 220
World Intellectual Property Organization (WIPO), 220
World Property Intellectual Property Organization (WIPO), 123

Y

Yelp.com, 193

Z

zoning, 165–168, 173–174, 220
  attorney, 168
  business, 165
  commercial, 166
  cottage industries, 166–167
  equipment, 166
  federal regulations, 166–167
  local restrictions, 165–166
  permit or license, 166
  remodeling, 166
  residences, 165–166
  sheltered workshops, 166
  square feet, 166
  telecommuting, 167–168

**Books
from
Allworth
Press**

Brand Thinking and Other Noble Pursuits
by Debbie Millman with foreword by Rob Walker (6 × 9, 336 pages, paperback, $19.95)

Branding for Nonprofits
by DK Holland (6 × 9, 208 pages, paperback, $19.95)

The Copyright Guide (Fourth Edition)
by Lee Wilson (6 × 9, 304 pages, paperback, $19.95)

Effective Leadership for Nonprofit Organizations
by Thomas Wolf (6 × 9, 192 pages, paperback, $16.95)

Fund Your Dreams Like a Creative Genius™
by Brainard Carey (6⅛ × 6⅛, 160 pages, paperback, $12.99)

How to Win Grants
by Alan Silver (5½ × 8¼, 140 pages, paperback, $12.95)

Infectious
by Achim Nowak (5½ × 8¼, 224 pages, paperback, $19.95)

Intentional Leadership
by Jane A. G. Kise (7 × 10, 224 pages, paperback, $19.95)

Leadership in the Performing Arts
by Tobie S. Stein (5½ × 8¼, 252 pages, paperback, $19.99)

Legal Guide to Social Media
by Kimberly A. Houser (6 × 9, 208 pages paperback, $19.95)

The Pocket Small Business Owner's Guide to Building Your Business
by Kevin Devine (5¼ × 8¼, 256 pages, paperback, $14.95)

The Pocket Small Business Owner's Guide to Business Plans
by Brian Hill and Dee Power (5¼ × 8¼, 224 pages, paperback, $14.95)

The Trademark Guide (Third Edition)
by Lee Wilson (6 × 9, 272 pages, paperback, $19.95)

Website Branding for Small Businesses
by Nathalie Nahai (6 × 9, 288 pages, paperback, $19.95)

To see our complete catalog or to order online, please visit *www.allworth.com*.